# HOW TO SAY IT
## on Your Resume

# HOW TO SAY IT
# on Your Resume

A Top Recruiting Director's Guide
to Writing the Perfect Resume for Every Job

**BRAD KARSH**
with **COURTNEY PIKE**

Prentice Hall Press

**PRENTICE HALL PRESS**
**Published by the Penguin Group**
**Penguin Group (USA) Inc.**
**375 Hudson Street, New York, New York 10014, USA**
Penguin Group (Canada), 90 Eglinton Avenue East, Suite 700, Toronto, Ontario M4P 2Y3, Canada
(a division of Pearson Penguin Canada Inc.)
Penguin Books Ltd., 80 Strand, London WC2R 0RL, England
Penguin Group Ireland, 25 St. Stephen's Green, Dublin 2, Ireland (a division of Penguin Books Ltd.)
Penguin Group (Australia), 250 Camberwell Road, Camberwell, Victoria 3124, Australia
(a division of Pearson Australia Group Pty. Ltd.)
Penguin Books India Pvt. Ltd., 11 Community Centre, Panchsheel Park, New Delhi—110 017, India
Penguin Group (NZ), 67 Apollo Drive, Rosedale, North Shore 0632, New Zealand
(a division of Pearson New Zealand Ltd.)
Penguin Books (South Africa) (Pty.) Ltd., 24 Sturdee Avenue, Rosebank, Johannesburg 2196, South Africa

Penguin Books Ltd., Registered Offices: 80 Strand, London WC2R 0RL, England

While the author has made every effort to provide accurate telephone numbers and Internet addresses at the time of publication, neither the publisher nor the author assumes any responsibility for errors, or for changes that occur after publication. Further, the publisher does not have any control over and does not assume any responsibility for author or third-party websites or their content.

HOW TO SAY IT ON YOUR RESUME

First edition: January 2009

Library of Congress Cataloging-in-Publication Data

Karsh, Brad.
  How to say it on your resume : a top recruiting director's guide to writing the perfect resume
for every job / Brad Karsh with Courtney Pike.
    p. cm.
  Includes index.
  ISBN 978-0-7352-0434-8
  1. Resumes (Employment)   I. Pike, Courtney.   II. Title.
  HF5383.K378 2009
  650.14'2—dc22
                                                                              2008039374

PRINTED IN THE UNITED STATES OF AMERICA

10  9  8  7  6  5  4  3  2  1

Most Prentice Hall Press books are available at special quantity discounts for bulk purchases for sales promotions, premiums, fund-raising, or educational use. Special books, or book excerpts, can also be created to fit specific needs. For details, write: Special Markets, Penguin Group (USA) Inc., 375 Hudson Street, New York, New York 10014.

*To my son, Milo.*
*So much happiness in so little time.*

# ACKNOWLEDGMENTS

This book is a reflection of all that we have accomplished at JobBound.

First of all, I'd like to thank all the wonderful clients who have allowed us to play a role in their career successes. A small sample of our work is represented in the pages that follow. As a career consultant, I've been inspired by their hopes, their dreams, and their accomplishments. It is truly what keeps me motivated. There is nothing more satisfying than hearing about the life-changing moments that often began with a resume.

Additionally, I would like to thank:

Matthew Carnnicelli from CLM for providing the guidance and direction that helped get this book published.

Maria Gagliano from Prentice Hall Press, whose wise counsel and even wiser editing helped make the book a reality.

Courtney Pike, not only for her help on the book itself—it would not have happened without her—but also for her dedication, commitment, and passion for JobBound.

Gloria Mueller from Glenbrook South High School for being my ultimate evangelist and for spreading the JobBound word.

Mike Sciola from Wesleyan University for providing some extraordinary career counseling well more than twenty years past my graduation date. The collective careers of my alma mater are in good hands!

Milo Karsh, my young son, who provided me with so many fun cuddle breaks during the writing of this book.

And most important, to my wife, Lisa, who supports, cares, and loves more than she can ever imagine.

# CONTENTS

# Appendices

# INTRODUCTION

When it's time to start looking for a new job, the first thing job seekers think about is their resume. For better or for worse, this single sheet of paper is one of the most important tools to getting a job. All of your work experience, all of your education, and all of the things that make you great have to be condensed onto this piece of paper. It's kind of scary when you think about it!

But have no fear. We are here to help.

In my career as a recruiting director at Leo Burnett Advertising—one of the largest advertising agencies in the world—I read tens of thousands of resumes. The sad truth is, most of the resumes I read were bad. In fact, I threw away about 50 percent of the resumes I received in less than five seconds! I know what you're thinking: "That wouldn't be my resume." However, chances are it would. No one sends out a resume assuming it will be pitched in the garbage in a few seconds.

The vast majority of the remaining resumes weren't as good as they could have been.

It's not enough just to have information on your resume if you don't tailor it to your specific situation. This book will not help you write a *good* resume. This book will help you write a *great* resume that is tailored to the exact job you want. We will help you realize the importance of thinking about where you are in your career, where you are going, and where you want to be.

Writing a resume is more than just dumping your previous jobs on a piece of paper. Writing a resume is crafting a sales and marketing pitch for *you*. Before writing an advertisement, the two main questions you must ask are:

1. Who am I selling to?
2. What makes what I'm selling different?

When you're writing your resume, you want to stay on track by remembering and answering those questions. You are marketing yourself to the recruiting director, so you want to keep the recruiting director's interests in mind at all times. Since each company and each recruiting director wants something a little different, you will have to tailor your resume for each job you apply for. In creating your resume, you want to focus on the employer's needs, not yours. One size does not fit all when it comes to resumes. If you are serious about the job search, you will have a few variations of your resume, targeted to different companies.

You also want to think about what makes you different and special, to tailor your resume to market yourself successfully. What makes you stand out from hundreds of candidates? What unique experiences, situations, or skills do you have to sell?

This book will walk you through the process of creating and tailoring an amazing resume that presents you as the best possible hire for the exact job that you want.

Your resume is your most important job search tool. You know that, though. That is why you are reading this book. Our goal is to make your resume one of the select few that get noticed and chosen as the best of the best.

**Why are resumes so important?** The simple truth is that your resume is your introduction to a company—in essence, your calling card. It isn't logistically possible for companies to meet every single person who applies for a job, so they rely on the resume to do the work for them. A recruiting director has to make a snap judgment about you before he or she makes the commitment to an interview. That's why the resume is so important. It is literally the only means you have to get selected by a company.

**What exactly do recruiting directors want to see when they look at a resume?** I can't tell you the number of times I've been asked that question. Figuring out what will get you hired is the holy grail of the job search.

Today is your lucky day, because you are about to hear from inside the recruiting department the secrets that most people never get a chance to learn.

# What Qualities Are Recruiting Directors Looking for in a Resume?

## 1. The essential job qualifications

Can you do the job? That is the question that all recruiting directors ask when looking at a resume. If they want someone with five years of sales experience, they are looking for at least five years of sales experience on your resume. It sounds simple, but you would be shocked at how many people fail to highlight the basic job requirements on a resume.

Recruiting directors are looking for the "easy" hire. They want to fit a round peg into a round hole. When they are tasked by their internal teams to hire someone, the first thing they are looking for is someone who matches up well with the job description. Now, that is not to say that they will not take a risk every now and then. They may hire the person with just four years of sales experience, but the person with the essential job qualifications is always in a good spot.

## 2. Achievement

It is one thing to do a job, and it is another to do a job well. Recruiting directors want to see proof of your success. When they're looking at a stack of resumes, many of them start to look the same—especially if candidates simply are listing job descriptions and not a sample of their job accomplishments. If I am hiring for a senior financial analyst and most of my candidates are current financial analysts, I want to see what makes each candidate unique. Unfortunately, the first bullet point on virtually every resume for a financial analyst says:

- Prepared financial reports

Of course you did! You are a financial analyst. Here is what recruiting directors want to know:

- Did you save the company money?
- Did you improve any processes?
- Did you win any awards or commendation?

Show your individuality by taking the opportunity to spell out your accomplishments in your resume.

## 3. A strong career path

Continuous growth and advancement without too many company changes sends a compelling signal of potential to a recruiting director. Job hopping, year after year, is usually viewed negatively by recruiting directors. If you've had six jobs in four years, then you are basically saying that you don't commit. You may have great excuses as to why you left each job, but recruiting directors assume that you would likely leave their company as well. You do not need to work at only one company for twenty years, but some level of stability and growth is important.

That being said, you're not doomed if you have held several different jobs throughout your career. Even if numerous companies dot your work history, there are compelling ways you can package and sell yourself. Fortunately, this book will help provide tangible tips for making the most out of your career path. Check out the chapter dedicated to the "Frequent Job Changer," which begins on page 75.

## 4. Well-rounded attributes

Although it is a broad term, it is always nice to find a candidate who is "well rounded." In other words, beyond your career history, what else do you bring to the party? Where you went to college becomes less important as you climb the corporate ladder, but a good education from a quality school never hurts. In addition, involvement outside of the office is a positive aspect. Perhaps you volunteer at a charitable organization, sit on the board of your condo development, or play the trumpet in a weekend orchestra. These extracurricular or professional development endeavors present you as a balanced, driven individual.

In summary, you will do well in the job search if you can show these four traits:

- Job qualification
- Achievement
- Strong career path
- Well-rounded attributes

In a perfect world, you would have the ideal mix and balance of all of these traits. But the truth is that it's not a perfect world out there. Many of us are not overqualified, highly accomplished, well-rounded, and driven superheroes. Maybe you hated your last job, so you don't have countless achievements to showcase. Maybe you want to change careers, so your qualifications are lacking, or maybe you like to ring in every new year with a new job.

We feel your pain. Fortunately, this book has advice for each person and every different situation. Even if you are lacking in one of the areas listed above, you can create a resume that demands attention and showcases your qualifications.

And for all the superheroes out there reading this book, don't assume you have it made, either. It is one thing to have the background and the skills to do the job, but you also have to make sure you exhibit that on your resume.

Let's talk specifically about how to write a great resume.

# How Do You Write a Great Resume?

## 1. Do your homework and craft a plan

You may have thought that you were done with homework once you entered the working world, but you have to do some prep work before writing a great resume. First, you want to research the company you're applying to and read the job description thoroughly. Check out the specific skills and attributes they are looking for. Do you have the qualities that they mention? Do you have the experiences that will make you an easy hire?

After getting a good idea of what the company is seeking, do a brainstorming exercise that will help you match your credentials with the job description and required skills. Write one job description or job responsibility at the top of a page, and then begin brainstorming things you have accomplished or experienced that match that qualification. For example:

**MUST HAVE EXCELLENT VERBAL AND WRITTEN COMMUNICATION SKILLS**

Presented new marketing plan to 15 members of management—

    J. Pope Marketing

Wrote four proposals that won company new business—

    J. Pope Marketing

Maintained client relationships in four different regions—

    Jonah & Sky, Inc.

Prepared quarterly status reports for executive management—

    Jonah & Sky, Inc.

**LOOKING FOR MANAGER TO CREATE CULTURE**

**OF ACCOUNTABILITY AND TEAMWORK**

Responsible for twelve direct reports—J. Pope Marketing

Team won four out of five pitches and awarded biggest account—

    J. Pope Marketing

Received 2008 "Best Boss" Award—Jonah & Sky, Inc.

Promoted to manager after five months—Jonah & Sky, Inc.

Managed 40 volunteers for charitable gala event—St. Jude Children's

    Hospital volunteer

During your brainstorming, you don't need to word everything perfectly. You just want to get your thoughts flowing on how you can tailor your resume and be the perfect fit for the job. This material will serve as the fodder for your resume. Remember that you can pull some experiences from your extracurricular or volunteer activities as well.

If you are making a career change, then this stage is especially important. You need to be creative in thinking about what you did in your past jobs that will apply to the job requirements of the new position you are seeking. There are lots of great examples on how to do this in the "Career Change" chapter.

Again, recruiting directors want to put a round peg into a round hole. They want to hire someone they know, from the first glance, can handle the basic job responsibilities. By going through this planning stage—for whatever job you are applying for—you can make sure your resume is tailored to the job you want. The recruiting director is not going to look twice at your resume if it doesn't reflect the qualifications that the company needs.

## 2. Keep it short and powerful

Short is better than long. Here's the problem: You have a lot to say, but recruiting directors don't have the time to hear it. Rarely would I pick up a resume and say, "Wow, I really wish this resume was one page longer!" However, I often would pick one up and say, "Wow, this is way too long, there is no way I am going to read all of this."

A resume does not need to be your life story. You simply need to tell recruiting directors enough information to get you hired. You don't have to tell them *everything*.

Think about it like a print advertisement you would see in a magazine. When you see an ad for a product like Tide detergent, it does *not* say the following:

- Tide comes in a powder.
- Tide comes in a liquid.
- Tide is available at grocery stores.
- Tide is available at convenience stores.
- Tide is available at Target and Wal-Mart.
- Tide works on colors.
- Tide works on whites.
- Tide smells nice.
- Tide was invented in 1887 by Milo Jay Tide III.
- Tide will get your clothes clean.

The ad just tells you why you should buy Tide detergent. It might be nice to know all that other stuff, and some of it may be meaningful to the folks at Tide. However, going into it all is not relevant or prudent given the space restrictions and limited time Tide has to catch your attention in an ad.

Think about your resume in the same light. You may have accomplished a lot, but you only have a limited amount of time to present your message to recruiting directors. Determine what you want them to know and see in their fifteen-second scan. In general, that means you should put the greatest emphasis on your most recent and most relevant experiences.

If you have twenty years of work experience, the recruiting director does not need to know the details of your administrative job after college. If one of your past jobs is irrelevant to the job you are seeking, you don't have to include any bullet points under the position. There is no rule that says you must describe every detail of your work history.

More seasoned job seekers will want to focus a majority of their resume on the most recent ten to fifteen years—unless of course they have some extremely relevant experiences that go beyond fifteen years. Now, that's not to say you shouldn't list any jobs from beyond the past dozen years or so. It means you should simply list those jobs on your resume but not include any bullet points.

Recent graduates and students will want to think of their resume as a rolling four-year document. As such, seniors in college should not list anything from high school. If you've been working full-time for two years, you'll only want to include college internships from junior and senior year. Of course, the obvious exception would be an experience that is incredibly relevant from beyond four years.

**You should not write full sentences on your resume.** Recruiting directors want to see bullet points that quickly and succinctly detail your work experiences. Remember, recruiting directors are scanning hundreds of resumes—all at once—and they are looking quickly to see if you merit more than an initial fifteen-second glance.

You should never use first person or third person on your resume. Full sentences make your resume overwhelming to review and difficult to read.

Each bullet point in your list of experiences should start with an action verb, and each action verb should be different and powerful. We've included a list of action verbs in the appendix as a reference.

You can use commas to your advantage to make the bullet points crisper and more concise. Here's an example of how you can make a wordy description succinct and potent:

**Bad:** I was in charge of the charity event for the entire city attended by 800 people that was so successful we raised $21,000

**Good:** Orchestrated citywide charity event attended by 800 people, raising over $21,000

Which one is easier to read? Which is more powerful? Bullet points and impact words make accomplishments jump out in the recruiting director's quick scan.

**Your resume should not be more than two pages** (with a rare exception). A curriculum vitae or CV is usually longer than two pages, but it is used primarily when applying for academic or scientific positions when all course work, publications, and presentations must be listed.

For a resume, this is a solid guideline to follow: If you have worked less than four years, you should have a one-page resume. After you have gained more than four years of experience, you can (but don't have to) use a two-page resume.

Even most Fortune 500 CEOs have only a one- or two-page resume. Once again, recruiting directors do not want to read a resume novel. Short and concise writing is more powerful than long, flowery prose.

## 3. Focus on your accomplishments and results

Most people's resumes are actually lists of job descriptions. This is the single biggest mistake that virtually all job seekers make. In essence, they describe not specifically what they did in each job they've had, but what anyone would have done in that position. Here is an example:

**Sales Representative**, *Drab Shark, LLC,* Middletown, CT, 2007–Present
- Sold manufacturing components to clients throughout
  New England
- Developed and maintained solid relationships with all customers
- Created call lists and scheduled in-person visits
- Managed personal budget and prepared reports

Now, that may sound good, but unfortunately, every sales representative in the history of Drab Shark—or any company for that matter—does those exact same things! The author of this resume simply wrote a job description for a sales rep. Undoubtedly, the reader of the resume will be familiar with what a sales rep does.

The key to a great resume is to focus on what *you* specifically accomplished. What did *you* do that was unique, special, different, or distinctive? What made *you* stand out?

The best way to do this is by thinking about your achievements. Accomplishments come in two forms: scope and results.

*Scope*

How big?

How much?

How many?

How often?

*Results*

Did you grow sales?

Did you save the company money?

Were you recognized for your achievement?

Did you create something new?

As you can guess from these questions, you get accomplishments through numbers, data, and tangible facts. You want to be as specific as you can in everything you write.

Let's look at a new version of the sample above. Same person, same job, but a very different resume:

**Sales Representative,** *Drab Shark, LLC,* Middletown, CT, 2007–Present

- Sold $35 million in manufacturing components to more than 1,200 clients throughout New England
- Ranked third out of 29 national sales representatives
- Exceeded company mandated goals by 9%
- Personally secured more than 400 new customers through dedicated cold calling and in-person visits
- Managed a budget of $35,000 annually, decreasing spending by 13%
- Prepared dozens of comprehensive summary reports delivered monthly to national VP of sales

Sounds quite a bit better, doesn't it? This is the number one key to writing a great resume.

**Don't be afraid to toot your own horn.** The job search is no place to downplay your accomplishments. If you aren't going to showcase your accomplishments, then no one will. Of course, you shouldn't be blustering and arrogant, but you should present a confidence and assurance in your abilities. If you worked with big-name clients or high-profile accounts, drop the names on your resume. You shouldn't be timid in saying you worked on the GE account, that you were a consultant for IBM, or you booked a client on *The Oprah Winfrey Show.* Dropping big names simply catches the recruiting director's eye and prompts a more in-depth review of your resume.

**Keep notes on your job accomplishments.** Ideally, you should update your resume at least every six months. But how many people actually do it? Not many.

It is so easy to forget about your accomplishments if years go by without any updates. I can't tell you how many times we work with clients that say they did some amazing things in the past—but just can't remember any of the details.

When that next offer comes along, you definitely want to have your resume ready to go. You never know when a friend, family member, or colleague might tell you about the opportunity of a lifetime. If you have to spend days and weeks trying to put your resume together, you could miss out.

Especially if you work for the same company for numerous years, it's easy for the years and your achievements to blur. If you don't update your resume, you should keep notes on all of your duties, projects, and achievements—particularily the numbers. That way, when it's time to update your resume or change jobs, you have all the necessary information on hand and top-of-mind.

• • •

Now that you know what you should and should not write on your resume, let's talk about the different sections.

# Sections of Your Resume

## 1. Contact information

All of your contact information should be at the top of your resume. Obviously, you want a recruiting director to be able to get in touch with you. You want to include:

**Your name.** You don't have to give your birth name if that's not the name you use. If your name is Mary Kate Elliot, but you go by Katy, then you should put Katy Elliot on your resume. If you have a two-page resume, it's a good idea to include your name on the second page as well.

**Your current address.** If you are a college student, you should choose one address—either your school address or your home address.

**Your cell or home phone number.** You want to include the best number where you can be reached. A recruiting director will be calling you, so make sure your voice-mail message is appropriate and professional.

**Your personal email address.** Do not include your work email address! Make sure your email address is professional-sounding. A recruiting director doesn't want to hire sportychick22@hotmail.com or whiskeydude@yahoo .com.

## 2. Objective

In most cases, you don't need an objective on your resume. If you are applying for a specific job at a specific company, you do not need an objective. Obviously, your objective is to get that job. Yet time and time again, we see long, flowery objective statements like this:

> Hardworking strategic thinker looking to use my exceptional communication, leadership, and creative problem-solving skills in a growing and dynamic organization

On the surface, that may sound good, but let's really think about what's written there. That statement is full of "self-ascribed attributes."

According to *you*, you are a hard worker, a strategic thinker, and a great communicator. In truth, anyone can write that on a resume. There is no test you take to prove that you are a hard worker.

As a result, these personal manifestos mean absolutely nothing to recruiting directors looking at your resume. They simply don't believe you. If you were not a hard worker, would you write this:

> Lazy worker looking to do the least amount of work for the most amount of money. Prefer boss that stays out of my face and lets me do what I want.

That being said, you will need an objective if you are applying for a job at a company and you don't know if they have an opening. In those instances, you should have a very specific and simple objective, such as:

To obtain a position as an IT Specialist at Pepsi

That way, whoever receives your resume will know where to forward it.

## 3. Summary of qualifications

Sometimes you need one, and sometimes you do not. Students, and professionals with less than four years of full-time work experience, should not have a summary. At the risk of being obvious, there is not much to summarize!

The only job seekers who need a summary are those with a two-page resume or those who are thinking about a career change and their most recent work experience is not directly related to the job they want.

A summary statement can work to the benefit of those who have been working for a while, especially if they have great experiences that occurred prior to their last job. In other words, you can highlight the good stuff that is on page two of your resume.

Just as with an objective statement, you must avoid the self-ascribed attributes. Make sure you back every statement up with support for your claim.

**Bad:** Great communication skills

**Good:** Great communication skills having delivered more than 50 presentations to audiences as large as 100

**Bad:** Strong and proven leader

**Good:** Seasoned manager with experience managing diverse groups of up to 12 associates across two branch locations

The key to a summary section is to keep it short, relevant, and results-oriented. We recommend you list four or five summary points. Here's a little trick when it comes to deciding which ones. Look at the job description and match up your experiences with that description. As we mentioned before, recruiting directors want to make the obvious and easy hire. If they say they are looking for someone with nine years of IT experience, then your first summary point can say:

> Seasoned IT professional with more than ten years of experience working for Fortune 500 companies

If they say they want a track record of success in launching new software programs internally, you say:

> Successfully launched and implemented company's largest-ever Microsoft upgrade spanning more than 2,500 units in less than 2 weeks

Do you get the idea?

Now, of course, you can't lie if you don't have the experience, but if you do, try to make yourself look like the perfect person for the job from the start.

You will see some great examples in this book, but that is how you want to think about a summary of qualifications.

## 4. Experience

This is arguably the most important section of the resume. The key point is the one we constantly highlight: focus on accomplishments rather than job descriptions. We can't stress that enough. Force yourself to make sure your resume is full of accomplishments and achievements.

Now the details:

Make sure you use headings in your list of jobs, and order them from most to least important.

Often, people start with the dates:

April 2004–June 2009 Eos Entertainment, Los Angeles, CA, Director of
Marketing

The fact of the matter is, dates are the least important thing; they should be listed last.

No one will pick up this resume and say, "Wow, April 2004 to June 2009." However, they may pick it up and say, "Wow, Director of Marketing . . . we're looking for this."

List headings all on one line. Begin with what is most important to the reader—either your title or the company. Choose the one that is most relevant, but make sure you keep it consistent throughout the resume. It should be either your title always first or the company always first. Bold the first of them, underline the second, and leave the rest of the entry in regular type.

Here is an example:

**Director of Marketing**, <u>Eos Entertainment</u>, Los Angeles, CA, April 2004–June 2009

There is no magic number of bullet points necessary for each job. You will, however, go into more detail and have more substance for the most recent and/ or most relevant jobs.

If you have been working at least ten years, you put fewer (or no) bullet points for jobs in your distant past. At this point, recruiting directors do not care that you spearheaded your company's IT migration to Samna Pro word processing in 1984!

The key for the experience section is to unearth "nuggets" that are specific and relevant for the jobs you are pursuing.

- What are you most proud of?
- What special projects did you do?
- What did you accomplish that is different from the person who did the job before you or after you?

For example, if you wrote press releases, how many did you write? What publications were they sent to and did anybody pick them up? Instead of a point that says:

Wrote press releases

have one that reads:

Wrote eight press releases distributed to more than 15 regional and local papers, securing placement in the *Chicago Tribune*, *Chicago Sun-Times* and *Indianapolis Star.*

In many ways, the experience section is like an in-depth interview.

The experience section does not have to be chronological, nor should it only include paid jobs or internships. Think about what the company is looking for and match that to what you've done.

Often, for students, leadership experiences in clubs and organizations are more important than being a waiter at Applebee's.

Likewise, professionals can also include volunteer and nonprofit activity in their experience section if the activity is notable and relevant.

## 5. Education

If you are a student, put your education information at the top of your resume. If you are a professional, your work experience trumps your education, so your education section should be at the end of your resume.

The only time that professionals should put their education first is if one of the following applies:

1. The major or degree is more relevant than the job experiences.
2. They returned to school to acquire an additional degree, and the new degree is the most relevant thing on the resume.

If you are a professional who has returned to school to get an MBA, a master's of another kind, or any relevant degree, then your education should be the first thing a recruiting director sees. You want to call attention to your new degree because, in many instances, it automatically qualifies you for a higher position or a higher salary. You can also include any prestigious awards and your GPA if it is over a 3.0.

Other professionals, who didn't recently get an advanced degree, should simply include their school name and degree at the end of their resume. If you are concerned about age discrimination, you do not need to include your graduation year. After you have been in the workforce for a few years, collegiate awards, scholarships, and GPA are less important.

If you haven't yet completed your degree, include all the education information and your expected graduation date.

## 6. Computer (and other) skills

Like the summary of qualifications, this section will work for some but not all of you. If you are going into a specialized field like IT or graphic design, then you definitely want to list your relevant computer skills. Similarly, if a job description asks for any specific computer skills, then you can list them.

At this point in history, you certainly do not need to list basic computer skills. Many resumes we receive will list Microsoft Word, PowerPoint and Excel, but let's be honest, for most jobs, the employer will assume you know those basic skills. Think about how we mentioned the limited amount of time someone has to read a resume and that person's desire to hit the "Wow" factor fast. I doubt anyone will pick up your resume and say, "Wow, she knows Internet Explorer!"

## 7. Activities, interests, boards, et cetera

The last section of your resume covers what you do outside of the office. This is an optional section. If you are involved in outside activities, it is typically a good idea to let your potential employer know that. It can be a plus to show how well rounded you are. Usually, this is a bullet point section with one item per line. Be wary of the activities you choose to list though. It can be risky to include political or religious groups. You also want to make sure you don't list potentially weird-sounding stuff like your membership in the Alien Worshipping Association of America! You will see some nice examples of how this works in our sample resumes.

This section is a clearinghouse for activities, clubs, associations, and volunteer work. Simply list the organization, the role, and the year.

• American Advertising Federation, Member, 2005–Present

You can also use the last line of your resume to list your interests, to help "round you out" as a candidate. The last line could read:

• Interests include: hiking, adventure races, travel, and Audi sports cars

You can put in one "funny" one at the end as an icebreaker. If you are applying for a job in a conservative field or need the extra line on your resume, you can eliminate the interests line altogether.

## References

Do not waste a valuable line at the end of your resume to say "References Available Upon Request." Well, of course they are. Don't use that space to state the obvious. If the employer wants references, they will request them whether you have that line on your resume or not.

# Resume Format and Visual Impact

Your resume needs to be easy to read. Sure that seems pretty obvious, but you'd be shocked at how few resumes we receive that are well designed and laid out correctly.

There are a few techniques you can employ to make sure your resume is formatted professionally and in a visually pleasing manner.

## Beware the resume template

There are many resume templates using Word or fancy applications that seem to make the resume writing process seamless. Unfortunately, the majority of those templates are bad.

First, most templates do not maximize space, and you end up with a resume that is overflowing with white space. You don't want your resume to be too cluttered, but you want every line and space to count.

Second, resume templates are difficult to alter. Often, they format the cells to begin with the dates of employment as the first item listed on the left. However, you now know that that the dates are the least important part of the entry and should go on the right. Just try rearranging the cells; it's a nightmare!

## White space

You don't want too much white space on your resume, or you'll end up with a four-page resume. However, too little white space makes your resume difficult to read. You can expand the margins to maximize space, but you never want to make the margins less than .75". You also want to break up your jobs and resume sections with a line of white space. It gives the eye a rest, makes the resume visually appealing, and carries you to the next point.

## Font

You do not have to use a certain font type, but the serif fonts are usually the easiest to read and the most professional. A few safe bets are:

Times New Roman
Garamond
Century
Goudy Old Style

Each font looks different, so the type size should be adjusted according to the font style. For the most part, anything smaller than a 9-point font is too small, and anything larger than a 12-point font is too big. The best test is to print it out and let a few people read it.

Use bold, italics, and underlining to make items on your resume pop. You can bold your titles, underline your company names, and italicize accounts you worked on or a description of the company you worked at. These are personal decisions; you just want to remain consistent throughout your resume, and you certainly don't want the resume to look like you went crazy with the **B**, *I*, and <u>U</u> buttons. Our sample resumes throughout the book will give you a solid idea of what works.

## Avoid

Gimmicks, fancy paper, and odd layouts. Laminated resumes on purple paper with glitter tell the recruiting director that there isn't much substance in the content. Print your resume on a nice quality paper of a modest hue—white, light blue, beige, or soft gray, for example.

## Fifteen-second test

To test the readability of your resume, give it to a friend or colleague to view for only fifteen seconds. What does your friend notice? Did your friend catch what you want the recruiting director to catch? This is a great technique to make sure you are getting your main points across.

# Special Tips for Online Resumes

When it was time to get my first job, I took my typed resume to a printer who had to set the type and make one hundred hard copies. Gone are those days! With online job postings, job boards, online company career centers, and email, most resumes are submitted digitally. What are some of the rules for electronic resumes?

## 1. Be wary of formatting issues

Most online resumes are uploaded in plain text, so all your beautiful bold, italic, underscored, and bulleted words will not be formatted. It is safest to use a standard style font, and always preview or email yourself before sending your resume to the recruiting director. Here are some more suggestions:

- Use UPPERCASE letters in place of **bold** headings.
- Create bullets by using dashes—or stars *.
- Save your resume in Notepad or plain text.

## 2. Include your cover letter in the body of the email and attach your resume as a Word document

As soon as you write the word "attached" in the body of your email, attach your resume! There is nothing worse than having to send a second email with the heading "Oops. Here it is."

## 3. Check the site's policies before posting

There are some very trusty job board sites like Monster, CareerBuilder, Yahoo! HotJobs, Dice, and so forth. However, there are a lot of schlocky sites as well! Be wary if the website says they will "blast" your resume out to all the hottest job boards. You do not want them blasting your resume and contact information to just anyone.

## 4. Always follow up with a phone call to make sure the person received your resume

Spam filters are abundant these days. When applying for a job, it's appropriate to follow up in a week to ensure that the employer received your resume. A simple call or email will suffice. However, do not fret when the company does not get back to you, and do not continue to call and email after the first contact. Given the flood of resumes, it's impossible for a recruiting director to reply to all those calls and emails.

## 5. Make sure your online profiles on social networks are professional

Many employers are using the Internet to help them make hiring decisions. Resumes aren't the only job screening tool, since ample information can be discovered on Google, Facebook, MySpace, and LinkedIn. Social networking sites can be wonderful tools for your job search and your career. Connecting with colleagues, future business partners, and potential employers is a great way to use social networks to your advantage. On the flip side, just as you may seek out potential employers online, companies are using social networks to check you out as well. Make sure your photos, interests, and personal information present you in a professional light.

•　•　•

Now that you have a solid background on what makes a good resume, let's jump into the real deal! What follows are some of the absolute best resumes that we have written at JobBound. They represent a variety of different fields, experience levels, and designs.

That is one thing you notice about JobBound resumes—each one is custom-tailored for the individual job seeker. While the fonts may look similar, the content is always different. We look at each person's situation and craft the single best resume for it. Some examples in the following pages represent people looking for a career change, while others represent those simply seeking an internal promotion.

With each resume, we reveal both the *before* AND the *after* version. We point out what we did and why we made the changes. You may notice that the *before* version is written just like your current resume. The changes between the versions are significant. With the new and improved resumes, candidates were able to secure a new job faster, gain a promotion, and get a higher starting salary.

Thoroughly read each resume to see the differences. Put yourself in the shoes of a recruiting director. Would you want to interview this candidate? How does the resume sound? What specific skills can you see in that person? By thinking about these questions, you will recognize the dramatic differences between the *before* and *after* versions.

You can learn something from each and every resume. We divided the resumes according to some specific job search situations, but we employ universal techniques for improving a resume. We all have different reasons we are looking for a job, and we all have different obstacles, goals, and experiences. Each situation and each resume presents a unique learning opportunity.

You may find that you relate most specifically to a few of the situations, so read those sections with special care. Also know that we add tips and overarching themes so you can learn from each and every *before* and *after* resume.

Let's take a look!

# THE CAREER CHANGE

Years ago, there were not many job changes, much less many "career changes." Most people got a job and worked at that company for thirty-five years until they retired with their gold watch.

People worked to have money to pay the bills, and there wasn't this idea that you were defined by your work. Today, we're more likely to search for meaning, fulfillment, and purpose in our jobs. People try on numerous different jobs and careers searching for that dream job that brings them happiness and fortune.

Nowadays, it is not odd for a person to have several different careers in one lifetime. Recruiting directors are becoming more attuned to and aware of this trend, so it is not as difficult to make a career change if you go about it the right way.

As I've said before, a recruiting director wants to put a round peg in a round hole. Hiring has high costs in terms of both time and money. Recruiting directors have neither the time nor the financial resources to hire people that cannot get the job done.

There are a few secrets to making a successful career change:

## 1. Gain relevant experiences

You want to get experiences outside of your current line of work that directly relate to the job you want. If you know you want to leave your banking job to write for your favorite travel magazine, start writing on the side and building your portfolio. If you want to switch from teaching to event planning, plan your class's graduation event to gain relevant experience. And if you want to leave journalism for marketing, look into your newspaper's marketing department before heading out.

You can also take classes, pick up new hobbies, or join industry organizations to acquire relevant skills and get in tune with the environment of your new field.

## 2. Create a summary section on your resume or highlight transferable skills

A summary can be a great way to show relevant skills when you don't have the exact background a company is seeking. If you list your most recent job first, you may throw off the recruiting director. By starting with a summary, you can actually match what you have done with the job description.

You also want to pinpoint the skills you gained in your past experiences that you can directly parlay into the job you want. Paint a clear picture for recruiting directors. You want them to see the skills and assets you have that transfer smoothly to their industry.

## 3. Make the best out of the experiences

Even if you don't have perfectly relevant experience, you want to sound as good as possible. In addition to hard skills, employers are also looking for soft skills. Things like strong work ethic, accomplishment, communication skills, management skills, and so on. If you show that you have done well in your past jobs, potential employers will see that you can be an asset to their organization.

• • •

Recruiting directors take chances every now and then. Even if you apply for a marketing job with no prior marketing experience, they may hire you if you show the potential. Of course, you are competing against candidates with marketing experience, so you have to go above and beyond to get noticed.

Since career changes are so common today, we've included several *before* and *after* resumes of people who were trying to make a successful one. Read each scenario and then examine how we sell and position the candidate in the *after* version.

# The Career Change

After twelve years of working primarily in corporate America, Mara wanted to move into the not-for-profit world. It's always tough when you want to change careers as a more experienced worker, but it can be done.

This is the JobBound strategy we used for Mara.

## 1. Highlighted not-for-profit experience

Mara had done some wonderful things for the Harbor Emergency Center for Girls, but she hadn't even listed it on her resume! Often, job candidates think that if they didn't get paid to do something, they can't put it on their resume. If they place it on their resume, they usually shove it in at the bottom in an obscure section called "other experience."

This is simply not the truth. Especially in the case of Mara, she needed to highlight her volunteer work in the "meat" of her resume. Remember, recruiting directors read a resume just like you read anything—top to bottom. Since they scan resumes quickly, if the first few entries do not appeal to them, they throw the resume away. We could not take the chance that they would miss Mara's great volunteer work. We put it right at the top.

## 2. Created a summary

By starting with a summary, we were able to match Mara's experiences with the job description. Even through she didn't have the extensive background they were seeking, we showed her relevant skills right at the top.

## 3. Emphasized her transferable skills and achievements

Although Mara didn't have perfectly relevant experience, we wanted to make it sound as good as possible. Mara was a team player, a solid communicator, and a natural leader. She had the soft skills to excel at any job. Also, because we showed that she did well in her jobs, potential employers could see that she could be an asset to their organization.

• • •

Take a look and see for yourself. The *after* version looks quite a bit better.

# Mara Malone

5267 North Kilpatrick Kansas City, Kansas 57834 (556) 227-3489 (H) (556) 987-3345 (W)

## OBJECTIVE

To secure a position that will give me the opportunity to develop new skills and strengthen my problem solving, evaluation and fundraising skills.

## Education

University of Tennessee
Knoxville, TN
      Masters of Science in Social Work, Administration and Planning Concentration,
May 1995

Towson State University
Towson, MD
      Bachelor of Science in Psychology, Counseling Concentration.
      September 1990

Institute for Communication Improvement–The Grant Institute
      Received a certificate in Professional Grant Proposal Writing
      April 2004

## Professional Experience

**CK,** Chicago                         March 2000–Present
      Assistant Media Planner

- Assist with publication research for the agency's clients.
- Conduct research to garner information about competitors
- Assist with developing the competitive analysis
- Monitor the cost of placed advertisements and resolve any discrepancies
- Ensure the proper placement of our client's advertisements

**State of Illinois**                March 1997–March 2000
Illinois Department of Human Services, Chicago
      Special Projects Coordinator (November 1997–March 2000)

- Plan and supervise special events for the Secretary of the Department of Human Services and write talking points
- Developed programs to assist disadvantaged families statewide
- Write responses to complaint letters
- Write informational brochures for medical assistance recipients
- Develop relationships with local employers on behalf of disadvantage families

Central Management Services, Chicago, IL
      Public Administration Intern, (March 1997–November 1997)

- Plan and attend outreach programs
- Schedule and coordinate bi-monthly board meetings
- Provide bid information to business owners
- Manage the daily operations of small office, and the activities of the Executive Director.

**Jewish Federation of Metropolitan Chicago, Chicago, IL**

      Program Specialist, (August 1995–March 1997)

- Disseminate information to Consortium Agencies

- Issues statewide request for proposals
- Review Federal and State legislation related to refugee issues
- Develop recommendations concerning technical assistance, funding and program design for Consortium agencies
- Review request for proposals for funding

## Knoxville Area Urban League, Knoxville, TN

Student Intern, (August 1994–May 1995)
- Develop program policies
- Grant writing
- Develop agency newsletter
- Conduct evaluations of agency programs
- Provide management assistance and board development for local day care center
- Network with community organizations

## Grassroots Crisis Intervention Center, Columbia, MD January 1992–July 1993

Transitional Housing Counselor (August 1992–July 1993)
- Connect clients to housing resources
- Provide financial management assistance
- Assist clients in obtaining career goals
- Connect clients to social service agencies
- Manage daily operation of 6 room shelter

Emergency Shelter Counselor (January 1992–July 1992)
- Conduct Intake Interviews
- Network with agencies providing long term affordable housing
- Provide crisis intervention

## Fellowship of Lights, Baltimore, MD

Youth Counselor (September 1990–January 1992)
- Supervise evening activities of one to 14 teenagers
- Network with agencies that provide foster care
- Answer hotline calls

Professional Accomplishments _____
- Develop programs from conception to completion
- Wrote information for distribution to the general public
- Assisted with the development of internal communications procedures

Skills _____
- WordPerfect and Microsoft Word
- Quattro Pro and Excel
- Grant writing and research
- Power Point

REFERENECES FURNISHED UPON REQUEST

# Mara Malone

5267 North Kilpatrick ♦ Kansas City, Kansas 57834
556.227.3489 ♦ mmalone@yahoo.com

## SUMMARY

- Passionate, 12-year, not-for-profit professional with Masters in Social Work
- Seasoned administrator with extensive background working for state, local, and privately funded not-for-profit organizations
- Exceptional written communication skills with history of grant writing, grant writing certificate, and more than 50 examples of brochure, newsletter, and other written work
- Dedicated "agent of change" having launched more than seven new programs and successfully sold dozens of new ideas

## EXPERIENCE

**CK,** ASSISTANT MEDIA PLANNER, Chicago, IL, 2000–Present
*Hyatt Hotels, AirTran Airways, La Quinta*
- Help compile magazine demographic composition information for more than 15 publications, used to determine Hyatt magazine buy
- Prepare quarterly competitive analyses tracking all media activity for 17 key brands
- Reconcile more than $245,000 in annual billings for four clients resolving all invoice discrepancies across 130 media vehicles
- Insure accurate placement of more than 200 executions across print, broadcast, and online
- Provided competitive support data used on winning La Quinta new business pitch

**THE HARBOR EMERGENCY CENTER,** COUNSELOR, Chicago, IL, 2002–Present
- Plan dozens of events for teenage girls in need
- Work part-time overnight shift in addition to full-time day job
- Counsel girls on variety of topics including personal issues and careers

**STATE OF ILLINOIS,** Chicago, IL, 1997–2000

*ILLINOIS DEPT. OF HUMAN SERVICES*, SPECIAL PROJECTS COORDINATOR, 1997–2000
- Planned, organized, and executed three special events throughout the state attended by Secretary of Human Services
- Created and implemented agency's first-ever customer service program providing local office jobs for long-term welfare recipients
- Overhauled medical assistance communication efforts writing 20-page brochure used statewide
- Contacted more than 20 local companies seeking employment for disadvantaged families
- Developed unique department resource fair, educating more than 100 constituents about services, jobs and day-care options

*CENTRAL MANAGEMENT SERVICES*, PUBLIC ADMINISTRATION INTERN, 1997–1997
- Planned two outreach program events for potential minority state contractors
- Prepared four bid requests totaling $750,000 distributed to minority business owners statewide
- Managed the daily operations of an office of six and the activities of the Executive Director

**JEWISH FEDERATION OF CHICAGO,** PROGRAM SPECIALIST, 1995–1997
- Wrote employment, funding, and regulatory materials disseminated to 16 consortium agencies
- Issued and reviewed proposals helping distribute funding across several statewide agencies
- Reviewed dozens of pieces of refugee-related federal and state legislation creating "call to action" letters distributed to local legislators
- Developed job-related recommendations for consortium agencies helping them employ more than 200 refugees over two years

**KNOXVILLE URBAN LEAGUE,** INTERN, 1994–1995
- Developed organization's first-ever policies and procedures manual outlining all program operations for agency serving community of several thousand
- Wrote grant requesting funding from Levi-Strauss to help support 24-hour day-care center
- Created a monthly agency newsletter distributed to organizations throughout the city
- Prepared and launched agency's first evaluation tool surveying program participants on a host of organization initiatives
- Provided management assistance and board development for local day-care center

**GRASSROOTS CRISIS CENTER,** TRANSITIONAL COUNSELOR, Columbia, MD, 1992–1993
- Connected more than 100 clients to dozens of housing resources citywide
- Developed training program to provide financial management assistance to shelter residents
- Managed all daily operations of six-room shelter
- Promoted from Emergency Shelter Counselor after only seven months

**FELLOWSHIP OF LIGHTS,** YOUTH COUNSELOR, Baltimore, MD, 1990–1992

## EDUCATION

**UNIVERSITY OF TENNESSEE**–KNOXVILLE, TN, 1995
- Master of Science in Social Work; Administration and Planning Concentration

**TOWSON STATE UNIVERSITY**–TOWSON, MD, 1990
- Bachelor of Science in Psychology; Counseling Concentration

**INSTITUTE FOR COMMUNICATION IMPROVEMENT—THE GRANT INSTITUTE,** 2004
- Certificate in Professional Grant Writing

# The Career Change

Sally received a degree in education and was an elementary school teacher. After a few years, she decided she needed a break from teaching. Because she enjoyed helping people, Sally acquired a job in human resources.

After working in human resources at GAP, Sally realized that she loved the industry. Sally wanted to stay in HR, so we really focused on her most recent job experience in her resume.

In fact, we kept the resume to one page and eliminated most of her other jobs that were not relevant to what she wanted to pursue. Even though Sally did a lot of great things while teaching, they weren't compelling to a recruiting director looking for an HR professional.

This is a great lesson: **Remember your target.** You are writing this resume for a recruiting director at a company where you want to work. What you think is relevant and important doesn't matter. All that matters is what that recruiting director thinks is important. Short, direct, and to the point is the way to go.

We beefed up Sally's HR experience by going from seven to eleven bullet points for GAP. Additionally, we also focused on her specific accomplishments. She had done some great things, and we wanted to draw the reader's attention to them.

# Sally Sadofsky
sallysadofsky@hotmail.com

776 Seymour Street #22
South Shire, IL 50621
(212) 539-7132

## Related Job Experience
GAP Assistant Manager, Human Resources, Des Moines, Iowa, 2002–present
- Hiring and training of all new employees
- Organizing, maintaining and updating all employee files
- Informing all employees concerning company policies and procedures
- Serving as liaison between GAP Corporate and retail outlet regarding employee issues
- Resolving personnel conflicts among employees
- Managing payroll for all store employees
- Creating small teams of sales coaches for relaying new product information to new employees

## Other Experiences
Eason Elementary Second Grade Student Teacher, Waukee, Iowa, Spring 2003
- Planned and implemented creative lessons
- Created lessons for a specific math group
- Organized and utilized a science center
- Helped students create stories while introducing the writing process

Heartland Area Education Agency, 2000, 2001, and 2002
- Coordinator for the Physics Olympics

Eason Elementary, Waukee, Iowa, Fall 2001
- Helped tutor students with their book words

Des Moines Public Schools, Summer 2001
- Assisted in planning a science distribution center

## Education
Drake University, Des Moines, Iowa
Bachelor of Science in Elementary Education, May 2003
Endorsement: Elementary Science and Coaching

## Honors, Awards, Licenses
Drake University President's List
Drake University School of Education Dean's List
K-6 Teacher Elem. Classroom and K-6 Science Basic Initial Teaching License, State of Iowa
Athletic Coaching Endorsement, State of Iowa

# Sally Sadofsky

**776 Seymour Street #22 ♦ South Shire, IL 50621**
**212.539.7132 ♦ sallysadofsky@hotmail.com**

## Experience

**Human Resources Assistant Manager,** GAP, Des Moines, IA, 11/02–Present

- Serve as liaison between corporate human resources and local store with more than 30 employees on all HR issues including benefits, recruiting, compensation, training, and workman's compensation
- Recruited and hired more than 40 full-time and part-time staff across three different job titles
- Manage store's entire training program spanning new hire orientation, benefits, sales, and operations for a staff of 36
- Oversee benefits plan including medical, dental, flexible spending, retirement, long and short term disability, employee stock purchase plan, and life insurance
- Overhauled and customized new GAP corporate training program enhancing learning among newest employees
  - Revised format now used at all eight district stores
- Help manage complex payroll process tracking store sales to align goals with weekly employee payments
- Developed "action plans" for four employees addressing a variety of performance issues
- Created and manage store's sales coaches overseeing two associates/trainers teaching all store operations
- Coordinate comprehensive year-long "GAP Giving" program featuring food drives, heart walks and holiday family "adoption"
- Promoted into HR role after beginning as sales associate
- Worked 20–40 hours per week while attending school full time in 2002–2003

**Student Teacher,** Eason Elementary School, Waukee, IA, Spring 2003

- Created specific lesson plans for a math group spanning two classes of second grade students
- Taught six weeks independently following six weeks of student teaching

## Education

**Drake University**—Des Moines, IA, May 2003

- Bachelor of Science in Elementary Education
- Coaching and Elementary Science Endorsement
- Major GPA 3.8/4.0
- President's List for students with semester GPA of 3.5 or above
- School of Education Dean's List

## Activities/Interests

- Coordinator, Physics Olympics, 2000–2002
- State of Iowa Athletic Coaching Endorsement
- Elementary Classroom/Science Basic Initial Teaching License, State of Iowa
- Interests include: travel, hiking, sports, and movie trivia

# The Career Change

First, Taryn's *before* resume really isn't a resume at all. It is simply a listing of her job titles. That is a huge mistake. Companies want to hire people, not simply job titles. Her first resume doesn't distinguish her from any other person who did those exact same jobs. No wonder she had trouble landing a job before she came to JobBound.

Second, Taryn was considering moving into public relations, so we highlighted her writing and media training skills. We didn't use a summary for Taryn because she was moving to a field in which the recruiting director would be very familiar with her previous jobs. She was going from a producer to a PR job. In the PR industry you "pitch" producers to get your story on the air. That was a real benefit for her since she was coming from the "inside." We wanted to make sure the recruiting director saw those jobs first thing in the resume.

We tried to showcase as many of her transferable skills as possible. Even though Taryn did not work at any PR firms, we were able to paint a picture of how she could easily segue into the industry. We highlighted all of her writing and communication skills—not something that's all that typical for a TV producer. From reading the *after* resume, it is easy to see that Taryn has superior communication skills and strong writing skills, and she is able to manage teams and important accounts with success.

In the *after* version, we really focus on what makes Taryn great. We mention all the famous people she booked. We talk about ratings for the show, and we even indicate that she was promoted extremely quickly. Wouldn't you want to hire a superstar if you were a recruiting director?

# *Taryn Swarmer*

123 Jason Drive, Apt. 9        Walker Colorado 60412        982.138.2903

## EXPERIENCE

Mar. 1997–Present

WMAQ-TV (NBC Affiliate)—Chicago, Illinois
**NEWS PRODUCER**
- 10:00 p.m. & 5:00 p.m. weekend producer
- fill-in producer (4:30, 5:00, 6:00)
- field producer
- special projects producer
- 11:00 a.m. producer (2000–2003)
- weekend morning producer (1997–2000)
- Columbia College professor of broadcast news writing (2000–2001)
- Drake University School of Journalism alumni advisor (current)

Sep. 1995–Mar. 1997

WHO-TV (NBC Affiliate)—Des Moines, Iowa
**NEWS PRODUCER**
- 10:00 p.m. TV newscast producer (Dec. 1996–Mar. 1997)
- 5:00 p.m. TV newscast producer (Sep. 1995–Dec. 1996)

Jul. 1994–Sep. 1995

WKJG-TV (NBC Affiliate)—Fort Wayne, Indiana
**NEWS PRODUCER**
- 10:00 p.m. TV newscast producer

Mar. 1993–Jul. 1994

WANE-TV (CBS Affiliate)—Fort Wayne, Indiana
**NEWS PRODUCER**
- weekday 10:00 p.m., hour-long 5:00 p.m., and noon show
- weekend 6:00 p.m., 10:00 p.m., and half-hour Sports Magazine Show

**ASSISTANT NEWS PRODUCER**
- 5:00 p.m. and noon show

Aug. 1992–Jan. 1993

KWWL-TV (NBC Affiliate)—Waterloo, Iowa
**DUBUQUE BUREAU INTERN**
- reporter     • photographer     • editor

Fall 1991

WHO-TV (NBC Affiliate)—Des Moines, Iowa
**PRODUCER INTERN**
- assisted in writing and editing nightly news

## EDUCATION

**B.A. in Journalism** (1992)   Minor: Speech
Emphasis: Radio, TV, and Broadcast News
Drake University—Des Moines, Iowa
*Student Body President Award*
(Founder of Alpha Phi Omega, a national service fraternity)
**Nominated for Midwest Regional Emmy Award 2002 & 2003**

# Taryn Swarmer

123 Jason Drive, Apt. 9 ♦ Walker, CO 60412
982.138.2903 ♦ tarynswarmer@aol.com

## *EXPERIENCE*

**WMAQ -TV (NBC),** NEWS PRODUCER, Chicago, IL, March 1997–Present
- Senior ranking producer for weekend evening news programs, overseeing hundreds of newscasts
  - Manage entire on-air and production staff including anchors, reporters, editors, and writers
  - Determine all show content, scheduling, and running order
  - Write show content, approve all copy, and handle breaking news stories
- Maintained station's strong position among key 18–49 adult demographic by enhancing overall programming
- Promoted three times, from weekend morning producer to midday producer to weekend evening news producer
- Weekend morning show rated #1 from 1997–2001, and ratings grew 56% in 1999–2000
- Work closely with public relations firms including Edelman, Golin/Harris, Hill and Knowlton, and Ketchum assessing potential stories and features, and booking talent
- Led media training sessions for 25 members of the Chicago Veterinarians Medical Association
- Co-produced 30-minute Emmy-nominated Dell's "DELL'S, OH WHAT A NIGHT" musical special show
- Booked and scheduled hundreds of guests including Bill Murray, John Lithgow, and Dr. Phil McGraw
- Created a special segment/report with Sun-Times columnist Bill Zwecker featuring interviews with Tim Kazerinski of Saturday Night Live, and Dennis De Young of Styx
- Produced new pilot program for "Mom TV" hosted by Allison Rosati airing several times in Chicago
- Developed and launched FashionFive—weekly fashion session with Barbara Glass
- Introduced series of live weekend musical performances by bands Edwin McCain, Styx, and All-4-One
- Nominated for Midwest Regional Emmy Awards in 2002 and 2003 for breaking news programs on Edens flooding and for interactive media segment on High School Hazing

**TODAY'S CHICAGO WOMAN,** FREELANCE WRITER, Chicago, IL, 1998
- Wrote six articles published by leading magazine for women

**WHO-TV (NBC),** NEWS PRODUCER, Des Moines, IA, September 1995–March 1997
- Lead producer for 5pm, and then 10pm weekday new broadcasts
- Managed dozens of live remote handling all details for group of 8–10 news staff at each event
- Reinvigorated broadcasts by launching a series of creative live events and website tie-ins, helping station maintain #1 ranking in 5pm time slot

**WKJG-TV (NBC),** NEWS PRODUCER, Fort Wayne, IN, July 1994–September 1995
- Served as Executive Producer on weekday 10pm newscasts
- Helped station move from #3 to #2, by overhauling quality and content of news programming

**WANE-TV (CBS),** NEWS PRODUCER, Fort Wayne, IN, March 1993–July 1994
- Promoted rapidly from associate, to noon, to 5pm, and ultimately 10 pm producer

**KWWL-TV (NBC),** REPORTER/PHOTOGRAPHER/EDITOR, Waterloo, IA, August 1992–January 1993

## *EDUCATION*

**DRAKE UNIVERSITY—DES MOINES, IA, 1992**
- B.A. in Journalism, Radio, TV, and Broadcast News Emphasis; Speech Minor

## *ACTIVITIES*

- Columbia College, Professor of Broadcast News Writing, 2000–2001
- Drake University School of Journalism, Alumni Advisory Board, 2004–Present
- Chicago Symphony Orchestra, Holiday Show Extra, 2003

# The Career Change

Garrett was in a position that may be familiar to some of you. He had started his own company and achieved success, but now he wanted to return to working in the corporate world. We did two key things to make him as marketable as possible.

First, we beefed up what he had accomplished running his own company. You will notice that we went from two bullet points in the *before* version to thirteen in the *after* version. Many entrepreneurs tend to downplay what they have done since it was not "corporate." We also tried to translate what he had accomplished into impressive skills a potential employer would value.

Second, we made his corporate experiences at HP and IBM much easier to read. We complemented the more entrepreneurial skills he developed at his own company with some "standard" corporate skills from these two well-recognized businesses.

The key to this resume was to balance his entrepreneurial skills with those of the traditional corporate world. By showing off the best of what he'd done, we made Garrett a very attractive candidate.

Starting with his new summary and moving throughout the resume, you get the impression that Garrett is ready to move to the next level and make a successful career change.

# Garrett Richards

1127 Aimee Lane
Houston, TX 82911
958.944.3359
*hulmer@hankel.com*

---

**SUMMARY** More than 11 years of professional services and market development experience dealing with fast-paced, rapidly expanding companies. Expertise includes diverse global experience in business development, relationship-based sales, strategy development and program/project management. Adept in bringing emerging products & services to market, building new businesses, strategic relationship management and navigating complex organizational environments.

---

## PROFESSIONAL EXPERIENCE

**2003–Present**    **HANKEL INTERNATIONAL INC.** .                                    **HOUSTON, TX**
*Co-founder/CEO*
Responsible for building and leading 55 person business process outsourcing (BPO) firm with service center in Bangalore, India to deliver Finance and Accounting (FA) services to middle market CPA firms. Since 2003 launch, responsibilities include strategy & business development, sales, and solution architecture. Established global best practices Citrix infrastructure, collaborating with leading consulting firms and enterprise hardware/software vendors. Currently oversees daily operations. Highlights include:

- **Business Startup-** Authored StaffLeader business model, plan and strategy. Secured venture funding and set valuation. Built strong team of top managers. Established technology architecture. Led initial clients through the BPO process.
- **Executive Leadership-** Leads the StaffLeader management team. Acts as primary spokesperson for the firm. Provides vision and motivation. Leads engagements with clients.

**1997–2003**    **HEWLETT PACKARD CORPORATION (VIA COMPAQ ACQUISTION)**    **HOUSTON, TX**
*Director, Strategy & Business Development–Enterprise Systems Group*
Responsible for identifying, developing and executing growth strategies for the $4B Intel-based server and storage business unit. Conducted analysis of new markets including assessing market size and desirability. Defined and sized the opportunity (TAM, SAM, SOM) and projected potential long-term revenues. Monitored key market and technology trends within the ecosystem and reported on competitors' alliances & partnership activities. Built and managed a team of 5 BDMs while growing additional revenue streams of $160M annually. Some of the highlights include:

- **Key Strategic Deals with Broadcom & Adaptec**—Successfully sourced and negotiated multimillion dollar complex deals with Broadcom's Serverworks Division and Adaptec. The Broadcom deal included licensing of storage technology for inclusion in Serverworks chipsets. The Adaptec deal included the licensing and integration of ICs and storage management software. These deals increased the addressable market for these technologies by 3x, creating a royalty stream to fund future development.
- **Business Strategy**—Managed strategy development for senior management. Conducted market segmentation and competitor analysis, which included conducting customer interviews, research, and analysis. Based upon the competitive landscape and economic value analysis (EVA), recommended and prioritized iSCSI, Infiniband, SAS/SATA portfolio strategy. Analyzed potential entry strategies including partnerships, licensing, and M&A. Developed and evangelized business plan to realign goals post-HP merger.
- **Venture Capital Community Alignment**—Identified and managed relationships with leading VC's such as Austin Ventures, InnoCal Ventures, Bessemer Partners, and Intel Capital. This provided a platform by which Compaq could influence early stage companies developing next generation technologies via direct equity investment or roadmap rationalization. Advisory Board Member for Platys Communications, an iSCSI silicon startup (since acquired by Adaptec).
- **Venture Funding**—Evaluated 75+ startups, ultimately invested in two strategic deals totaling $8M. Recommended not to develop a new business joint-venture for Portable Data Center Security (Secure Site) based upon analysis of business case, market sizing, and corporate strategy. Start-up soon after filed for bankruptcy protection; decision saved Compaq over $7M in proposed investment.

*Manager, Marketing & Business Operations- Storage Products Group*
Promoted in only 9 months (typical promotion was 2-4 yrs). Responsible for managing marketing and business operation activities with specific focus on enterprise HDDs, fabric switches, and storage arrays

---

in a highly matrixed environment. Led the organization of 17 individuals (5 direct line managers) to produce consistent growth-oriented results during Digital acquisition. Successfully led integration team efforts and reduced attrition as compared to other similar organizations in the company. Ability to manage via influence to achieve objectives. Responsibilities included:

- **Business Operations**—Managed 8 worldwide operations HC to hit quarterly execution to financial targets. Drove short-term forecasting and closed supply/revenue gaps with sales Geo's. Redesigned forecasting model and process yielding 30% increased accuracy and reducing end-of-life (EOL) inventory. Developed a complete product pricing strategy for 3,000 SKUs and multiple distribution channels. Produced 18-month rolling forecasts and life-cycle mgmt process for product transitions.
- **Business Planning**—Worked closely with senior executives to develop and get buy in on the business plan and product strategy for network attached JBODs. The plan included analysis of the market opportunity, customer needs, product features, and positioning. Validated market potential on a global scale through focus groups and customers interviews.
- **Business Development**—Established key partnerships with library and software vendors such as HP, Quantum, Overland Data, and other automation vendors. Explored partnerships with key vendors like Brocade and Gadzooks to launch integrated Wintel storage platform.

*Product Manager, Data Products Business Unit*
COMPAQ DLT family PMM (tape storage products for backup and disaster recovery solutions)—Successfully drove all aspects of product marketing. Responsibilities included:

- **Product Marketing**—Developed MRDs including market sizing, pricing and positioning strategy for the DLT products. Led worldwide launch and Go-to market activities.
- **Product Management**—Aligned product development team to focus on customer requirements. Defined product requirements for the next generation of DLT (SDLT). Recruited 150+ early adopters and customers for the beta program all over the world including Europe, Japan, Australia, and Asia. Conducted a detailed competitive analysis of key players in Near-line and Hierarchical Storage Management space.
- **PR/ MarCom**—Developed the branding and messaging for the product. Successfully launched the product to global customers and partners through a successful media campaign. Worked and communicated with several key industry analysts like Giga, Gartner, and IDC for positive write-ups on the product. Also, promoted the product at several Compaq and industry trade shows.

**1995–1997**  **INTERNATIONAL BUSINESS MACHINES**  AUSTIN, TX
*Business Planning Analyst, Server Group*
Consolidated, analyzed, and communicated worldwide revenue forecasts and targets with senior management; collaborated with development teams & line managers to create product portfolio.

- Performed financial analysis and due diligence on various development projects.
- Evaluated numerous engineering, operations and manufacturing financial strategies.
- Developed and supported business case for proposed $400 million R&D laboratory.
- Investigated options for consolidating manufacturing sites and combining development laboratories.

## EDUCATION

**1993-1995**  **UNIVERSITY OF TEXAS, MCCOMBS GRADUATE SCHOOL OF BUSINESS**  AUSTIN, TX
*Master in Professional Accounting (Magna Cum Laude)*
**1990-1993**  **UNIVERSITY OF TEXAS**  AUSTIN, TX
*Bachelor of Business Administration (Accounting Major)*

## PERSONAL

Avid tennis-player, cyclist, and runner. Enjoy traveling and photography. Volunteer with Houston Habitat for Humanity. Coach youth soccer teams.

# Garrett Richards

1127 Aimee Lane ♦ Houston, TX 82911
958.944.3359 ♦ garett@aol.com

## SUMMARY OF QUALIFICATIONS

- Seasoned outsourcing/offshoring professional with experience analyzing, transacting, implementing, managing, optimizing, and overseeing all aspects of O/O lifecycle
- Dedicated project manager with responsibility for recruiting, training, supervising, and retaining a team of more than 50 professionals both in the US and abroad
- Proven analytical and strategic thinker having researched, synthesized, and recommended action plans for dozens of $1MM+ projects at HP, Compaq, and IBM
- Passionate O/O advocate having created, positioned, and developed market for unique outsourcing practice used by dozens of CPA firms across the country

## EXPERIENCE

**HANKEL INTERNATIONAL INC.,** CEO/CO-FOUNDER**,** Houston, TX, 2003–Present
- Created and manage best-in-class, 55-person business process outsourcing firm providing finance and accounting services to several of the leading middle-market CPA firms nationwide
- Grew company to more than $1MM in revenue in first year
- Authored business model, plan, and strategy, set valuation, and solicited and secured venture funding
- Developed all components of corporate strategy including pricing, work flow process, market strategy, candidate identification, and IT infrastructure
- Strategically analyzed multidimensional issues including market trends, globalization, currency rates, financial macro trends, brand psychology, industry cycles, and competitive landscape intelligence to launch concept and maximize shareholder value
- Positioned company as providing value-added strategic long-term outsourcing solution beyond price
  - Minimize staff turnover by dramatically reducing mundane tasks for newer US-based associates
  - Focus US staff on growth, acquisition, and high-level customer service
- Secured majority of new business by reaching out to the country's leading mid-tier CPA firms
- Established all operations at service center in Bangalore, India for more than 30 full-time employees
- Virtually eliminated all off-shore staff turnover by instituting industry-leading retention programs
- Processed more than 10,000 corporate, partnership, individual, and sales returns in first year of operation, and project 40,000 returns for 2006
- Traveled more than 250,000 miles worldwide during the course of the year

**HEWLETT PACKARD/COMPAQ,** Houston, TX, 1997–2003
DIRECTOR, STRATEGY AND BUSINESS DEVELOPMENT–ENTERPRISE SYSTEMS GROUP
- Identified, developed, and executed growth strategies for the $4B Intel-based server and storage business unit
- Launched company's first-ever IP-centric VC tour, partnering with leading Venture Capitalists in Silicon Valley to align tech investments with Compaq's overall tech strategy
  - Sourced and secured relationships with leading VCs including Austin Ventures, InnoCal Ventures, Bessemer Partners and Intel Capital
  - Selected as Advisory Board Member for Platys Communications (later acquired by Adaptec)
- Ultimately grew additional revenue streams more than $120MM while building and managing a team of five Business Development Managers
- Sourced and negotiated multimillion-dollar complex deal with Broadcom's Serverworks division to license storage technology for inclusion in Serverworks chipsets
- Secured major partnership with Adaptec, licensing and integrating Ics and storage management software to help increase the addressable market to more than 3 million servers representing 60% of the market

- Key team member developing comprehensive market communication plan to realign goals for $5B unit post-HP merger
- Conducted customer interviews with leading companies including Procter & Gamble, Citibank, and Chase to help segment marketplace and analyze competitive activity
- Performed in-depth scenario analysis to recommend iSCSI, Infiniband, and SAS/SATA portfolio strategy within $2B disk storage industry
- Analyzed potential entry strategies across several segments including more than 30 mergers and acquisitions, partnerships and licensing deals in $4B Intel division
- Recommended and secured $8MM in two strategic VC deals after evaluating more than 75 startups
  - Saved Compaq $7MM by recommending against investment in Portable Data Center Security– company later filed for bankruptcy protection

MANAGER, MARKETING AND BUSINESS OPERATIONS–STORAGE PRODUCTS GROUP
- Managed a team of 17 producing consistent growth across HDDs, fabric switches, and storage arrays
- Dramatically reduced employee attrition following Digital acquisition by developing comprehensive personnel integration strategy
- Increased accuracy 30% and significantly reduced end-of-life inventory by overhauling forecasting model
- Developed a complete product pricing strategy for 3,000 SKUs and multiple distribution channels, representing $3B in annual sales
- Conducted dozens of focus groups and customer interviews to help validate $700MM global market potential for key unit
- Established key partnerships with tape library and software vendors including HP, Quantum, and Overland Data representing $150MM in incremental revenue
- Promoted in only nine months versus typical two- to four-year time frame

PRODUCT MANAGER–DATA PRODUCTS BUSINESS UNIT
- Led all marketing activities for fully-integrated $400MM worldwide launch of COMPAQ DLT products
- Overhauled product development team to better align structure with customer requirements
- Managed highly successful beta program recruiting more than 150 early adopters from five continents

INTERNATIONAL BUSINESS MACHINES, BUSINESS PLANNING ANALYST, Austin, TX, 1995–1997
- Developed and supported comprehensive business case for proposed $400MM R&D laboratory
- Performed financial analysis on more than 10 development projects representing $65MM in investments
- Worked closely with senior management to consolidate, analyze, and communicate $2.5B in worldwide revenue forecasts and targets

## EDUCATION

UNIVERSITY OF TENNESSEE GRADUATE SCHOOL OF BUSINESS—KNOXVILLE, 1995
- Master in Professional Accounting
- Magna Cum Laude Graduate

UNIVERSITY OF TENNESSEE—KNOXVILLE, 1993
- Bachelor of Business Administration; Accounting Major

## ACTIVITES/INTERESTS

- Avid options, derivatives, and stock trader since 1991
- Habitat for Humanity volunteer
- Youth soccer coach
- Enjoy tennis, cycling, running, traveling and photography

# The Career Change

Most people have hobbies, interests, and activities outside of work, or at least we hope you do! Sometimes, people get so much enjoyment and excitement from these hobbies that they decide to make their passion their new career.

I've known a fisherman who started a charter boat business, a great chef who wrote a series of cookbooks, and a fine artist who began a photography company. Every day people are turning their hobbies and interests into money-making businesses.

Like many of these people, our next client, Flora, was looking for a change of pace. Interestingly, she wanted to pursue her passion for volunteer work. She wanted to go from the corporate office to the not-for-profit field.

As we have mentioned, mid-career changes can be tricky. As a job seeker, you have a lot of experience, but typically not in the area you want to enter. That is why crafting a resume that focuses on your transferable skills is critical.

Here's what we did for Flora:

1. We moved her volunteer experience with Slow Foods USA to the second entry on her resume. She had it buried under volunteer experience, and as you can see, she did some pretty amazing things with the organization. She sat on the board of directors, and she even wrote a book about the movement!
2. We highlighted her volunteer involvement as the first entry in the summary section of the resume so a recruiting director would see her strong involvement immediately.
3. We focused her bullet points in her other jobs on the types of accomplishments and activities that would be most relevant for a not-for-profit: skills like growing a brand, leading teams, and networking with other organizations.

Since there is so much time and money involved in hiring and onboarding, recruiting directors typically don't like to take a lot of chances. With an abundance of candidates for each job, it can be easy just to cast aside any resume that isn't spot on. That's why the goal of any good resume is to make you the "safe, easy hire." The best thing you can do on your resume is try to match up your experiences with the company's needs. A great way to do this is to look at the job description and then try to focus your resume on what they want to see (without lying, of course)!

**Flora Flurston**
545 Ferry 5th Street
Boston, MA 13238
728.379.9981 or 728.882.9015

## PROFILE

A versatile marketing and communications professional with experience developing and implementing successful integrated marketing campaigns. Skilled at using a full complement of marketing and communications vehicles and practices. Effective manager of people, agencies and budgets. Proven ability to identify who's who and what they can do. Motivated team player.

## PROFESSIONAL EXPERIENCE

**CountryTime Lemonade**  Chicago, IL  1997–present
**Director, Marketing (1999–present)**
**Director, Public Relations (1997–1999)**

- Oversaw annual dollar volume increases of 10% against a declining category
- Developed business strategies for product line extension; managed launch planning and sales support for staged roll-out
- Supervised first-ever logo and package design restaging to increase shelf impact and update brand image
- Provide collaborative leadership with multiple groups, including sales, operations and finance
- Manage multiple agency relationships, including media, advertising, interactive, packaging, research, public relations and customer service
- Identify opportunities for and supervise company's involvement in sponsorships, special events and trade shows
- Develop marketing communications and sales programs for retail and business-to-business channels to ensure full sell through

**Roberts Public Relations**  Chicago, IL  1996–1997
**Vice President**

- Provided strategic public relations counsel to CPG clients on brand positioning and product launches
- Managed several teams totaling 12 individuals
- Oversaw close to $1 million in fees
- Created and presented new business plans and budgets
- Clients and accomplishments included: successful launch of Johnson & Johnson's Acuvue contact lenses, resulting in doubling of program fees to $600,000; launch of J&J's Uristat OTC analgesic, supported solely by public relations; reintroduction of James River Corporation's Dixie Riddle Cups; and Radio Flyer's 80th Anniversary, which generated unprecedented media coverage for the company; the Milk Mustache program

**Golin/Harris Communications**  Chicago, IL  1991–1996
**Group Supervisor**

- Developed, managed and implemented brand-positioning public relations programs, new product launches, cause-related marketing, special events, and corporate communications

- Planned and implemented strategic media relations programs, including national media campaigns (print, television, and radio), press conferences, satellite media tours, video news release and b-roll production, junkets, and celebrity spokespersons
- Clients included: Jim Beam Bourbon, and the Small Batch Bourbon Collection, Midas International, DowBrands Consumer Products, Bays English Muffins, Tioxide Americas

**Edelman Worldwide**          **Chicago, IL**          **1988–1991**
**Senior Account Executive**
- Clients included: Sara Lee Corporation, Ore-Ida Foods, Inc., Beatrice Hunt/Wesson, National Live Stock and Meat Board

**ThornLeaf Productions**          **Chicago, IL**          **1987–1988**
**Program Coordinator**
- Provided liaison between Rotary International and video production company for production of video newsmagazine targeting worldwide membership
- Researched and developed story ideas and visuals; wrote scripts
- Developed communications strategy to promote newsmagazine

**Larry N. Deutsch Interiors**          **Chicago, IL**          **1984–1987**
**Project Coordinator**
- Project coordinator and client liaison for interior design firm

## OTHER
**Co-Author,** "The Slow Food Guide to Chicago Restaurants, Bars and Markets" (Chelsea Green Publishing, 2004)
**Member**, **Board of Directors,** Slow Food USA
**Co-Founder,** Slow Food Chicago
- Founded Chicago chapter of national non-profit organization, which grew to 300 members (the fourth largest in the country)
- Worked with local and international officials, chefs, producers and the media to coordinate special events that raised both awareness and funds for the organization
- Supervised large-scale events and initiatives with all-volunteer force

## PROFESSIONAL AWARDS
Silver Anvil (2)
Golden Trumpet (3)
Golden Quill (1)

## EDUCATION
**The University of Iowa**, Iowa City, IA
Bachelor of Liberal Arts, Art History, 1984

**Institute for American Universities**, Aix-en-Provence, France
- **Continuing Education:** Northwestern University, Marketing
**References Available Upon Consideration**

# Flora Flurston

545 Ferry 5th Street ♦ Boston, MA 13238
728.379.9981 ♦ fflurston@gmail.com

## SUMMARY

- Passionate supporter of the Slow Food movement, serving as national Board Member, Regional Director, and Co-Founder of Chicago Chapter
- Dedicated marketing executive having rebranded, overhauled, and invigorated one of America's iconic Lemonade brands
- Seasoned public relations professional with 10 years experience crafting fully-integrated PR plans for some of the world's biggest brands including J & J, Jim Beam, DowBrands, and Sara Lee

## EXPERIENCE

**DIRECTOR OF MARKETING,** COUNTRY TIME LEMONADE, Chicago, IL, 1997–Present
- Reinvented targeting efforts contemporizing brand and contributing to 10% dollar volume increases in a declining category
- Launched a series of targeted sponsorship and sampling events with Y-Me and Lincoln Park Zoo Winter Lights Festival among key consumers raising awareness of product attributes
- Introduced multimedia campaign across print and radio targeting younger female audience as means to highlight new product benefit and usage ideas
- Work directly with company president developing strategic marketing programs and integrated sales efforts impacting organization with $12MM in sales annually
- Manage company's syndicated marking data, analyzing competitive dynamics and performance, and preparing comprehensive quarterly sales team briefings
- Introduced and rolled out new honey wheat line extension including first-ever logo and package design restaging, exceeding penetration expectations
- Overhauled agency relationships with seven key vendors saving $10,000 in agency fees, streamlining efficiencies, and identifying new partners
- Developed dozens of marketing communications and sales programs for more than 340 retailers, brokers, and food service accounts nationwide
- Promoted from Director of Public Relations to Director of Marketing in 1999

**BOARD OF DIRECTORS,** SLOW FOOD USA, Chicago, IL, 1997–Present
- Elected to Board representing 11,000 members nationwide for organization devoted to preserving traditional foodways and educating people about food as a center of community
- Co-Author of "The Slow Food Guide to Chicago Restaurants, Bars and Markets" (Chelsea Green Publishing, 2004)
  - Managed team of 50 contributing writers reviewing more than 100 establishments
- Co-founder of Slow Food Chicago growing chapter to 300 members–fourth largest local chapter out of 130 nationally
- Selected as Midwest Regional Governor overseeing 10 local chapters with 300 members
- Won *Chicago Tribune* "Good Taste" award for starting chapter in Chicago

**VICE PRESIDENT,** ROBERTS PUBLIC RELATIONS, Chicago, IL, 1996–1997
*Johnson & Johnson, Milk Mustache, Radio Flyer*
- Managed a total staff of 12, and oversaw $1 million in fees
- Successfully launched both Acuvue and Uristat for Johnson & Johnson, resulting in incremental $600,000 in program fees
  - Introduced and established Uristat as category leader with PR-only plan featuring national media tour, b-roll, and media events

- Supported Acuvue introduction with fully integrated campaign featuring sports celebrity spokespeople, traveling kiosks, targeted sampling, and b-roll
- Received dedicated coverage on CNN, NBC/CBS/FOX (all national), Conan O'Brien Show, and USA Today featuring world's largest wagon built for Radio Flyer's 80th anniversary
- Reached 245 million consumers in 1996 through comprehensive PR campaign for Milk Mustache efforts

**GROUP SUPERVISOR,** GOLIN HARRIS COMMUNICATIONS, Chicago, IL, 1991–1996
*Jim Beam Bourbon, Midas International, Bay's English Muffins*
- Launched Jim Beam Small Batch Bourbon Collection connoisseurs product line, quickly becoming national category leader
- Promoted "Project Safe Baby" for Midas including national press event with National Transportation Safety Administration and Washington DC mayor Marion Berry
- Celebrated 200th anniversary of Jim Beam Bourbon with a consumer contest reaching millions of customers nationwide, generating hits in the *New York Times*, *USA Today*, and *Bon Appetit*
- Won Golden Trumpet (2x), Golden Quill, Silver Trumpet and Bronze Anvil awards for national, industry-recognized PR campaigns

**SENIOR ACCOUNT EXECUTIVE,** EDELMAN WORLDWIDE, Chicago, IL, 1988–1991
*Sara Lee Corporation, Beatrice Hunt/Wesson, National Livestock and Meat Board*

**PROGRAM COORDINATOR,** THORNLEAF PRODUCTIONS, Chicago, IL, 1987–1988

**PROJECT COORDINATOR,** LARRY DEUTSCH INTERIORS, Chicago, IL, 1984–1987

## EDUCATION

**THE UNIVERSITY OF IOWA**—IOWA CITY, IA, 1984
- Bachelor of Liberal Arts; Art History

**INSTITUTE FOR AMERICAN UNIVERSITIES**—AIX-EN-PROVENCE, FRANCE, 1983

**NORTHWESTERN UNIVERSITY**—EVANSTON, IL, 1988
- Continuing Education in Marketing

# SEEKING INTERNAL PROMOTION

Some people who come to JobBound love their current company, but they are seeking an internal promotion. They enjoy the environment and the corporate culture, but they are ready for "bigger and better" responsibilities.

At many companies, you aren't promoted automatically when you reach certain benchmarks. Some openings are very competitive, so you have to apply and be considered against your colleagues and outside applicants as well.

In this case, it's imperative that you really sell yourself. Your immediate manager may not be the one making the decision, and the higher-ups may not be fully aware of the great things you have accomplished. You can't assume that just because people know of you that they know all the amazing things you did on the job.

Here are some recommendations:

## 1. Take the application process seriously

External candidates may not have a job to fall back on, so they can be a competitive force. In addition, companies often see the benefit in recruiting a new person with a different perspective and skill set. That being said, you have to do yourself and your work justice. You can't assume you'll get the job just because you're on the inside.

## 2. Find out as much about the new job as possible

If you have the job description, use it just as you would for a position outside of your company. Match up your skills to those of the new position. If there isn't a job description, then it's incumbent upon you to learn what the new job entails. One of the benefits you have versus an outsider is that you know the company and the culture. Talk to folks at the company, and use your connections to your advantage.

## 3. Showcase what makes you great

Average employees do not get rewarded. A+ employees do. Show how you went above and beyond your call of duty, and illustrate how you can easily rise to the next level.

## 4. Tell the right people that you are seeking the promotion

Do not be shy about telling your manager or department head that you are interested in the opening. Make your career goals clear, and use your company network as leverage.

• • •

Check out the next few resumes, and see how we painted each client as an accomplished candidate who was ready for the next step.

# Seeking Internal Promotion

Dan's ingoing resume was not too bad. That being said, you never want to hand over a so-so resume, especially if you want a promotion!

You will notice that we specified his accomplishments on his *after* resume. We got to the root of his achievements and created points like the following:

- Generating $200,000 in revenue
- Saving 90% of man-hours
- Serving as company guru to 600 employees

Each of these points paints a clear impression that Dan gets results and Dan makes things happen. Obviously, Dan deserves a promotion and more money; look how much money he has generated!

In his summary section, on his *before* version, Dan made a lot of claims that could or could not have been true. In the *after* version, we quantified all of them to prove to the internal recruiting director that he is an amazing candidate. Dan is definitely someone that the company wants to keep and reward.

471223 Diamond Square, Detroit, MI 48362
home phone: (442) 572-8912; business phone: (883) 832-8931; email: ddarduno@yahoo.com

# *Dan Darduno*

**JOB OBJECTIVE**

System Programmer/Analyst

**BACKGROUND SUMMARY**

* Nineteen years of experience in developing, debugging, testing and implementing large scale software engineering projects
* Strong mathematical and business application background
* Excellent logical problem solving skills
* Highly motivated and working independently
* Good leadership and team player skills

**QUALIFICATIONS**

Hardware
IBM Mainframe and PC

Operating Systems
OS/MVS, WINDOWS, MS/DOS

Software
TSO/ISPF, JCL, ControlM, SyncSort, FileAid, Quick, Excel, Visio

Databases
IMS, dBase, DB2, Access, Alpha III/IV

Programming Languages
PL/1, COBOL, Assembler, Pascal, Visual Basic, PL SQL, C, Fortran

**WORK EXPERIENCE**

1996–present
Elite& Co., Northfield, MI. Senior Programmer/Analyst

* Led a four-member team in developing and implementing Statistical Analysis System for General Motors Corporation
**In just one year, the number of dealers purchased the system, increased from 20 to more than 200**
* Created, realized and supported various business applications for Ford, Daimler Chrysler and Asian Imports manufacturers
**Generated combined revenue in excess of $100,000 per year**
* Re-designed, coded and enhanced Marketing Vehicle Registration System that produces hard copies and on-line monthly reports. **Decreased production run time from 3 days to less than 6 hours**
* Developed and maintained IMS/VS application program that updates batch and on-line hierarchical databases during annual automobile conversion
**Saved more than 90% of man-hours by computerizing process**
* Quickly learned application software; analyzed and updated both open and mainframe systems

*Environment:*
PL/1, SyncSort, Quick, Assembler, IMS, ControlM, Visual Basic, SQL, C, Excel, Access, Visio

HOW TO SAY IT ON YOUR RESUME

**471223 Diamond Square, Detroit, MI 48362**
**home phone: (442) 572-8912; business phone: (883) 832-8931; email**: ddarduno@yahoo.com

# *Dan Darduno*

| | |
|---|---|
| 1995–1996 | Ohio National Financial Services, Cincinnati, OH.Programmer/Analyst |
| | * Specialized in programming support of administrative systems in life insurance and annuities |
| | * Developed several applications and computer reports to meet customer's requirements |
| *Environment:* | PL/1, COBOL, SyncSort, FileAid, SQL, DB2, Access |

| | |
|---|---|
| 1992–1995 | Tri-State Sleep Disorders Center, Cincinnati, OH.  Senior Programmer |
| | * Developed, tested and supported computerized systems for complex sleep studies. Systems are being used on a daily basis to work with pre- and post-treated patients |
| | * Originated and implemented set of user graphic interfaces to enhance diagnostics of sleep disorders |
| | * Created and maintained data entry and reporting subsystems |
| *Environment:* | Basic, SQL, Excel, Alpha III/IV |

| | |
|---|---|
| 1989–1992 | Polytechnical Institute, Kharkov, Ukraine. Senior Programmer |
| | * Organized and supported full development cycle of the computer simulation software |
| | * Developed and implemented several mathematical models |
| *Environment:* | PL/1, Pascal, Basic |

| | |
|---|---|
| 1986–1988 | Institute of Radioelectronics, Kharkov, Ukraine. Programmer |
| | * Designed control system to check for the inconsistencies in initial models. The system used database (dBase) to access standard designs and produce new structures, based on computational engine performing operations on large matrices |
| *Environment:* | PL/1, Fortran, Pascal, dBase |

**EDUCATION**

| | |
|---|---|
| 1981–1986 | Kharkov State University, Kharkov, Ukraine |
| | Department of Applied Mathematics and Mechanics |
| | MS in Mathematics and Computer Science |

**CONTINUING EDUCATION**

| | |
|---|---|
| 1999–2001 | New Horizons Computer Learning Center, Cincinnati, OH |
| | Advanced Microsoft Access and Excel |

| | |
|---|---|
| 2002 | Northern Kentucky University, Covington, KY |
| | Visual Basic for Excel and Access |

| | |
|---|---|
| 2003 | Schoolcraft College, Livonia MI |
| | Visual Basic for Applications |
| **REFERENCES** | Available upon request |

---

# Dan Darduno
471223 Diamond Square ♦ Detroit, MI 48362
442.572.8912 ♦ ddarduno@yahoo.com

## SUMMARY OF QUALIFICATIONS

- Seasoned system programmer and analyst with 19 years of experience developing, implementing and supporting a diverse array of systems for clients including GM, Ford, and Chrysler
- Dedicated professional with a proven track record of virtually flawless work across hundreds of systems in a variety of environments
- Established leader and subject matter expert recognized by management as company "guru" on quality assurance, and several specific programs
- Results driven programmer having created programs generating millions in revenue and saving thousands of man-hours annually

## EXPERIENCE

### SENIOR PROGRAMMER/ANALYST, ELITE & CO., Northfield, MI, 1996–Present
- Developed, supported and delivered more than 2,000 cyclical and AD-HOC reports with revenue in excess of $13MM
  - Achieved unprecedented nine-year record of error-free reports with no customer complaints
- Led a four-member team in a six-month, $1.5MM project developing and implementing a statistical analysis system tracking all registration information for 200,000 used cars divided by zip code
  - Resulted in tenfold increase in systems sold to car dealers to more than 200 nationwide
- Generated more than $200,000 in revenue annually by creating, implementing, and supporting over 100 business applications for Ford, Daimler Chrysler, Honda, and Toyota analyzing sales, registration, and VIN operation information
- Overhauled complex Marketing Vehicle Registration System–customizable report tracking every single vehicle sold by every manufacturer
  - Decreased production run time from three days to less than six hours
- Automated comprehensive IMS/VS application program tracking every vehicle sale in America back to 1979 covering more than 350 million vehicles
  - 250,000 records can be updated in minutes, saving 90% of man-hours on a system used by 40 staff members across the company
- Selected by management as subject matter expert in PL/1 serving as company guru for 600 employees
- One of 15 out of 170 moved from Cincinnati to Southfield selected to train a staff of 10 on all aspects of production and statistical support responsibility at new IP programming practice
- Transferred three major company processes for Mercedes, GM, and Chrysler from mainframe to open system by utilizing Oracle Database using PL/SQL
- Operate in environment with PL/1, SyncSort, Quick, Assembler, IMS, ControlM, Visual Basic, SQL, C, Excel, Access, and Visio

### SENIOR PROGRAMMER, TRI-STATE SLEEP DISORDERS CENTER, Cincinnati, OH, 1992–1996
- Developed, tested, and supported computerized systems automating all aspects of complex sleep studies conducted on 1,000 patients annually

- Modified existing system devised to analyze patient's sleep patterns, dramatically reducing minor study variations, resulting in better diagnostics
- Created and maintained data entry reporting systems with more than 10,000 entries
- Operated in environment with Basic, SQL, Alpha III/IV, and Excel

**SENIOR PROGRAMMER,** POLYTECHNICAL INSTITUTE, Kharkov, Ukraine, 1986–1992
- Designed more than 30 computerized mathematical control system simulation processes used to check for electrical engineering inconsistencies
- Wrote program organizing unique system showing how production processes would work in physical environment
- Worked one-on-one with physicist, helping devise more efficient industrial fuses
- Operated in environment with PL/1, dBase, Pascal, Basic, and Fortran

## COMPUTER SKILLS

- Hardware: IBM Mainframe, and PC
- Operating Systems: OS/MVS, WINDOWS, MS/DOS
- Software: TSO/ISPF, JCL, ControlM, SnycSort, FileAid, Quick, Visio, Excel
- Databases: IMS, dBase, DB2, Alpha III/IV, Access
- Languages: PL/1, COBOL, Assembler, Pascal, Visual Basic, PL SQL, C, Fortran

## EDUCATION

**ORACLE UNIVERSITY**—TROY, MI, 2005
- Oracle, SQL, Oracle PL/SQL

**SCHOOLCRAFT COLLEGE**—LIVONIA, MI, 2003
- Visual Basic for Applications

**NORTHERN KENTUCKY UNIVERSITY**—COVINGTON, KY, 2002
- Visual Basic for Excel and Access

**KHARKOV STATE UNIVERSITY**—KHARKOV, UKRAINE, 1986
- M.S. in Mathematics and Computer Science

# Seeking Internal Promotion

Matthew wanted to make the big jump from product management to marketing director at his company. In essence, he was looking to get a fairly major promotion.

This brings up a very interesting point when putting together a resume. It is always better if you know what your next move will be. You don't *have* to know, but it helps to have an idea in order to make the resume as relevant as possible.

One of the tricks that we use is to ask the canditate to give us the job description for the job opening. Here is the key point:

*You are writing your resume for the next job, not for the job you have.*

In other words, all that matters is how you position yourself for the next job. Remember, a recruiting director wants to hire the person who most accurately fits the job description. As you craft your resume, try to match up what you have done with what the company is seeking.

In the case of Matthew, we highlighted all of his relevant experiences to make him look like a marketing director. We focused on how he had grown brands, how he had gone well beyond the call of duty, and how he was a visionary marketer with solid results and an MBA.

The beauty of this resume is that he seems well qualified for the higher position after reading only one-half of the first page of the resume.

**Matthew Doherty**
51 East Peterson
Pinesville, CO 36781
891.681.6781
ppollack@gmail.com

# Matthew Doherty

## OBJECTIVE

Director of Marketing position at Proofpoint.

## SUMMARY

Marketing professional with over nine years of experience, with seven in security, networking, and telecom services for the small and medium business market. Skilled at product marketing, management, and channel marketing:

- At SonicWALL–the leading SMB security appliance vendor–I am spearheading the outbound product marketing for all of SonicWALL's secure content management solutions, including email, web, and endpoint security products
- At Netopia–a leader in DSL equipment for small businesses and residential users–I played a key role in the company's turn-around after telecom industry downturn by the leading the RFP response initiative to some of the largest carrier and service provider customers in the world
- At NorthPoint–a nationwide DSL service provider to small and medium businesses and residential customers–I was selected to lead the marketing team at the company's European joint-venture
- At Sprint PCS, I devised the first online distribution of wireless service in the wireless industry

## EXPERIENCE

**SonicWALL, Inc.—Sunnyvale, CA**                                                          July 2005–Present

**Product Marketing Manager IV**

Reporting to the Vice President, Secure Content Management Business Unit, lead the outbound product marketing for SonicWALL's secure content management appliances and solutions:

- Contributed lead generation campaigns resulting in 40% quarter-over-quarter revenue growth (for three quarters running) for SonicWALL's Content Security Manager, a dedicated secure content management appliance for companies with 1,000 employees or less
- Led a comprehensive channel partner recruitment campaign for SonicWALL Email Security, growing selling partner base from 250 to 1,000 selling partners in four months
- On a quarterly basis, develop the presentation content, speaker notes, and demos for SonicWALL's worldwide partner roadshow series, which occurs in 40 cities worldwide, with 1,000 channel partner participants
- Grew SonicWALL's worldwide Channel Partner Web Seminar participants from 350 to 1,500 in Q206; also increased overall geographic, product, and editorial coverage for the Partner Web Seminar series

**Netopia, Inc.—Emeryville, CA**                                                          March 2001–June 2005

**Senior Product Marketing Manager**

Reporting to the Senior Vice President of Sales and Marketing, led the product marketing effort for Netopia's Broadband Equipment division, which supplies carriers and service providers targeting the small and medium business and residential markets:

- Led the product launch of four business-class router and residential gateway product families designed for residential and small business applications
- Positioned and marketed Netopia business-class routers around their security feature set, including VPN, firewall, and secure remote management capabilities
- Supported the sales and marketing effort to strategic accounts, such as US and European carriers and service providers; was instrumental in key customer wins, including EarthLink, BellSouth (SMB division), AT&T (SMB division), Covad, Belgacom, Eircom, and Swisscom
- Coordinated the RFP response process, working with senior management and sales teams on strategic account opportunities; quarterbacked over 40 RFPs from major customers over three years
- Launched new family of small business Wi-Fi products at key service provider accounts; at BellSouth, I personally led a product launch that resulted in a ten-fold annual increase in revenues at the account
- Managed a $2.0 million marketing budget for a $100+ million (sales) company
- Responsible for all product related content development, such as sales collateral, white papers, product literature, online media and product/strategy briefings

- Served as the company's competitive intelligence and market research expert
- Represented the company at industry speaking events and to the IT analyst community

## NorthPoint Communications—San Francisco, CA                    November 1998–February 2001

NorthPoint was a nationwide DSL service provider targeting small and medium business and residential markets. The company also launched a European joint venture.

### Senior Manager, Product and Channel Marketing                    May 2000–February 2001

VersaPoint was a pan-European broadband provider formed by NorthPoint and Versatel in Amsterdam, The Netherlands. As a key member of the expatriate start-up team, I managed a team of four personnel that handled all the product and channel marketing for one of the leading pan-European, DSL-based, broadband providers:

- Led the marketing effort to acquire, build, and manage a pan-European ISP channel (Netherlands, Germany, France, and UK)
- Grew ISP partner base from zero to ten business-focused ISPs in the Netherlands and Germany; supported sales effort with selling tools (collateral and site-sellers), direct mail, seminars and events, and ISP lead generation
- Developed VersaPoint FastTrack and Business Builder, ISP channel support programs that helped ISP partners grow and manage their DSL businesses
- Results included "fast tracked" ISPs that have sold their first commercial line in under two months and 100% partner participation in the Business Builder end-user leads program
- Managed all end-user demand generation in the small business market, achieving end-user lines sales growth at 45% sequentially, month-over-month

### Product Manager, Residential DSL Products                    January 2000–April 2000
Product managed NorthPoint's first wholesale DSL product for the residential marketplace:
- Responsible for product definition, features and benefits, product documentation, and ongoing management and enhancement to the product
- Managed all product related interactions with Engineering, Legal, Sales, Finance, IT and other cross functional organizations
- Grew ISP partner base selling the product from 4 partners to 35 partners in four months
- Grew aggregate sales volume to 25% of NorthPoint's total line count

### Manager, New Channel Development                    November 1998–December 1999
Reporting to the Director of Channel Marketing, responsible for new sales channel development:
- Led the development of the strategy for new DSL sales channels through PC OEMs, retailers, VARs, and alternative channels, including Dell, Gateway, CompUSA and Office Depot
- Successfully launched NorthPoint Value-Added Reseller (VAR) Channel: developed strategy, sold to senior management, acquired and managed a two million dollar budget
- Implemented several strategic VAR marketing initiatives with equipment vendors such as 3Com, Netopia, and Efficient and ISPs such as XO, MegaPath, and UUNet; led, organized, and hosted VAR marketing events, encompassing more than 1,000 VAR participants, 50 ISP participants, in 20 cities across the US
- Managed direct mail, direct email, online media, and telemarketing to communicate with the VAR channel

## Sprint PCS—Irvine, CA                    June 1997–November 1998
Manager, Channel Strategy and Operations
Reporting to the Director of Distribution, responsible for all channel management and new channel development:
- Responsible for the formulation and the management of the company-wide channel strategy
- Conceived, negotiated, and led the launch of the first online distribution programs in the wireless industry

## Procter & Gamble—Rotterdam, The Netherlands                    MBA Summer Internship 1996
Assistant Brand Manager
Initiated a market leadership program for Ariel (Tide in the U.S.), the leading laundry detergent on the market

## FreeNet, (Co-)Founder and President—Rotterdam, The Netherlands                    1996
Start-up company resulting from Rotterdam MBA Entrepreneurship Team, 1996
- 1st prize winners at the European Business Plan of the Year Competition, 1996

# Matthew Doherty
51 East Peterson ♦ Pinesville, CO 36781
891.681.6781 ♦ ppollack@gmail.com

## SUMMARY OF QUALIFICATIONS

- Seasoned Channel Marketing Executive with 10 years' experience building value propositions for value-added resellers targeting small and medium sized business customers
- Dedicated sales partner with a background developing enablement tools for worldwide sales teams helping facilitate business opportunities with companies including AT&T, BellSouth, Dell, and Gateway
- Visionary marketer having launched the nation's first-ever online mobile phone store for Sprint, and having created, sold, and launched several multi-million dollar marketing programs
- MBA trained professional with nine-year background leading teams working for three $100MM+ networking equipment and security companies

## EXPERIENCE

SONICWALL, INC., PRODUCT MARKETING MANAGER, Sunnyvale, CA, July 2005–Present
*World's #1 security appliance vendor for small/medium sized companies: $175MM in annual sales*
- Lead the outbound product marketing for secure content management appliances and solutions, targeting channel partners worldwide
- Increased quarterly revenue growth 40% for SonicWALL's Content Security Manager
  - Petitioned management for additional funds to create integrated outbound campaign through 75 reselling partners throughout the world
- Quadrupled channel partners to 1,000 resellers in just four months by spearheading a recruitment campaign for SonicWALL Email Security
  - Developed content for 45 "Road Shows" across the globe giving away free trial version of software and promoting full range of security products
- Prepared a 50-page comprehensive quarterly summary report outlining business analytics and metrics for meeting with Executive Board and CEO
- Launching an extensive research program tapping into insights from both end-users and partners formalizing market research cycles for the company
- Overhauled content and logistics for quarterly Channel Partner Web Seminar increasing participation 400% to 1,500 partners worldwide

NETOPIA, INC., SENIOR PRODUCT MARKETING MANAGER, Emeryville, CA, March 2001–June 2005
*Leading supplier of broadband equipment working with carriers and service providers targeting small/medium businesses and residential market: $100MM in annual sales*
- Spearheaded high visibility product launch of new family of small business Wi-Fi products to BellSouth resulting in tenfold annual account revenue increase
  - Convinced company CEO to spend $100,000 to sponsor national BellSouth sale meeting to introduce new products
  - Developed proprietary "Desktop Wireless Guide" to assist 1,200 sales reps at 25 call centers to better sell Netopia products
- Introduced completely new strategic decision to create a dedicated RFP process helping company win 12 accounts representing $50MM in business annually
  - Major wins included EarthLink, BellSouth, AT&T, Covad, and Eircom
- Partnered closely with sales and marketing teams supporting strategic accounts in Europe and the US
- Created all product related content including sales collateral, white papers, direct mail, online media, and product/strategy briefings used by a sales force of 40 and thousands of frontline partner sales reps
- Represented the company at several national industry speaking events and to the IT analyst community

**NORTHPOINT COMMUNICATIONS,** San Francisco, CA, November 1998–February 2001
*Nationwide DSL service provider targeting small/medium business and residential markets*

SENIOR MANAGER, PRODUCT AND CHANNEL MARKETING, May 2000–February 2001
- Worked in The Netherlands to launch VersaPoint–pan-European joint venture formed by NorthPoint and Versatel providing broadband throughout Europe
- Managed a team of four as key member of expatriate start-up team overseeing $100MM product and channel marketing efforts
- Grew partner base from zero to 10 business-focused ISPs by creating and executing a fully integrated marketing effort spanning direct mail, targeted collateral/on-site selling tools, and interactive live events
- Increased end-user sales growth 45% monthly by creating a unique program to target small business market

MANAGER, NEW CHANNEL DEVELOPMENT, November 1998–April 2000
- Developed strategies to sell product through some of the nation's most prominent PC OEMs, Retailers, and Value Added Resellers (VARs) including Dell, Gateway, CompUSA, and Office Depot
- Introduced NorthPoint's first-ever VAR selling channel, developing business case presented to senior management, securing $2MM in funding, and developing strategic plan
- Created and executed a series of innovative marketing programs using direct mail, online media, telemarketing, direct email, and special events to reach thousands of VARs nationwide

**SPRINT PCS,** MANAGER, CHANNEL STRATEGY/OPERATIONS, Irvine, CA, June 1997–November 1998
- Conceived, negotiated, and launched the wireless industry's first-ever online distribution program–The Sprint PCS Store on AOL
  - First time a consumer could purchase a mobile phone online
- Responsible for all channel management and new channel development including company-owned stores and mall units

**PROCTER & GAMBLE,** ASSISTANT BRAND MANAGER, Rotterdam, The Netherlands, Summer 1996
- Initiated a market leadership program for Ariel (Tide in the US) as part of MBA summer internship

# EDUCATION

**ROTTERDAM SCHOOL OF MANAGEMENT**—ROTTERDAM, THE NETHERLANDS, 1997
- Masters of Business Administration—Erasmus Graduate School of Business
- MBA Exchange Program: IESE, Barcelona, Spain, Fall 1996
- 1st prize winner—European Business Plan of the Year Competition, 1996
  - Defeated teams from 15 other European business schools with free dial-up ISP concept

# INTERESTS

- Fishing, cooking, golf, and history

# Seeking Internal Promotion

I have said it before, and I will say it again: specifics, specifics, specifics.

Job seekers have a difficult time understanding the perspective of the resume reader. In your mind, you know exactly what you did on the job. In your mind, you understand the scope of your accomplishments. In your mind, everything on the resume makes perfect sense.

However, you must realize that the recruiting director knows none of this. In Richard's case, he was seeking a promotion, but the person who would promote him was not even in his department. He had to make sure he marketed himself effectively.

Look at what we did to make Richard's resume more specific.

## 1. We dropped a few names

Sprint, Verizon, AT&T, Carrier, Rheem, Trane, and so on. Since Richard worked on a few smaller accounts, we included familiar names that were the backbone of the company to show that he had interacted with the top clients.

## 2. We talked numbers

Whether it is billions, millions, thousands, or even just a few, notice the specific numbers we included throughout the resume. When a recruiting director reads the statement below, he or she might assume it refers to two or three agency partners:

> • Mentoring international and domestic agency partners

In the *after* version, we made sure the recruiting director knew it was forty clients and seventy-five agency partners.

## 3. We highlighted results

From increasing sales and creating new processes to driving interest in a product or service, we included it all.

• • •

There is no way you can read this resume and not know that Richard is an accomplished professional who gets things done with excellent results. Richard undoubtedly deserves a promotion.

**Richard Pike**

richard@aol.com

1005 Dale Street
Malvin, IL 60629

(712) 421-8511 H
(712) 428-8823 M

## Objective

To obtain a senior level marketing management position within the sports/entertainment industry where I can utilize past experiences in building brands through the development of insightful business/messaging strategies and executing successful, integrated communications

## Professional Experience

**BKR Chicago**—*Chicago, IL*                                                    *June 2003–Present*
*Senior Account Manager*

*Riley Corporation*

Accountable for the marketing communications management of an international B2B technology and engineering conglomerate at the corporate, platform and divisional levels

- Developing global corporate communications and media strategies that target Fortune 500 CEOs and investors
- Formulating integrated platform and divisional messaging strategies that support the Riley global brand
- Facilitating market research to determine appropriate targeting and messaging relating to new product launches
- Leading prominent media partner to develop high-impact, cost effective media strategies that include TV, print, radio, on-line, and outdoor on an international scale
- Mentoring international and domestic agency partners to understand communication goals and deliver on-strategy creative executions
- Managing client relationships for more than 8 different platforms and divisions within Riley
- Responsible for overseeing all execution and production, including TV, radio, print, web and outdoor

*ALLTEL*

Involved in the daily account management and tactical execution of advertising efforts for the nation's largest regional consumer wireless communications provider

- Guided the development of new product/promotion launch strategies
- Worked extensively to and facilitate the execution of TV, radio, and print advertising
- Instituted protocols and procedures to track competitive advertising
- Developed a monthly newsletter for distribution to both the client and agency that included competitive telecommunications advertising, the latest industry news and trends, and implications and recommendations

- Hosted weekly agency/client status meetings to track work progress and manage deadlines
- Participated in several new business pitches and advertising award submissions

**The Brinson Foundation**—*Chicago, IL* *March 2002–May 2003*

*Marketing Communications Consultant*

Guided the design and production of all annual reports, informational brochures, office signage, and website production for a Chicago-based, international charitable foundation

- *Managed the creative development and execution of all foundation collateral*
- *Supervised outside vendors throughout production process*
- *Directed grantee content development for inclusion in collateral*

**Backspin Productions, Inc.**—*Irvine, CA* *August 2000–October 2001*

*Account Manager*

Responsible for managing all accounts consisting of national golf course management companies including American Golf, Heritage Golf Group, Western Golf Properties, and Environmental Golf

- *Developed branding initiatives and marketing strategies, integrating traditional print mediums with Web, CD Rom, and eCommercials*
- *Conducted in-depth market research to ascertain needs and demands of clients and users of end products*
- *Drafted and negotiated service contracts for all accounts*
- *Oversaw the development of digital direct mail*
- Supervised the formulation of web/multimedia architecture and user experience models and evaluated client/user feedback for content continuity and flow

**Western Golf Properties, Oak Creek Golf Club**—Irvine, CA *August 1996–July 2000*
Director of Marketing and Tournament Sales

*Urban Arena Landscape Architecture*—Newport Beach, CA *August 1998–September 2001*
Illustrator/Designer

**Gary Roger Baird Golf Design International**—Santa Ana, CA *April 1997–March 1998*
Draftsman/Illustrator

*Related Skills, Activities, Honors*
- *BKR "Better Ideas. Better Results." Leadership Award Recipient 2005*
- *Golf Professional 1996–2000*
- *Class President, Sigma Chi Fraternity*

*Education*
**Bachelor of Science, Landscape Architecture** *June 1996*
**California Polytechnic State University, San Luis Obispo**
- *Dean's List for Academic Achievement*

# Richard Pike

1005 Dale Street ♦ Malvin, IL 60629
712.421.8511 ♦ richard@aol.com

## SUMMARY

- Seasoned marketing professional with 10 years' experience building brands across an integrated platform spanning traditional media and cutting edge technology
- New brand specialist with extensive background researching, developing launch strategies, and creating communications plans in the golf, wireless, and technology industries
- Dedicated manager and partner , worked as key group leader with diverse agency and client teams as large as 40
- Proven performer formally recognized for leadership achievements at DDR

## EXPERIENCE

**BKR CHICAGO,** SENIOR ACCOUNT MANAGER, Chicago, IL, June 2003–Present

Riley
- Manage communications strategy, production, and execution of global brand campaign for $16 billion B-to-B technology company, coordinating efforts across 20 countries
- Serve as brand's consultant developing business strategies, product strategies, and go-to-market strategies for Emerson brand spanning 85 distinct divisions
    - Continually sell Emerson "overbrand" concept encouraging portfolio efficiencies and managing integrated communications strategy across all sub-brands
- Primary liaison for 40 clients worldwide encompassing all business units, and for a total of 75 agency partners and vendors
    - Work with team members and clients in China, Brazil, Great Britian, France, and more
- Helped launch Ultratech Home System–integrated suite of heating, ventilation, and air conditioning (HVAC) products revolutionizing the way contractors and OEMs purchase equipment
    - Increased sales 45% in less than one year
    - Products sold to nation's largest OEMs including Carrier, Rheem, and Trane
- Launched marketing effort for unique plant automation platform for process management product that dramatically increases plant uptime
    - Developed comprehensive communications strategy encompassing new plans and procedures
    - Launched campaign globally for $12 billion product–company's most profitable
- Key contributor to several research studies including brand study research, demography, and consumer test
    - Participated in extensive qualitative and quantitative naming research interviewing 560 HVAC representatives to determine new name for worldwide product launch
- Awarded prestigious BKR "Better Ideas. Better Results." Leadership Award for outstanding accomplishments

ALLTEL
- Manage business for largest regional wireless company in the country with $7B in sales and $40MM in agency revenue

- Repositioned brand, dramatically increasing consumer consideration from 26% to 32%—exceeding goals more than threefold
- Increased nationwide net sales by more than 20% in seven of first eight quarters
- Developed hundreds of TV, radio, and print advertisements for fast-paced $11MM retail account
- Initiated account's first-ever competitive advertising protocols and procedures evaluating marketing efforts for nation's largest wireless companies including Sprint, Verizon, and AT&T
  - Prepared a monthly competitive newsletter distributed to entire ALLTEL marketing department and company CEO providing agency POVs to help guide brand strategy
- Helped extend BKR relationship to include Mur BKR, Del Rivero BKR and BKR Matrix increasing holding company revenue up to $7MM

**THE BRINSON FOUNDATION,** MARKETING CONSULTANT, Chicago, IL, March 2002–May 2003
- Guided the design and production of a wide variety of collateral material for international charitable foundation donating $5MM annually
- Produced a series of informational brochures distributed to leading cultural and civic groups throughout the nation including The Field Museum, Metropolitan Museum of Art, and the Art Institute
- Designed format for 50-page annual report still in use today, and crafted organization's first-ever website

**BACKSPIN PRODUCTIONS,** ACCOUNT MANAGER, Irvine, CA, August 2000–October 2001
- Marketed several new golf courses from pre-opening to opening, establishing initial market presence and dramatically exceeding year one sales goals in all instances
- Developed a series of innovative technology based marketing programs including CD-ROM programs and eCommercials
- Prepared fully integrated marketing programs spanning traditional and non-traditional advertising media based on extensive consumer research

**WESTERN GOLF PROPERTIES,** DIRECTOR OF MARKETING, Irvine, CA, August 1996–July 2000

**OAK CREEK GOLF CLUB,** FREELANCE GOLF PROFESSIONAL, Irvine, CA, May 1996–May 2000

## EDUCATION

**CALIFORNIA POLYTECHNIC STATE UNIVERSITY**—SAN LUIS OBISPO, 1996
Bachelor of Science in Landscape Architecture

# Seeking Internal Promotion

The changes we made in Susan's resume provide an excellent example of the "less is more" philosophy. In her *before* resume, she had listed too many jobs from college, and she had too many different titles and positions in her most recent employment section.

She was hoping to secure a promotion within her current company, so many of her past experiences were no longer relevant. We cleaned it up.

We consolidated her titles for her advertising agency job and for her contract position. Again, the recruiting director does not need every single detail of your past. While you think the distinction is important, that doesn't necessarily mean the recruiting director will. Take a look at what Susan wrote in her *before* version for the McDonald's and DDB jobs and see if you can tell what she did when. It definitely had me confused. Keep it short and focused.

We also eliminated her college internships. Since she had been working for several years, those positions were no longer relevant.

The one-page resume works well for her and showcases her hard work at DDB. Susan is positioned well to move up in the agency.

# SUSAN SPRINGS

EMAIL: *springs@aol.com*

456 SILVER AVE. # 8 S ♦ SACRAMENTO, CA 204819       PHONE: (416) 361-8921

## OBJECTIVE

Open to opportunities as a seasoned Senior Account Executive or entry Account Supervisor position.

## PROFESSIONAL EXPERIENCE

**MCDONALD'S CORPORATION**—Oakbrook, Illinois                                     8/05–present
*BRAND MANAGER (CONSULTANT)*—MCDONALD'S MENU MANAGEMENT TEAM      9/04–10/04
- Co-managed market tests on Sampling to see if results were successful. Resulted in first ever National QSR Sampling Event
- Co-managing development of new product slated for National Launch in back half of 2006. Work in conjunction with cross-functional departments and responsible for management of all agencies in assignments, provide project updates and presentations to Senior Management and Leadership teams.

**DDB CHICAGO**—Chicago, Illinois                                                       2003–present
*ACCOUNT MANAGER*—MCDONALD'S MENU MANAGEMENT TEAM                     2003–8/05
- Managed 10 new product Advertised Sales Tests in various markets throughout the United States, resulting in the National Launch of 5 new products.
- Managed 3 fully-integrated National Launches of new products including TV, Radio, Print, OOH, Direct Mail and Digital.
- Managed R & D and initial strategic planning on additional 4 new products in pipe line for National Launches slated in 2006
- Managed over 24 TV productions: 12 Live Action and 12 Food Shoots.
- Managed first ever National QSR sampling program with Chicken Selects resulting in a lift of (trying to get % from client)
- Represented DDB Menu Management team at over 15 Client Iterative Research groups that affected development of new product initiatives .
- Responsible for managing annual $7MM+ production budgets for Menu Team.
- Co-authored 8 Creative Briefs with Planning Department
- Member of the Competitive Task Force—responsible for competitive analysis of largest competitor, Burger King
- Responsible for all facets of marketing plan: R&D, strategy, positioning, production, on-air marketing tactics

*ACCOUNT MANAGER*—MCDONALD'S YOUNG ADULT TEAM                           6/05–present
- Managed $ Menu National OOH program
- Managing first ever college-targeted OOH program
- Managing a renaming/rebranding initiative for one of the largest sales drivers of our business

**DAILEY & ASSOCIATES ADVERTISING**—West Hollywood, California                2001–2003
*ASSISTANT ACCOUNT EXECUTIVE*—WEYERHAEUSER, LEGOLAND CALIFORNIA
- Successfully collected over $1.3MM+ in over-due invoices from client in a 4-week period.
- Generated two annual agency bonuses in excess of $40,000 by keeping all jobs within $7MM+ budget.
- Coordinated the Agency's successful new business pitch for the largest portion of the Weyerhaeuser account including spearheading competitive research, analyzing marketplace dynamics, compiling all presentation materials and managing pitch timeline.
- Helped manage three television commercial productions and eight print productions from creative development through final client approvals.
- Wrote three creative briefs and helped produce fully integrated campaigns including TV, print, radio, outdoor, direct marketing and business to business.
- Coordinated all components of LEGOLAND California''s 2003 summer promotions including partner relationships, on-site efforts and ticket giveaways.
- Created comprehensive competitive analysis for LEGOLAND California tracking the travel and tourism industry both locally and nationally.
- Responsible for creative rotation schedules, traffic instructions, talent contracts, weekly status reports, and production timelines.
- Chosen as one of five nominees out of staff of 280 for Dailey "Bright Light" award based on attitude and achievements.

**AAAA**—INSTITUTE FOR ADVANCED ADVERTISING STUDIES PROGRAM—Los Angeles, California 2/2003–5/2003
*ACCOUNT MANAGEMENT TEAM*—POWER RANGERS
- Chosen as one of five nominees to represent agency based on accomplishments and achievements.

- Created fully integrated $10MM marketing plan presented to Client and Industry Executives.
- Developed creative strategy, target insights and brand positioning.
- Presented Interactive Media and Promotional concepts to Executive panel.

**SUE PROCKO PUBLIC RELATIONS**—Beverly Hills, California                                    2000–2001
*INTERN*—**HOME ENTERTAINMENT PR AGENCY**
- Coordinated and manned the pressroom at the largest trade show in the industry held in Las Vegas, Nevada.
- Successfully organized national radio promotion for largest client, resulting in 150,000 DVDs shipped in 11 days, dramatically exceeding expectations.

## EDUCATION

**CALIFORNIA LUTHERAN UNIVERSITY**—Thousand Oaks, California
Bachelor of Arts, Marketing Communications, Magna Cum Laude                              5/2001
Overall GPA 3.78/4.0, Dean's List all Semesters
Presidential Scholarship Recipient—Academic Excellence Award funding 35% of college education at CLU.

**PEPPERDINE UNIVERSITY**—Malibu, California                                                        Study
Abroad Participant—Buenos Aires, Argentina; Madrid, Spain                                1999

## ACTIVITIES AND INTERESTS

Volunteer for Off the Street Club in Chicago                                              2005
Co-Chair of the First Annual "Dailey Golf Day"                                            2003
Co-Chair of the Advertising Association of Los Angeles "Career Day" at Dailey            2002
American Cancer Society's Relay for Life–Participant                                      2000–2002
Screen Actors Guild—Member in good standing                                              1983–present

Interests include: Traveling, movies, competitive ballroom dancing, photography, and making homemade Italian pizza.

# SUSAN SPRINGS

456 SILVER AVENUE # 8 S ◆◆ SACRAMENTO, CA 204819 ◆◆ (416) 361-8921 ◆◆ springs@aol.com

## PROFESSIONAL EXPERIENCE

**MCDONALD'S CORPORATION**—(August 2005–present / September 2004–October 2004)    Oak Brook, IL
*BRAND MANAGER (CONSULTANT)*—MCDONALD'S MENU MANAGEMENT TEAM

- Requested by McDonald's management to fill in for a Director on a Field Training assignment to serve as full-time Brand Manager for two separate stints
- Managing all aspects of new breakfast product launch including: test market evaluation, product development, pricing and sales, marketing plan, operations test, and advertised sales test
- Leading a cross-functional team comprised of five agencies: General, African-American and Hispanic Consumer market segments, merchandising and packaging, and internal McDonald's departments consisting of: Culinary, Operations, Equipment, Business Research, Sales Analysis, Supply Chain and Creative
- Overseeing logistics for six store operations test in preparation for 1,000+ store advertised sales test
- Organized successful Chicken Selects sampling market test leading to McDonald's national sampling launch–first-ever in Quick Service Restaurant category

**DDB CHICAGO**—(September 2003–present)    Chicago, IL
*ACCOUNT MANAGER*–MCDONALD'S MENU MANAGEMENT TEAM/YOUNG ADULT TEAM

- Managed 10 new product advertised sales tests in more than 20 markets throughout the United States
  - Developed concepts, attended 50+ focus groups, worked extensively with local markets to develop all aspects of integrated marketing campaigns
  - High success rate resulting in 5 products launching Nationally within a two year timeframe
- Spearheaded advertising efforts for 13,000 store National launches of: Chicken Selects, Premium Chicken Sandwiches and Fiesta Salad
  - Lead integrated advertising efforts for Premium Chicken Sandwiches resulting in 114% increase in unit volume
  - Managed fully integrated campaign for launch of Chicken Selects resulting in $9,000—$12,000 annual incremental profit per store
- Successfully managed more than $14 million in production budgets across 24 television productions spanning two years
- Planned and executed all advertising for first-ever National Quick Service Restaurant sampling program with Chicken Selects resulting in a volume lift of 115%
- Co-authored eight creative briefs in conjunction with Planning Department–worked closely with a team of over 24 creatives
- Prepare quarterly comprehensive analysis of Burger King as member of DDB/McDonald's Competitive Task Force
- Managing creative development, production and logistics for McDonalds's first ever college-targeted out-of-home program covering over 850 college campuses Nationwide

**DAILEY & ASSOCIATES ADVERTISING**—(August 2001–July 2003)    West Hollywood, CA
*ASSISTANT ACCOUNT EXECUTIVE*—WEYERHAEUSER, LEGOLAND CALIFORNIA

- Championed collection of $1.3+ million in overdue invoices from client in a 4-week period
- Generated two annual agency bonuses in excess of $40,000 by keeping all jobs within $7+ million budget
- Selected as one of five nominees to represent agency at the AAAA Institute for Advanced Advertising Studies Program
- Chosen as one of five nominees out of staff of 280 for Dailey "Bright Light" award based on attitude and achievements

## EDUCATION

**CALIFORNIA LUTHERAN UNIVERSITY**    Thousand Oaks, CA
Bachelor of Arts, Marketing Communications, Magna Cum Laude; Graduated May 2001

**PEPPERDINE UNIVERSITY**    Malibu, CA

## ACTIVITIES AND INTERESTS

Volunteer for Off The Street Club in Chicago (2005)
Co-Chair of the First Annual "Dailey Golf Day" and the Los Angeles "Career Day" at Dailey (2002–2003)
Interests include: Traveling, movies, photography, and making homemade Italian pizza

# FREQUENT JOB CHANGER

As we mentioned in the "Career Change" chapter, switching jobs or careers is more common these days. Job seekers switch jobs for a variety of reasons—maybe they have a horrible boss, or they need a shorter commute, or they want more money or less stress. The reasons vary, but it is definitely common to see several companies in a person's job history.

A recruiting director obviously wants to hire a great employee who will be dedicated to the company. Hiring, training, and onboarding a new employee is a costly expense, so the recruiting director wants to hire someone who will show a little loyalty. There is nothing worse than taking the time and resources to hire and train new employees just to have them leave after three months. From the employer's perspective, it's kind of like breaking up with a significant other just when the relationship is getting good!

With that perspective in mind, you can see why a "job hopper" might raise the eyebrows of recruiting directors. They will not throw your resume in the garbage automatically, but they will be a little concerned about why you changed jobs so many times. They might be afraid you will leave their company in six months.

Here are some tips and techniques that you can use on your resume to help with this situation:

## 1. Address the job changes in your cover letter

If you held numerous jobs in the last couple years, you have the opportunity to explain your story in your cover letter. If you address your situation, this may prevent recruiting directors from thinking "Taboo!" when they look at your resume.

Now, you have to be careful when using this technique. You want to mention your reasons briefly in one or two sentences, and then move on. You don't want to call more attention to your job hopping by dwelling on the topic, and you don't want to drag up any dirt or baggage. A recruiting director doesn't want to hear sad stories about the last five nightmare bosses you had. Since this is such a fine line to walk, we have included a sample cover letter at the end of this book to show you how to clarify your job hopping in a professional, explanatory manner. Here are a few ideas for sharp first sentences for your cover letter:

*My career path has been a winding road, and I never realized how many skills I could gain from taking the scenic route.*

*Jobs have taken me across the country from Oregon to South Carolina, but now I am ready to settle down in Austin, Texas.*

*You have to try on a lot of hats to find the perfect fit.*

## 2. Eliminate jobs that are not relevant to the job you are pursuing

For example, if you held three jobs in 2007, you don't have to mention the interim retail job that you picked up for two months.

## 3. Focus on the positive

Changing jobs and environments frequently equips you with some skills that employers are seeking: versatility, experience, adaptability, resourcefulness. Highlight the wide breadth of skills and experiences you have gained by working at numerous companies.

• • •

If you absolutely hate your job, then you shouldn't remain miserable for three years simply because you do not want to be seen as a job hopper. Just employ some of our tips listed on the following resumes to make the best of what may not be an ideal situation.

# Frequent Job Changer

We used a little JobBound trick on Ethan's resume. You are getting the inside scoop, so feel free to incorporate this tip on your resume. Ethan had some great experience, but you will see that he did a lot of contract work. He ended up spending just a few months at each of several different companies. That can be a challenge on a resume. As a job seeker, you run the risk of appearing to move to a lot of different jobs and to hold no employer loyalty.

Here's what we did. Instead of listing both the month and the year for each job, we simply listed the year. That allowed us to exclude a couple of his jobs, so it doesn't appear as if he moved around so much. This trick works both for people who have done contract work as well as for those of you who have changed full-time jobs quite a bit.

Now, this is not advocating lying or being deceptive on your resume, but your resume doesn't need to be a daily chronicle of your experiences. You never want to lie or present false information on your resume, and you also need to be prepared if an interviewer asks you specific questions about dates. Of course, you want to be open and honest in this case.

You can simply state, "I had a number of contract jobs during the year, so I only focused on those that were most relevant."

Check out the new resume. It highlights Ethan's great qualifications, and it makes him look like a more stable employee.

# Ethan Everest

8831 E. Eastwick Street
Eastbay, CA 44862

Phone: (416) 378-5671
Email: ethaneverest@yahoo.com

## Professional Objective

Accomplished human resources professional seeking a position in a medium to large company that would apply advanced degrees in human resource and business management, along with eight years of business and benefits administration experience.

## Experience

**SUA Insurance Company,** Chicago, Illinois

1/2005 to Present

### *Human Resources Administrator*
Manage the overall human resources function of a start-up Property and Casualty insurance company in downtown Chicago, which has since doubled in size. Responsible for lifecycle recruiting, benefits administration, and employee relations. Developed the compensation program and performance management policy.

- Oversee all drug screening, background checks, and reference verification.
- Provide benefits orientation and enrollment support to organization, which includes medical, dental, STD & LTD, life insurance, and leave of absence.
- Responsible for maintaining vendor relationships for benefits and payroll.
- Maintain personnel files to ensure completeness and compliance with federal and state laws.
- Facilitate internal training and coordinate outsourced training programs to meet the needs of the company or regulatory requirements.
- Conduct exit interview and process termination of employees.

**BeneTemps,** Needham, Massachusetts

11/2004 to 1/2005 (Contract position)

### *Implementation Support Representative*
Contracted to assist with the implementation of new clients for ADP TotalSource, which is one of the largest Professional Employer Organizations in the world. Maintained client data, reviewed employment materials of new client employees, and provided ongoing support to the implementation specialist in conducting audits and providing information to clients.

- Reviewed client New Hire booklets for accuracy.
- Handled client issues in the absence of the implementation specialist.
- Responsible for fulfillment of Welcome Packages, Client Source Binders, and Orientation Packages.
- Maintained information on new clients in tracking system and reported issues to the implementation specialist for further resolution.

**Kelly Services,** Florence, Alabama

6/2004 to 9/2004 (Contract position)

### *On-Site Supervisor*
Managed a temporary staff of over 450 employees for Sara Lee's food processing facility. Responsible for lifecycle recruiting, safety orientations, plant tours, employee relations, and client relations with Sara Lee management.

- Conducted New Hire Orientation; completed and verified all new hire paperwork (i.e. I-9's , W4's).
- Conduct exit interviews and made recommendations to upper management for process and work flow improvements.
- Workers Compensation-- First report of injury.
- Represented organization at unemployment hearings.

**FlexBen Corporation,** Lombard, Illinois                                    2/2004 to 5/2004

*Account Manager*

Responsible for COBRA plan administration for 10 clients. Acted as the subject matter expert in responding to client inquiries and escalated participant calls.

Trained customer service department on client specific policies and procedures.
- Counseled client and participants on COBRA regulations and Plan procedures.
- Generated client specific letters in relation to billing, terminations, and enrollment.
- Resolved issues at the client and customer level.
- Designed and developed client communication.

**Human Resources International,** Chicago, Illinois          9/2003 to 2/2004 (Contract position)

*Benefits Analyst*

Contracted to administer benefits for over 3,500 staff, associate and partner attorneys of Mayer, Brown, Rowe & Maw LLP, which is among the 10 largest law practices in the world. Drafted policies and procedures for the benefits analyst role, acted as the lead analyst as the firm changed its LTD policy for over 200 partner attorneys, and participated in the analysis and research of companies to potentially outsource its COBRA benefits.

- Resolved benefit related issues for employees.
- Conducted benefit orientations for current and new employees.
- Premium billing reconciliation.

**Follett Corporation,** River Grove, Illinois                            3/2001 to 9/2003

*Benefits Specialist*

Administered corporate benefits for over 5,000 active employees, retirees, and former employees. Also responsible for administering COBRA, and the corporate leave of absence policy for six divisions.

- Administered benefits programs such as: health insurance, dental insurance, life insurance, long-term and short term disability insurance, retiree health plan, domestic partner benefits.
- Resolved benefit related issues for employees.
- Consulted with field HR personnel regarding the proper procedures for leave of absences, and short/long-term disability.
- Manually processed weekly payroll for leave of absence employees.
- Drafted policies and procedures for benefits specialist position.
- Assisted in organization of health fairs and other special health & welfare vendor functions.

## *Education*

**Roosevelt University,** Chicago, Illinois

Walter E. Heller College of Business Administration, Masters of Science in Human Resources Management (Expected graduation 5/2009)

**DePaul University,** Chicago, Illinois

Bachelor of Arts, Business Management, June 2003

---

# Ethan Everest

8831 E. Eastwick Street ♦ Eastbay, CA 44862
416.378.5671 ♦ ethaneverest@yahoo.com

## EXPERIENCE

**HUMAN RESOURCES SPECIALIST,** SUA INSURANCE COMPANY, Chicago, IL, 2005–Present
- Sole HR representative for a growing organization with 69 full-time employees
- Hired 43 full-time professionals in 2005 ranging up to Director level across all company departments, more than doubling the size of the company
- Proactively sought out unique low cost recruiting techniques saving organization thousands of dollars in executive recruiter fees
- Helped craft job descriptions for 40 job titles across eight different departments
- Manage relationship with Professional Employer Organization (PEO), handling all payroll, benefits, workers' compensation, unemployment, and more
- Overhauling compensation program revamping job bands and updating salary structure for rapidly expanding organization
- Established company's first-ever performance management process insuring annual assessment compliance for all employees
- Launched new hire orientation program spanning medical and dental benefits, short/long term disability, life insurance, and leave of absence processes
- Seeking out cost effective benefits program to eventually replace PEO
- Coordinate training program, selecting content and sourcing training vendors
- Oversaw two office location moves in less than one year

**ON-SITE SUPERVISOR,** KELLY SERVICES, Florence, AL, 2004
- Managed a temporary staff of more than 450 employees for Sara Lee food processing facility
- Screened and hired hundreds of candidates for several different high-turnover plant positions
- Coordinated New Hire Orientations for more than 200 full-time temporary employees
- Recommended to upper management revised payment disbursement process for temp employees
- Oversaw weekly performance appraisal process for dozens of workers
- Managed and tracked strict attendance policy resulting in several terminations
- Represented Kelly Services at several disputed unemployment hearings

**BENEFITS ANALYST,** HUMAN RESOURCES INTERNATIONAL, Chicago, IL, 2003–2004
- Contracted to administer benefits for more than 3,500 staff, associates, and partner attorneys at Mayer, Brown, Rowe and Maw LLP—one of the world's largest law firms
- Managed a comprehensive five-tiered benefits program across the firm
- Created organization's first-ever policies and procedures document outlining all activities for the benefits analyst role
- Partnered with outside vendor to overhaul firm's LTD policy for 200 partner attorneys

**BENEFITS SPECIALIST,** FOLLETT CORPORATION, River Grove, IL, 2001–2003
- Administered corporate benefits to more than 5,000 active employees, retirees, and former employees across the country
- Worked closely with Senior Management and HR Director/Managers at six different corporate divisions
- Communicated with up to 50 employees weekly concerning COBRA eligibility for employees in more than 100 locations nationwide

- Maintained contact with dozens of employees regarding short and long-term leaves of absence, and FMLA
- Handled all aspects of retiree benefits for more than 50 former employees
- Crafted company's first-ever policy and procedure manual for benefits specialist position
- Administered company's new domestic partner benefits program–overseeing and verifying all documentation

## EDUCATION

**ROOSEVELT UNIVERSITY**—CHICAGO, IL, May 2009
- Masters of Science in Human Resource Management; Walter E. Heller College of Business Administration

**DEPAUL UNIVERSITY**—CHICAGO, IL, June 2003
- Bachelor of Arts; Business Management

# Frequent Job Changer

Nicholas had a number of great experiences at a number of businesses. Just as we did for Ethan, we only included the years—and not the specific months—for Nicholas's employment dates. We also removed the bullet points from his earliest experiences to deemphasize his multiple jobs.

Additionally, we had to teach Nicholas that it was okay to be a name-dropper. He was faced with an interesting dilemma. He had worked at the forefront of the digital marketing field, but most of the companies he worked for had gone out of business, changed names, or were not all that recognizable to mainstream marketers.

We took a different approach to highlight his skills and accomplishments. First of all, we highlighted his past clientele. He had helped manage the online marketing efforts of some of the world's biggest brands—GM, Kraft, and Sony. We put that as the first point in his summary. Now, that should turn a few heads.

We also showcased his job titles instead of his companies. You will notice that in the *before* version, he lists his company names first and bolds them. Have you heard of the companies L90 or Performics? Neither had we. Instead, we started with his titles. In his case, the titles were manager of business development and director of sales. That establishes his experience and credibility. It also takes the attention away from the company name, and the fact that he worked at a different company every two years.

This isn't necessarily the approach for everyone, but you want to start each entry either with your title or with your company—whichever is more relevant to the recruiting director. Just make sure you keep it consistent all the way through the resume.

**Nicholas Nickelby** 334 Newberry Ave.—Northbrook, IL 58634 H: (847) 668.3387 C: (847) 563.8751

Creative, result-oriented marketing communications professional with extensive experience in Internet marketing and media, traditional advertising and promotions. Superb writer, highly skilled in project management, strategic concepting, and event planning for consumer and business to business applications. Self-starter, strong motivator, excellent communicator and skilled manager of people and projects.

## Performics, Inc (Chicago, IL)
Sr. Manager Business Development—September 2002–Present
**Email Marketing**
- Responsible for the development of all internal processes and reporting for email marketing initiatives
- Manage relationships with over 30 email marketing vendors executing campaigns for clients including, Bose, Sony, Kraft & Kohl's
- Developed internal reporting tool to track campaign results and determine ROI of email campaigns
- Act as Performics privacy officer on matters related to SPAM legislation and it's effect on email marketing

**Lead Generation**
- Project Manager for the launch and execution of a Performics lead generation platform
- Executed Performics first ever lead generation campaigns for Bose, hpshopping, J.Jill, A&E and History Channel online
- Generated $80,000 in incremental revenue for Q3 & Q4 of 2003 through the execution of lead generation campaigns

## L90 Online Media & Direct Marketing (Chicago, IL)
Director of Midwest Sales—March 2001–January 2002
Director of L90 Direct—March 2000–March 2001
- Managed five person sales staff to 105% of regional goal for 2001 fiscal year ($3.1 Million)
- Interacted with agency Senior level media and account staffs in an eight state region selling L90 capabillities
- Consulted with Fortune 500 companies in online marketing strategy at the brand management and director level; clients included Sears.com, Tropicana, Quaker Oats, Chrysler & Discover financial services

## Keith Kriegler & Associates (Chicago, IL)
Account Supervisor—June 1999–March 2000
**The Maytag Corporation**
- Oversaw all facets of agency business in relation to the four million dollar Maytag appliance account; Responsibilities included management of assignments with Maytag corporate & regional offices and Maytag International
- Consulted Maytag's Retail Merchandising Director & Category Vice Presidents on the development of retail marketing initiatives pertaining to their four core appliance categories
- Coordinated cross promotions between The Maytag Corporation and Kraft to provide value-added incentives to consumers in the retail and on-line environment

## UPSHOT (Chicago, IL)
Sr. Account Manager—May 1997–May 1999
**The Coca-Cola Company**
- Developed innovative marketing programs to leverage and extend brand equities for Coca-Cola
- Generated strategic promotional concepts for core brands including Coca-Cola Classic, SURGE and Fruitopia
- Managed client relationships with Coca-Cola internal promotions unit including development of budgets and program timing

**Southwestern Bell Communications (SBC)**
**SmartMoves**
- Managed day to day operation of the SBC SmartMoves channel marketing initiative
- Oversaw the development of program tactics including sales aids, quarterly newsletters and on-premise events to increase revenue through the channel

## UPSHOT (Chicago, IL)—Cont'd

Sr. Account Manager—May 1997–May 1999
**Diversity Mobile Unit**
- Project manager on the creation and deployment of the Southwestern Bell Diversity Mobile Unit
- Coordinated 14 vendors for the development of mobile unit accessories including: a video wall & bilingual video, interactive computer programs, bilingual website, branded inflatables & digital photography
- Managed the mobile unit tour staff and a development budget in excess of $800,000

**College Marketing**
- Assisted in the implementation and execution of the SBC College tabling promotion
- Oversaw all facets of media including placement of 30 college newspaper ads and ten radio remotes
- Managed a customer acquisition initiative targeting collegiate consumers at Oklahoma University and Texas Tech

## Sport & Social Clubs of the U.S. (Chicago, IL)

Director of Marketing—March 1994–March 1997
- Supervised a five person staff for execution of national marketing plans, including promotions, public relations, advertising, direct mail and data base management
- Project leader on programs related to the internet and other electronic media; coordinated inclusion of Chicago Social Club pages on www.cyberchicago.com
- Coordinated on-premise marketing efforts for national sponsors, Anheuser-Busch and Jack Daniels
- Administered national on-premise bar sponsorship program; managed an average of 60 accounts per quarter

## Campbell Mithun Esty Advertising (Southfield, MI)

Account Executive—December 1991–January 1993
**Jeep & Eagle Division—Chrysler Corporation**
- Project leader in creation of promotional and technical four color brochure and binders for distribution to over 1,500 Jeep/Eagle dealerships
- Managed the inclusion of all Jeep/Eagle vehicle information on the Prodigy computer network
- Assisted in merchandising programs with regards to the launch of the Jeep Grand Cherokee and Eagle Vision

## Ross Roy Communications (Bloomfield Hills, MI)

Assistant Account Executive—January 1990 to November 1991
**Chrysler Corporation**
- Responsible for the monthly production and distribution of the Jeep/Eagle technical service program "Video Tec" to over 1,500 Jeep/Eagle dealers nationwide
- Interacted with Chrysler Corporation training personnel in the development of "Video Tec" including conceptualization of topics, material scripting, video & print production and distribution

---

**EDUCATION:**    Michigan State University-BA / Advertising May 1989

**INTERESTS &**    Two term Vice President—Michigan State University Alumni Association
**HONORS:**    Member of Chicago Interactive Marketing Association (CIMA)

---

# Nicholas Nickelby

334 Newberry Ave. ♦ Northbrook, IL 58634
847.668.3387 ♦ nnickelby@aol.com

## SUMMARY

- Dedicated interactive marketing professional with considerable experience managing online efforts for some of the world's biggest brands including GM, Kraft, and Sony
- Successful new business developer helping secure several million dollars in new client activity
- Seasoned leader with more than 10 years experience managing, training, and developing diverse teams
- Tireless "agent of change" helping launch several significant, revenue-generating new programs

## EXPERIENCE

**MANAGER, BUSINESS DEVELOPMENT,** PERFORMICS, INC, Chicago, IL, 2002–Present
*USA Today, Sony, General Motors, Kraft, Kohl's, Bose, Spiegel*

- Sourced concept and project managed development of company's first-ever lead generation platform creating $500,000 in gross revenue
- Overhauled firm's entire email marketing effort, revamping operations, testing, and business development resulting in $165,000 in sales
  - Coordinated all new business activity facilitating relationships with more than 120 clients including GM, Kraft, and Sony
  - Solicited and secured more than 15 email partners representing 100,000,000 opt-in names
  - Created proprietary campaign performance summary reports for every company client tracking effective CPM, opens, click throughs, and sales
- Quadrupled leads and revenue for Graduate Loan Center by identifying and securing better and stronger relationship partners
- Added 250,000 qualified names to Bose database in less than four months through aggressive operations and management
- Act as company's privacy officer, educating dozens of clients on legislative email marketing issues
- Managed operations for all processes related to lead generation and email marketing, including all client communication pieces, partner direction, and internal protocol

**DIRECTOR, MIDWEST SALES,** L90 ONLINE MEDIA/DIRECT MARKETING, Chicago, IL, 2000–2002

- Managed five-person staff generating $3.1MM in sales in 2001, exceeding year ago figures by 12%
- Sold Tropicana on first-ever online media effort—a $200,000 sale—ultimately comprising development of micro site and game/sweepstakes component
- Ranked second in nation behind Yahoo! in online program sales to Starcom media buying company
- Developed and sold $125,000 integrated program to Kraft featuring content and online presence
- Trained staff of five in comprehensive S.P.I.N selling techniques
- Called on several Fortune 500 companies including Sears.com, Quaker Oats, Chrysler, and Discover

**KEITH KRIEGLER & ASSOCIATES,** ACCOUNT SUPERVISOR, Chicago, IL, 1999–2000

- Oversaw all facets of agency business, and staff of three for $4MM Maytag appliance account
- Led production of quarterly local store marketing kits across four key appliance categories distributed to more than 130 retailers nationwide
- Presented dozens of advertising/promotion retail strategy concepts to four key "C-level" directors

**SENIOR ACCOUNT MANAGER,** UPSHOT, Chicago, IL, 1997–1999
*Coca-Cola, SBC*
- Prepared comprehensive promotion book compiling all point-of-purchase for Coca-Cola brands, annually distributed to 60 bottlers nationwide
- Managed SBC Diversity Mobile Unit comprised of video wall, bilingual website, and branded inflatables traveling to 30 markets and seen by more than 20,000 people
- Helped implement and execute SBC College program handling all media including newspaper and radio at 30 campuses throughout the country

**DIRECTOR OF MARKETING,** SPORT AND SOCIAL CLUBS OF THE US, Chicago, IL, 1994–1997
- Developed turnkey marketing programs helping club expand presence from 12 to 23 markets in less than three years
- Led a staff of five executing marketing plans including promotions, public relations, advertising, direct mail, and database

**ACCOUNT EXECUTIVE,** CAMPBELL MITHUN ESTY ADVERTISING, Southfield, MI, 1991–1993
*Jeep and Eagle Division, Chrysler Corporation*

**ASSISTANT AE,** ROSS ROY COMMUNICATIONS, Bloomfield Hills, MI, 1990–1991
*Chrysler Corporation*

## EDUCATION

**MICHIGAN STATE UNIVERSITY**–EAST LANSING, MI, 1989
- Bachelor of Arts in Advertising

## ACTIVITIES/INTERESTS

- Board Member, Chicago Interactive Marketing Association (CIMA), 2001–Present
- Vice President—two terms, Michigan State University Alumni Association, 2001–2003
- Referee, Various Basketball Leagues, 1994–Present
- Interests include: athletics, travel, cooking, and reading

# Frequent Job Changer

First, before we go any further, please take thirty seconds right now and read the MJK Worldwide job in both the *before* and *after* versions of the resume that follows. Pretty amazing, right?

On the *before* version, Tina is practically screaming, "Look at me, look at me, I'm a job hopper!" The way she places her dates all the way to the left in the white space really calls attention to her job mobility! Again, dates are least important, so they should be included last in the entry—especially if you do not want them to stand out.

There was also another problem; Tina didn't like her current job. When we asked her what she had done she replied, "Not much." It took some time to pull out her accomplishments and successes. As we have said before, you *must* focus on those accomplishments to get your resume to stand out, even if you hate your job!

We hope one thing you are learning is to take good notes. We work with many clients who have simply forgotten what they have done in the past. They don't remember how many people received the newsletter they wrote, what their department did in sales, or by how much they exceeded the company's goals. This is very important information to have, so make sure you keep your resume up-to-date. You should update it every four to six months, or take great notes and keep a resume dossier.

By employing a few formatting techniques, we were able to take the focus away from Tina's job hopping and highlight her credentials and skills.

# TINA TALUPA
2891 Teatery Avenue
Tallahassee, FL. 89210
782.128.9283 (cell 782.291.8933)
TinaTalupa@netscape.com

**EXPERIENCE:**

October 2002 to
Present

**MJK Worldwide;** Chicago, IL
**Senior Vice President, Event Marketing**
- Research and plan trade shows for clients to include booth space, collateral, message branding
- Create annual Public Relations and Event budgets
- Created brand awareness through experiential marketing

October 2000
June 2002

**FREEDRIVE, INC.**, Chicago, IL
**Director of Public Relations and Special Events**
- Created and released all press releases, press conferences and media relations material
- Built relationships with a variety of journalists both local, national and international markets
- Implemented all community relations effort as well as a Corporate Partnership Marketing Program
- Researched trade shows and planned them from start to finish;
- Booth space, collateral, all marketing materials and corporate messaging, travel and budget
- Created annual public relations and special events forecast
- Wrote a marketing plan and implemented a sales action plan
- Positioned FreeDrive as "The Leader in Web-Based Storage"

September 1999
October 2000

**JAM PRODUCTIONS, PARK WEST.**, Chicago, IL
**Director of Sales**
- Generated Sales by building relationships with the Chicago Convention Bureau
- Updated Lighting and Production Staff
- Worked with owners on Budgeting and Profit and Loss Statements

March 1993
July 1999

**MICHAEL JORDAN'S RESTAURANT**, Chicago, IL
**Director of Special Events**
- Original opening team. Produced events for 25 to 5000 people for diverse market segments that included the President of the United States, various other public figures in the entertainment and sporting world, corporations, fundraisers and social business
- Streamlined record keeping system to include monthly pace reports, labor reports, profit and loss statements. Coordinated sales effort

---

and mission statement to mirror the excellence of the name on the door
- Wrote and revised marketing plan to keep sales and marketing efforts uniform
- Positioned the restaurant as "The Place to Go"
- Created Streamline record keeping system

March 1991
To April 1993

**LEVY RESTAURANT @ McCORMICK PLACE**, Chicago, IL
**Sales Manager**
- Forecast to meet 4.5 million dollars in food and beverage sales
- Created booking, contract distributions and filing systems. Worked with convention trade show management on needs for exhibitors, as well as show management
- Produced events for 10-4000 people. Created outside sales position to elevate sales

May 1990
NY
To March 1991

**BEAR MOUNTAIN INN, ARA LEISURE SERV.**, Bear Mountain,

**Director of Sales and Marketing**
- Responsible for increasing sales from $1 million in private dining sales to $2.7 million in less than one year
- Created menus and brochures for sales and marketing tools
- Worked within the community to create name recognition
- Directed sales staff of 5 and operational staff of 30

February 1988
May 1990

**THE 95th RESTAURANT, ARA LEISURE, SERV.**, Chicago, IL
**Private Dining Sales Director**
- Increased food and beverage sales by 25%
- Developed outside sales position
- Planned a variety of affairs for conventions, business meetings and social affairs
- Coordinated events with purveyors, chefs, staff, accountants and special suppliers, music, flowers, linens, etc

October 1983
To October 1987

**THE PUMP ROOM, LETTUCE ENTERTAIN YOU**, Chicago IL
**Manager/Maitre'd/Grande Dame**

**EDUCATION**:

Bachelor of Arts and Sciences, Communications and Marketing
University of Miami, Coral Cables, FL

**AFFLIATIONS**:

ISES—International Special Events Society
AMA—American Marketing Association
NACE—National Association Catering Executives
MPI—Meeting Planner International
CARA—Chicago Area Runner Association

# Tina Talupa

2891 Teatery Avenue ♦ Tallahassee, FL 89210
782.291.8933 ♦ TinaTalupa@netscape.com

## EXPERIENCE

**MJK WORLDWIDE,** SENIOR VP, EVENT MARKETING, Chicago, IL, 2002–Present
- Planned, organized, and executed more than 10 major events for clients including Merrill Lynch, Priester Aviation, and Chase Insurance
- Developed strategic, fully-integrated event marketing program for Priester Aviation comprising customer acquisition, customer retention, and overall brand awareness
  - Created intimate Polo Club event generating more than $75,000 in new business from existing clients
  - Attracted 500 high net worth individuals to client acquisition event soliciting sponsorships from Mass Mutual, Lake Forest Sports Cars, and the Buckingham Club
- Secured Dusty Baker as keynote speaker and planned inaugural Gilda's Club of Chicago event raising more than $200,000 for people living with cancer
- Presented dozens of comprehensive seminars to corporate executives on topics including networking, business etiquette, and brand ambassadorship

**FREEDRIVE, INC.,** DIRECTOR OF PR & SPECIAL EVENTS, Chicago, IL, 2000–2002
- Helped increase company users sevenfold from 500,000 to 3,500,000 by executing eight national trades shows and integrated public relations efforts
- Positioned Freedrive as leader in web-based storage through integrated marketing plan spanning radio, newspaper, and internet efforts
- Created and managed annual public relations and event budget of $500,000
- Developed more than 100 press releases distributed to publications worldwide and picked up by *USA Today*, the *Wall Street Journal*, and the *New York Times*

**JAM PRODUCTIONS/PARK WEST,** DIRECTOR OF SALES, Chicago, IL, 1999–2000
- Booked more than 20 events generating $250,000 in ticket sales including Bob Dylan, Elvis Costello, and Paul Simon
- Helped recast Park West from music-only venue into special events venue helping drive $240,000 in incremental revenue
- Oversaw production capabilities revamp including overhaul of sound, lights, and facilities
- Increased ticket sales 25% in one year

**MICHAEL JORDAN'S RESTAURANT,** DIRECTOR OF SPECIAL EVENTS, Chicago, IL, 1993–1999
- Part of original core team opening and running one of Chicago's most visible restaurants
- Planned opening-month events attended by 1,200 people including Michael Jordan, and more than 100 press from around the world
- Organized all restaurant functions for five-day Democratic National Convention in 1996 featuring appearances by Vice President Al Gore, Hillary Clinton, Bill Bradley and Kevin Costner
- Planned 750 special events annually, managed a staff of 30, and generated a peak annual figure of $2.2MM in special event sales
- Streamlined record system to include monthly pace and labor reports and P&L statements
- Crafted mission statement and integrated sales/marketing plan

**LEVY RESTAURANT @ MCCORMICK PLACE,** SALES MANAGER, Chicago, IL, 1991–1993
- Initiated Chicago Auto Show Gala Night—annual event now considered one of Chicago's premier celebrations
- Oversaw more than $4.5MM in annual food and beverage sales

**BEAR MOUNTAIN INN/ARA,** DIRECTOR OF MARKETING, Bear Mountain, NY, 1990–1991

**THE 95TH RESTAURANT/ARA,** PRIVATE DINING SALES DIRECTOR, Chicago, IL, 1988–1990

**THE PUMP ROOM,** MANAGER/MAÎTRE D'/GRANDE DAME, Chicago, IL, 1983–1987

## EDUCATION

**UNIVERSITY OF MIAMI—CORAL GABLES, FL**
- Bachelor of Arts and Sciences in Communications and Marketing

**CULINARY INSTITUTE OF AMERICA—POUGHKEEPSIE, NY**

## BOARDS/AFFILIATIONS

- Board of Directors, North Park Elementary School, 2004–Present
  - Director of Annual Giving efforts
- International Special Events Society (ISES), 1993–Present
- Meeting Planners International (MPI), 1993–Present
- Chicago Area Runner Association (CARA), 1987–Present

# THE GAP

Rejoining the workforce after an extended layoff is perceived to be one of the most difficult transitions in life. You may have been raising your children, caring for a relative, or—as one job seeker we worked with had done—won the lottery and then wasted all your money. In any case, it's a daunting proposition to pull out the business suit, polish up the resume, and start looking for a job.

It's certainly not an easy task, but if you prepare appropriately, and attack the search smartly, it's not as intimidating as you may think.

With the right mind-set, the proper downtime approach, and some specific strategies, you can get back out there and land work. Here are the guidelines:

## 1. The mind-set

You have a gap in your resume.

So what!

There is this perception that having a gap in your resume is a horrible sin. It's not. The fact is, it's incredibly common these days. Layoffs, unfortunately, are an everyday occurrence. There has been an increase in men and women staying home to raise their children. Work/life balance awareness has increased to the point where more people are taking time off for other personal reasons as well.

Thirty years ago, the typical job situation had the male breadwinner getting a job out of college or high school and spending the rest of his career working for one company until his gold-watch retirement party.

Those days are long gone.

There's no need for you to be shy about the fact that there's a gap in your resume. You are part of a large and growing population of job seekers that have taken time off for a variety of reasons. There's no need to fret.

## 2. The approach

The biggest issue that employers have with employees returning to the workforce is their perceived state of being "out of the game." Technology, industry trends, and job skills can all change rapidly over the course of a couple of years.

Therefore, you want to make sure that you can show your aptitude in some of these areas. Take computer classes, get involved with trade organizations, and stay abreast of industry happenings by reading trade publications during your time off. It does take some time, but not nearly as much as working full-time.

## 3. The strategy

Packaging your "gap" in a resume takes careful consideration. Don't try tricks like altering dates or writing about how you honed your managerial skills negotiating with three children under the age of ten. What recruiting directors want to know is that you're in the game and ready to contribute.

Of course, it's always ideal to be able to tell your story in person, but often you don't have the luxury of meeting someone face-to-face. Therefore, the cover letter becomes a great tool to let a potential employer know about your resume gap and why it's not a big deal.

- Mention why you're reentering the workforce now:

I had always wanted to return to the workplace, and now that my children are in school full-time, it's the perfect opportunity.

- Talk about how you stayed in the game:

I wanted to stay involved in advertising as much as I could after our company closed our office, so I've attended monthly meetings of the Chicago Advertising Federation and also took a class on advanced media skills.

When used correctly, a cover letter is a great complement to your resume. See our appendices on page 271 to understand other ways you can use a cover letter to your advantage. We've even included a few sample cover letters.

Ultimately, it is not going to be easy to rejoin the working world, but with the right game plan, it doesn't have to be as difficult as you think. Check out some of our tips and hints for the following candidates who were ready to get back into the workforce.

# The Gap

Muriel was looking to get back into the full-time workforce after working part-time and raising her children. She had a high-powered job at a big bank, with a great amount of responsibility, but she also worked long hours and had a lot of pressure. Now that her children were older, she wanted to get back in the game. She was seeking a good job with nice responsibility that would keep her mind sharp.

Many of you may find yourself in this boat: moving from freelance or part-time to full-time work. You may also be anxious about this move, and think that employers will look down upon you as a candidate that is not as qualified. Don't worry; it is simply not true.

These days, people come in and out of the workforce with much more frequency than in the past. Some leave to raise children, some get downsized, and some simply take time off to "discover" themselves. If this is you, it's okay to jump back into a job.

Here is what we did with Muriel. First of all, we removed the "part-time" reference to her previous job. There is no need to call that out. Sure, if someone were to ask, you could tell them, but it doesn't need to be flagged on the resume.

Second, we really focus on her accomplishments. Look at how her most recent job comes to life in the *after* version. There is no way that it sounds like a part-time job. We also pulled some bullet points out of her work experience back in the nineties. As you progress through your career, you can always do this "trimming" with earlier positions.

It worked. Muriel got a great, full-time job with the company of her dreams!

**Muriel Landry**
**290 Marble Square**
**Malibu, CA 20491**
**(958) 383-3696**
**muriel@yahoo.com**

**AUTONICS USA, INC., February 2003 to present, Vernon Hills**
North American sales office and distribution center for privately held South Korean manufacturer of electronic components.

Office Manager (part-time)
Responsible for inventory management, accounts receivable, accounts payable and payroll.
- Negotiated purchasing contract with General Electric; established minimum order quantity, improved payment terms and return of consigned material.
- Established new distributor discount schedule to provide higher discounts to top tier customers and simplify order process.
- Reported monthly financial performance trends to President.


**NORTHERN TRUST CORPORATION, May 1986 to June 2002, Chicago**
Provider of financial services including fiduciary and trust, banking, investment management services.

Business Process Analyst—Cash Movement System (Aug. 1994 to June 2002)
Subject matter expert for Cash Movement System used by staff to move trust clients' cash, $110 billion per month. Supported over 2,300 internal partners. Trained employees, coordinated enhancements to increase functionality. Established Business Requirements, Content Specifications and Screen Design for replacement system. Facilitated User Acceptance Testing (UAT) for replacement system.

System Project Coordinator—Cash Movement, Inquiry Tracking (Mar. 1992 to Aug. 1994)
Managed up to seven data entry clerks. Trained internal partners on cash movement for trust clients. Project Manager for Inquiry Tracking system, an in-house application used to send trust account inquiries.

Trust Fee Financial Analyst—Trust & Financial Services Fee Division (Sept. 1990 to Mar. 1992)
Managed five hourly employees. Reported monthly fee income and forecasted quarterly and annual fee income for each Trust Product. Established a database for retrieving current, forecasted and historical fee results.

Senior Financial Analyst—Trust & Financial Services Administration (Sept. 1987 to Sept. 1990)
Coordinated the 5 year strategic and 1 year profit performance plan for Trust and Financial Services (TFS), a business unit earning approximately 55% of Northern Trust's income. Analyzed income and expense results. Developed a more accurate and efficient model to allocate $145 million of internal expenses.

Investment Manager Liaison Representative—Trust Operations (May 1986 to Sept. 1987)

**ARLINGTON FEDERAL SAVINGS AND LOAN, December 1984 to May 1986, Arlington Heights**

Loan Processor (July 1985 to May 1986)
New Accounts Representative (Dec. 1984 to July 1985)


**EDUCATION**
MBA, 1991, International Business, DePaul University, Chicago
BS, 1984, Finance, University of Illinois, Champaign-Urbana
Internship, 1984, Meyer International, PLC and London School of Polytechnic, London, England

**VOLUNTEER**
Treasurer, 2001, Monica Balson Lincolnshire Village Trustee Campaign
Treasurer, 2001, 2002, Lincolnshire Swim Team
Treasurer, 2002, 2003, Lincolnshire Community Association
Treasurer, 2005, Stevenson Dance Connection

# Muriel Landry

290 Marble Court ♦ Malibu, CA 20491
958.383.3696 ♦ muriel@yahoo.com

## EXPERIENCE

### AUTONICS USA, INC., OFFICE MANAGER, Vernon Hills, IL, 2003–Present
- Responsible for inventory management, accounts receivable, accounts payable, and payroll at North American sales office and distribution center for privately held South Korean electronic components manufacturer
- Dramatically lowered past due accounts receivable by introducing a formal process to track delinquent payments and by creating a "no payment/no product" company policy
- Reduced accounts payable delinquencies from 24 months to less than 12 months by vigilantly managing cash flow and by launching company's first-ever automatic funds transfer payment process
- Renegotiated purchasing contract with General Electric increasing minimum order quantity 150% and improving net payment terms 20%
- Oversee inventory distribution of more than 150,000 units annually across 150 distributors in North America and Central America
- Saved organization $100,000 annually by recommending cost-cutting measures to combat company overages
- Established strategic new distributor discount schedule increasing sales 9% by providing deeper discounts
- Reported monthly financial performance trends to company President helping guide corporate direction

### NORTHERN TRUST CORPORATION, Chicago, IL, 1986–2002

#### BUSINESS PROCESS ANALYST—CASH MOVEMENT SYSTEM, 1992–2002
- Supported more than 2,300 internal partners as company's subject matter expert for proprietary Cash Movement System used to move $110 billion monthly in trust clients' cash
- Trained hundreds of employees at 10 offices throughout the U.S. and U.K.
- Coordinated dozens of system enhancements including major initiative allowing more than 100 locations nationwide to print checks locally versus all at one Chicago location
- Managed a team of up to seven data entry clerks

#### TRUST FEE FINANCIAL ANALYST—TRUST & FINANCIAL SERVICES FEE DIVISION, 1990–1992
- Reported $22 million in monthly fee income and forecasted quarterly and annual fee income for 15 distinct Trust Products
  - Created company's first-ever report automation process
- Worked closely with Controller's group to establish a comprehensive, user-friendly database for retrieving current, forecasted, and historical fee results

#### SENIOR FINANCIAL ANALYST—TRUST & FINANCIAL SERVICES ADMINISTRATION, 1987–1990
- Coordinated the five-year strategic, and one-year profit performance plans for Trust and Financial Services (TFS)–a business unit earning 55% of Northern Trust's income
- Analyzed income and expense results across personal and corporate accounts helping guide company performance and growth
  - Results presented to Chairman of TFS and several business unit heads
- Partnered with SVPs and Division Heads to develop a dramatically more accurate and efficient model allocating $145 million of internal expenses annually

#### INVESTMENT MANAGER LIAISON REPRESENTATIVE—TRUST OPERATIONS, 1986–1987

### ARLINGTON FEDERAL SAVINGS & LOAN, LOAN PROCESSOR, Arlington Heights, IL, 1984–1986

## EDUCATION

**MBA, INTERNATIONAL BUSINESS, DEPAUL UNIVERSITY**—CHICAGO, IL, 1991
**BS, FINANCE, UNIVERSITY OF ILLINOIS**—CHAMPAIGN-URBANA, 1984

# The Gap

Abigail had done it all. She was a major in the U.S. Air Force. She had led relief efforts halfway around the globe in places like Kosovo and Kiev, and she had managed huge public works and government construction projects in Alaska. Wow!

The problem was that her resume was all over the place. It lacked focus and was filled with a variety of small, short-tenured jobs with gaps interspersed throughout.

We cleaned it up a couple of ways. The first thing you will notice is a very compelling summary. We captured the essence of what she had accomplished, since her background was nontraditional and since she had more than twenty-five years of work experience. Importantly, we also tailored that summary to match her background with the job description for a position she was pursuing in logistics.

The next thing we did was eliminate some entries on her resume. Abigail made sure she listed every month and every experience she had dating back to 1980. Quite frankly, that is too much information. Most recruiting directors simply do not care that you took off a few months to travel in 1993!

Nowadays, a "gap" on your resume is not going to kill your career. If you have gap after gap, it will certainly raise a few red flags. Especially for very experienced job seekers with more than fifteen or twenty years experience, a few gaps simply don't matter that much.

That is why we only included years for her dates, and that is why we grouped a few jobs together. The result is a much "tighter" resume that tells her amazing story in a manner that is easy to read and understand.

**ABIGAIL ALBRIGHT**
**5605 Appleton Avenue, Apartment #5A, Albion, AK 90506**
**email: abigailalbright@gmail.com**
**Telephone: 550.336.0056**


## CAREER SUMMARY

*09/2005–Present*
After working 10 years both overseas and in Alaska, chose to take an opportunity to pursue a long delayed graduate degree.

*Property Manager, General Services Administration, Juneau, Alaska*
*09/2002–09/2005*
Responsible for all operations, logistical support, project management and support activities for five federal buildings. Ensured people, services and materials were where they needed to be, when they needed to be. Farsighted, strategic planner able to catch shortfalls and deficiencies before they disrupt operations. Managing a staff including building engineer and mechanics, responsible for:
- On-site Project Manager for projects contracted by other agencies such as U.S. Coast Guard. Ensured client's designs and expectations were properly identified, contract and procurement actions on track, and that the project was completed on time.
- Planned for large ($1M–$15M) capital improvements five to twenty years out.
- Managed third party vendor mechanical and custodial contracts.
- On-site Project Manager for large one-time projects such as a PCB abatement and lobby remodel.
- Working with Federal Protective Services and tenant agencies, ensured day-to-day security; planned for future security enhancements.
- Responsible for a $2.1M annual budget.

*Assistant Mission Director for Program Support, CARE International, Prishtina, Kosovo*
*09/2000–06/2001*
Responsible for all operations, logistical support, contractual and support activities for CARE's mission in Kosovo and Macedonia. Managing a staff of 40, responsible for:
- The daily operation of a diverse and far-flung mission in two countries, including all mechanical and emergency back-up systems.
- A procurement unit responsible for the procurement of equipment and supplies.
- A fleet of vehicles and staff of drivers.
- The movement of equipment, materials and people within country as needed, working with UNKFOR.
- The asset management of a warehouse of equipment, furniture and supplies as well as UN/USAID funded heavy equipment.
- The leasing and maintenance of all housing occupied by personnel.
- A human resources unit, administrative unit, travel and IT unit.
- The mission support budget.

*Deputy Executive Officer, United States Agency for International Development (USAID), Kiev, Ukraine*
*05/1997–07/2000*
Responsible for all operational and logistical support for a 130 person mission in Belarus, Moldova and Ukraine. In 1998, chosen by American Embassy to be "Transportation Control Officer" for Vice President Gore's trip to Ukraine; worked with Secret Service and White House staff on logistics. Additionally, assisted with logistical support for Secretary of State Madeleine Albright and First Lady Hillary Clinton delegations. Worked with Ambassador's staff to strategize vulnerability to the possible loss of Ukraine's power grids; designed an aggressive plan using engineers which resulted in the Ambassador's decision not to evacuate non-essential American personnel in Ukraine. Served as consultant to International Rescue Committee (IRC) by traveling to Moscow and refugee camps in Ingushetia (bordering Chechnya) to evaluate possible aid options as well as security risk to IRC personnel. Managing a staff of 50, responsible for:

- The operation of a commercial building and 45 residential properties.
- A procurement office responsible for all purchases for the agency.
- The asset management and warehousing of over $1M of equipment, vehicles, furniture and supplies.
- A fleet of vehicles and drivers.
- Oversight of security.
- Multiple residential properties identified for lease negotiations, refurbishment when necessary, and maintenance for the duration of the lease.
- Records management, IT and inter-office communications.

*Consultant, Greater Jewish Assistance and Relief Network (GJARN), and Winrock International, Ukraine*
*12/1996–02/1997*
Evaluated the after-project effectiveness of a large USAID funded project for GJARN; set up office operations for Winrock International in Ukraine.

*Co-Country Director, Counterpart International, Minsk Belarus*
*10/1995–10/1996*
Co-Country Director for a USAID funded initiative in support of social development and health programs in Belarus.

*Logistician, Hughes Technical Services, Kiev Ukraine*
*04/1995–08/1995*
Hired as a short term contractor providing logistical support towards the implementation of the Nunn-Lugar Program in Ukraine.

*Sales Manager, IntelNews, Kiev Ukraine*
*08/1994–02/1995*
Sales Manager for Ukraine's first post-Soviet English speaking newspaper for the diplomatic and foreign business community.

*Sabbatical, traveling around the U.S.*
*10/1993–07/1994*

*United States Air Force; departed with rank of Major*
*08/1980–10/1993*
Over the span of a 13 year career, acquired a wide range of management expertise with focus on operations, logistics, administration and people.

- Maintenance (Nuclear) Officer for a Munitions Squadron in support of NATO operations, Balikiser Turkey;
- Maintenance Officer for B-52, B-1 and KC-135 aircraft, Ellsworth AFB South Dakota. Operationally involved in the deployment of B-52 bombers and a maintenance squadron during the first Gulf War;
- Chief of Base Administration, Malmstrom AFB Montana. Responsible for all administrative functions for an Air Force Base supporting 6000 personnel;
- Nuclear Missile Launch Officer for Intercontinental Ballistic Missiles, Davis-Monthan AFB Arizona.

## EDUCATION

- How to Write Successful Grants, Juneau, Alaska, 2006
- Enrolled LLM program, University of London, 2005
- How to Manage Multiple Locations, Rockhurst University, 2005
- Simplified Acquisition Procedures, Federal Acquisition Institute, 2004
- Contracting Officer Representative Mentor Course, GSA, 2004
- Project Management, ESI International, Portland WA, 2003
- General Services Officer Training, USAID, Washington DC, 1999
- Contracting Officer's Technical Representative Training, USAID, 1999
- Program Activity Manager Training, USAID, 1999
- Supervisory Skills Training, USAID, 1999
- Bachelor of Arts Degree in Psychology, University of Massachusetts, 1977

# Abigail Albright

5605 Appleton Avenue, Apartment #5A ♦ Albion, AK 90506
550.336.0056 ♦ abigailalbright@gmail.com

## SUMMARY

- Seasoned operations and logistics expert with experience working on dozens of multimillion-dollar projects throughout the world
- Passionate creative problem solver with a proven background of resolving complicated issues with simple, logical solutions
- Seasoned manager leading teams as large as 200 for both the U.S. Air Force and at large governmental agencies
- Dedicated agent of change, specializing in identifying organizational shortcomings and thriving in environments where solid direction is needed

## EXPERIENCE

**PROPERTY MANAGER,** GENERAL SERVICES ADMINISTRATION, Juneau, AK, 2002–2007
- Responsible for all operations, logistical support, project management, and support activities across five federal buildings in five different Alaskan cities
- Served as on-site project manager working with 10 different federal agencies developing creative solutions to difficult problems across dozens of projects
- Managed a $500,000, three month abatement project, encapsulating lead paint throughout building garage and boiler room
- Oversaw $600,000 lobby renovation serving as on-site project manager for Seattle-based project management team
  - Dramatically enhanced building security, upgraded elevators, and renovated floors
  - Worked closely with Department of Homeland Security correcting a series of potential security oversights
  - Determined solution to complex building access issue, facilitating entrance/exit flow while maintaining rigorous security compliance
- Provided long-term strategic planning for capital improvement projects up to $15 million ranging from new ventilation systems, to upgraded boilers
- Overhauled and improved Department of Homeland Security remote border station housing in Haines, Alaska
- Supervised a staff including a building engineer and a team of mechanics across five locations
- Successfully oversaw a $500,000 mechanical and multi-year custodial contract
- Managed a $2.1 million annual budget spanning dozens of individual projects

**ASSISTANT MISSION DIRECTOR,** CARE INTERNATIONAL, Prishtina, Kosovo, 2000–2001
- Supervised a staff of 40 responsible for all operations, logistical support, and contractual activities for CARE's postwar mission in Kosovo and Macedonia
- Implemented organization's first-ever live auction of heavy equipment raising more than $100,000 for CARE
  - Followed all government disposal regulations, withstanding audit scrutiny
- Crafted unit's first procurement manual outlining policies and procedures based on US government guidelines
- Reduced operational rent costs by 1/3 by moving headquarters location
- Overhauled the asset management of a warehouse of equipment, furniture, supplies, and UN/USAID funded heavy equipment by introducing a new inventory system

**DEPUTY OFFICER,** US AGENCY FOR DEVELOPMENT (USAID), Kiev, Ukraine, 1997–2000
- Responsible for all operational and logistical support for a 130-person mission across Ukraine, Belarus, and Moldova, managing a staff of 50
- Selected by American Embassy to be "Transportation Control Officer" for Vice President Al Gore's trip to Ukraine in 1998
    - Partnered with Secret Service and White House staff on complex transportation logistics
- Assisted with logistical support for visits by Secretary of State Madeleine Albright and First Lady Hillary Clinton and their delegations
- Met with Deputy US Ambassador to craft Y2K readiness plan ultimately implemented by US embassy
    - Plan resulted in Ambassador's decision not to evacuate hundreds of nonessential American personnel from Ukraine prior to 12/31/99
- Developed plan to backup Y2K affected computer programs, saving two years' worth of data by utilizing a team of local tech experts to fix hundreds of hardware systems
    - Due to success, program offered to other USAID agencies worldwide
- Traveled to Moscow as consultant to International Rescue Committee (IRC) evaluating possible aid options and security risk to IRC personnel at refugee camps in Ingushetia
    - Recommended and implemented unique education program for entire camp using refugee teachers to work with children who had not had any education in more than a year
- Supervised refurbishment of dozens of antiquated former Soviet structures, transforming them into habitable Western housing units
- Oversaw a procurement office with a staff of three responsible for millions of dollars of vehicle, furniture, office equipment, and other purchases
- Managed security, maintained a fleet of 25 vehicles with 20 drivers, and led team handling all records management, IT, and interoffice communications

**CO-COUNTRY DIRECTOR,** COUNTERPART INTERNATIONAL, Minsk, Belarus, 1995–1996

**SALES MANAGER,** INTELNEWS, Kiev, Ukraine, 1994–1995

**UNITED STATES AIR FORCE,** 1980–1993
*Departed with rank of Major*
- Responsible for all administrative functions of Malmstrom AFB Montana supporting 6,000 personnel as Chief of Base Administration
- Secured three consecutive "Excellent" scores from Inspector General on behalf of base commander–first time ever in 45 year history of Strategic Air Command
- Offered commendation for preparing 150-page award package recognizing excellence of 1,000 person maintenance deputate
    - Award won for all of Air Force and competed in Department of Defense
- Deployed entire squadron in less than three weeks during first Gulf War
- Maintenance Officer for KC-135, B-52, and B-1 aircraft at Ellsworth AFB, South Dakota

# EDUCATION

- **How to Write Successful Grants**, Juneau, AK, 2006
- **How to Manage Multiple Locations**, Rockhurst University, 2005
- **Simplified Acquisition Procedures**, Federal Acquisition Institute, 2004
- **Contracting Officer Representative Mentor Course**, GSA, 2004
- **Project Management, ESI International**, Portland, WA, 2003
- **General Services Officer Training**, USAID, Washington, DC, 1999
- **Contracting Officer's Technical Representative Training**, USAID, 1999
- **Supervisory Skills Training**, USAID, 1999

**Bachelor of Arts Degree in Psychology**, University of Massachusetts, 1977

# The Gap

Shannon had a two-year gap sandwiched between two museum jobs. After she graduated with her second degree, Shannon job-searched in Louisiana and discovered that options were limited. She decided to move to New York, where she believed there would be more opportunities.

Once she moved to New York, Shannon realized it was more difficult to find a job there than she had expected. She was out of work for two years until she landed a museum job in New York. After working at that museum for about a year, she was ready to search for a new opportunity. This time, Shannon wanted to solidify a new job before resigning from her current position, but she was nervous that recruiting directors would think she lacked initiative and drive due to her past two-year hiatus.

First, we reassured Shannon that she shouldn't be worried. She currently held a job, and she was excelling in the position. We listed her accomplishment "Won Employee of the Year in 2006 out of a staff of 45 and won five Employee of the Week awards" to reinforce that Shannon was a star employee.

Shannon thought that she should not include any dates on her resume, in order to hide her gap. Dates are standard on a resume, so removing all dates actually raises more red flags than a simple gap.

We added the dates for her job experiences, and we also included the years that she attained her degrees. That way, the recruiting director could deduce that Shannon moved to New York after attaining her second degree from a college in Louisiana. This subtle addition offers an explanation and helps soften the gap.

We coached Shannon on ways to answer any questions about her two-year gap. We decided taking a slightly humorous approach could help deflect attention while still offering clarification. We focused on the inability to find a job in Louisiana rather than her struggles finding a job in New York:

*Louisiana has a lot of culture and character, but when it came down to finding a viable position in the arts, I came up empty-handed. That's why I decided to move to New York, where I knew I would have the opportunity to join a organization like yours . . .*

*Louisiana definitely has flair, but it lacks a strong arts community. I was having a difficult time finding a good fit after I graduated, so I decided to move to New York . . .*

Shannon was able to leverage her most recent experience and downplay her two-year gap through her new resume.

# Shannon McPhee

83081 Catz Road, New York, NY 10021, 212.121.1212
shannon@hotmail.com

**CAREER SUMMARY:** An administrative management professional with five years experience including communication development, event and meeting coordination, marketing, and customer service experience in publications, an international association, and museum work settings.

- Coordinates five teams who serve three museums; 25 Divisions.
- Communicates with all levels of employees, management, and donors.
- B.A. in French (Art, History, & Theatre); Minor: Communication.
- Awarded: Employee of the Year 2003; premier recipient.
- Trilingual: Highly fluent in French and Intermediate fluency in Spanish.
- Proficient in all aspects of office automation.

## WORK EXPERIENCE & ACCOMPLISHMENTS

### HARTS CONTEMPORARY MUSEUM, New York

#### Office Coordinator/Manager
- Assists the Facilities/Zone Manager in a wide variety of administrative, supervisory, quality assurance, and customer service functions.
- Receives, reviews, screens, and controls all incoming service actions, documents, reports, memoranda, etc.
- Delegates service calls to staff as appropriate; regular and emergency actions.
- Alerts Building Management Staff and schedules services of contractors to special problems and arrangements.
- Meeting Coordinator and Facilitator for Building Manager, BMD Staff, other Staff, and vendors.
- Establishes, organizes, and maintains files automated special events/reservations calendar.
- Secondary Staff contact for the Office of Human Resources; regularly updates all personnel actions and other related confidential documents.
- Employee of the Year Award—2003; multiple winner of Employee of the Week.

### RAE PORTRAIT GALLERY, Louisiana
#### External Affairs Assistant

- Assisted the External Affairs Director and staff in implementing development programs, planning and execution of Portrait Gallery events; performed administrative duties including updates and maintenance of NPG database, telephone calls, correspondence, timekeeping, and more.
- Helped define new External Affairs Assistant position.
- Managed/resolved numerous vendor relations and travel issues.
- Established 600+ New Donor & Foundation files.

**REGIONAL MUSEUM OF WOMEN IN THE ARTS,**
Louisiana
**Development & Event Assistant** (Summer Position)
Assisted the Development Manager researching potential donors, coordinated multiple Women's
Committee meetings/events, and the composition of donor solicitation and thank you letters.
- Strong internet research skill application.
- Developed two major Foundation Profile Reference Guides.
- Coordinated event volunteers.

**CP MAGAZINES, Buffalo, LA**
**Marketing Associate** (Summer Positions)
Assisted Marketing Manager of newsletter publishing company on various projects including
promotion on newly released newsletter and subscription renewal campaigns.

- Conducted cold calls to national subscribers.
- Achieved a 10% increase in subscription renewals.
- Completed high volume data entry projects.

**AMERICAN FRANCAISE, Buffalo, LA**
**Membership & Event Coordinator** (Summer Position)
Handled and directed incoming calls from international, multi-lingual members.
Performed office administrative duties; event attendance records, dues, and mailing lists.
Assisted in Alliance and French Embassy event coordination.
- Keyed the organization's first computerized member database.
- Hostess at French Embassy; Bastille Day celebrations.
- Edited, revised, and filed French documents.

**EDUCATION**

> Centenary College, Shreveport, LA
> Sorbonne University, Paris, FRANCE
> Centenary College, Shreveport, LA

**_TRAINING & CERTIFICATIONS_**

Millennium Development Management System
Peoplesoft/ Enterprise Resource Planning
Prevention of Sexual Harassment Training
Facilities Center Program
Notary Public (DC., MD., & VA.)

# Shannon McPhee

83081 Catz Road ♦ New York, NY 10021
212.121.1212 ♦ shannon@hotmail.com

## EXPERIENCE

**HARTS CONTEMPORARY MUSEUM–OFFICE OF FACILITIES MANAGEMENT**, NEW YORK CITY, 2006–Present

*Office Manager/Coordinator*

- Manage all facilities/operations for 100 events annually with audiences from 50–300
- Coordinate and execute more than 50 internal meetings annually for a staff of 45
- Liaison between dozens of outside vendors, clients, and internal departments overseeing all aspects of event setup and breakdown
- Extensive experience planning events including receptions, workshops, lectures, and exhibitions
- Help manage an annual budget of $55,000 including final year-end purchases
- Won Employee of the Year in 2006 out of a staff of 45 and won five Employee of the Week awards

**RAE PORTRAIT GALLERY**, BUFFALO, LA, 2000–2004

*External Affairs Assistant*

- Planned and executed three full-day commission VIP meetings to establish collection and donation funding throughout the year
- Commission events featured luminaries including Walter Mondale, William Rehnquist, and Ross Perot
- Managed communication program for campaign soliciting $30MM for portrait of George Washington
- Oversaw quarterly donor mailings and updated comprehensive contributor database with 500 names
- Created organization's first-ever foundation filing system tracking 600 donors contributing more than $60,000 annually

**REGIONAL MUSEUM OF WOMEN IN THE ARTS**, BUFFALO, LA, Summer 1999

*Event/Development Assistant*

- Helped organize and execute annual spring gala attended by 300 guests
- Coordinated team of volunteers at several event openings and programs
- Prepared extensive research summary tracking hundreds of potential donors

## EDUCATION

**CENTENARY COLLEGE,** SHREVEPORT, LA, 2004

- Event Management Certificate Program

**CENTENARY COLLEGE,** SHREVEPORT, LA, May 2000

- Bachelor of Arts in French; Communication Minor

**SORBONNE UNIVERSITY,** PARIS, FRANCE, Fall 1998–Spring 1999

- Studied art, history, music, and theater in French

## ACTIVITIES/SKILLS/INTERESTS

- Alliance Francaise, 1997–Present
- Regional Museum of Women in the Arts, 2000–Present
- International Club of LA, 2003–Present
- Fluent in French, proficient in Spanish

# LAID OFF

You were downsized, laid off, asked to leave, or maybe you were even fired for cause. Now what? This is certainly a tricky situation to manage, but fortunately, you do not have to wear a scarlet letter.

You do not write:

Director of Communications, Baton Rouge, LA, July 2006–Fired.

When recruiting directors pick up your resume, they don't know why you left your last job. Getting laid off is something that might have to be addressed during the interview.

It's never easy to transition into the idea of getting a new job after you lose your old one. But if the day arrives, what exactly do you do? Mere thoughts of the sudden job search can be immobilizing, and it's a problem that plagues many job seekers. Here is the inside scoop on exactly how to take the next step:

## 1. Put your house in order

Resume, cover letter, interviewing skills—you'll need to have all of them brushed up and in top-notch shape. Your resume may have been sitting dormant since you graduated college ten years ago, but trust me, the recruiting director no longer cares that you raised $370 for the "Cannes Car Wash '99" with the Advertising Club. Use this book as a guide to update your resume.

Don't assume that the title or company from your former job will speak for themselves either. Just because you were the account director on Unilever at Ogilvy New York doesn't mean you'll get any job you apply for. There are an abundance of well-qualified candidates out there. The more diligent you are with your preparation, the better your chances.

## 2. Reassess your career

Our first inclination is to get another job doing the same exact thing, as quickly as possible. We think like a robot: "Lost job as account director on car account at large multinational ad agency. Must get new job as account director on car account at large multinational ad agency."

Take some time to think. Do you like your career? Do you like the field you work in? What might make you happier? The earlier you do this in your career the better. One lament I hear from more experienced job seekers is that they feel trapped.

That doesn't necessarily have to be the case. Now that you're changing jobs, reassess your priorities and make sure you're not just blindly jumping into the next job. You can start your own company, go to work in a different city, or get training for another industry. Obviously, there are some constraints on what you can do, but take some time to really think about that next move.

## 3. Get out there

You have more tools than you think when it comes time to see what jobs are available. Take this short quiz to determine if you know the best way to land work. Please select which is the most effective way to score your next job:

**A.** Check out online job postings

**B.** Network

**C.** Work with an executive recruiter

**D.** Scour individual company websites

**E.** All of the above

Yes, folks, the answer is E. If you are serious about landing that next job, you want to go after it with vigor. Like anything else in life, the more effort you put into your job search the more you get out of it. Each method has its advantages:

- Online job postings are how most companies list their open jobs.
- Networking can get you access to hiring managers and recruiting directors with a recommendation from someone on the inside.
- Executive recruiters often are hiring for jobs that are not posted online.
- Company websites allow you to stay abreast of up-to-date job listings.

However, each approach can have its disadvantages as well. Going home one night and applying to twenty jobs online—and then wondering why you haven't heard from anyone—is not the best way to look for a job. Similarly, putting all of your eggs into the executive recruiter basket can be a risky proposition. It sounds like a cliché, but the wider you cast your net, the more likely you are to catch a fish (or in our discussion, land a job).

• • •

Looking for a new job after getting laid off can be an intimidating process. But if you go about it with a plan on how to do it the right way, it can be incredibly rewarding and breathe new life into your career.

Check out the next resumes and see how we worked with candidates who had been laid off.

# Laid Off

When Carrie came to JobBound, she had been let go by her previous employer and had been volunteering at a museum. For her next job, she was looking to go into the not-for-profit field. When we talked, she was embarrassed by the fact that she had been fired, so we placed the museum entry first on her resume, which made it less likely that a recruiting director would ask why she'd left Szabo Advertising.

Carrie also didn't think the museum job should be on her resume because it wasn't a paid position. That's a big mistake. Obviously, the museum job should be on there—especially since it was her field of interest. Many job seekers, especially students, relegate extracurricular activities or volunteer work to a lower position on the resume. Often, those experiences are incredibly meaningful. Now, you don't have to list all of them in the "meat" of your resume. But if you do have some relevant and compelling non-work experiences, don't be shy about listing them prominently.

You should also watch out for abbreviations and acronyms. On her *before* resume, Carrie lists RTEC, AOR, and TRU. Huh? Some acronyms were unique to her company, some to her account, and some to the field itself. Don't assume the reader knows all of them.

**Carrie Carmichael**
1607 West Carolton, Chicago IL 60611, 312.187.2258
312.789.2458  Email: CarrieCarmichael@aol.com

## SUMMARY

Senior Account Planner with 10 years of experience. Accounts include Consumer Packaged Goods and Retail clients, with a focus on women and children. To note, many qualitative studies conducted with young adult males. Experience with top agencies as well as with client side industry. In addition to work experience, also teaches "Planning 101" at the Chicago Portfolio School.

## PROFESSIONAL EXPERIENCE/ACHIEVEMENTS

**Szabo Advertising**                                                                              **April 2004–Oct 2005**
**Senior Planner**
*Client Responsibility: Kellogg USA*: **Kellogg's Frosted Flakes, Corn Pops, Apple Jacks, MiniSwirlz and new products.** *PMUSA:* **Marlboro (all varieties), Blend No. 27, Parliament and new products.**

- Develop and Protect Brand Positions, as well as Brand Repositioning on Corn Pops, Apple Jacks, and Kellogg's Frosted Flakes
- Work on innovation team to position up and coming products
- Conduct qualitative: focus groups, one-on-ones and ethnographies (hundreds)
- Develop/Conduct creative briefs/briefings
- Key client contact
- Mentor Jr. Planners
- Key player for Thought Leadership with Boomer Women
- Lead for Thought Leadership team against target of the future (multi-cultural)
- Consistently seek a variety of research (data) sources, both traditional and non-traditional
- Lead on insights project for discovery on Hip Hop. Gamer and BMX subcultures
- Key player working with TRU panel to develop insight for Kids RTEC
- Develop case studies as needed

**Build A Bear Workshop St. Louis, Missouri**                                          **March 2002–March 2004**
**Strategic Marketing Analyst**

- SWOT Analysis/Key Player in brand positioning process
- Took company from grassroots marketing efforts to a nationwide ad campaign
- Analyzed internal, syndicated consumer and trend data (TRU, Zandl, BABW Database, MRI, Simmons, etc.)
- Lead idea generation meetings
- Provided qualitative research service as well as Competitive Analysis
- Managed AOR to initialize on going National Communication, which lead to an 20% increase in sales
- Mentored other Marketing Associates and colleagues

**DARCY/MEDIAVEST WORLDWIDE, St. Louis, Missouri**                     **March 1998–March 2002**
**Account Planner**
**Media Supervisor**
*Client Responsibility:* **Masterfoods USA(M&M/Mars): Skittles Bite Size Candies; Uncle Ben's; and Seeds of Change. Total billings: $55 million.**

- Championed proprietary strategic planning tools to develop strategic platform for brand communication.
- Extended KPOV (Kid's Point of View) qualitative research program to include over 75 schools nationwide to provide diverse demographic constituent pool.
- Proposed and conducted research for a global new product launch

- Developed agency competitive analysis standards and process for St. Louis office
- Key player in developing communication strategies to align public relations, outreach and internal communications for clients.
- Designed and conducted national research study on Inner City teens.
- Lead for providing analysis and recommendations based on both traditional and non traditional research
- Trained, mentored and coached Assistant/Media Planners.
- Participated in successful new business pitches

**MOTTERT, KRIEGER & ASSOCIATES**      1996–1998
<u>Media Planner/Buyer</u>
*Client Responsibility:* **The Brown Shoe Company: Life Stride Naturalizer; Natural Sport and Buster Brown Total billings: $10 million.**

**UNITED STATES ARMY**      1992–2000
<u>Computer Logistic Specialist—92A</u>
- 2 years active and 6 years reservist

## EDUCATION/TRAINING

**Kansas State University of Manhatten, Kansas—BS/BA**      **1992–1996**

Burke Institute Training: Moderating, Brand Positioning, Specialized Qualitative      **2002–2004**
with Children, One-on-One interviewing
Account Planners Conference      **2002–2005**
Chicago Portfolio School teaching "Planning 101" to Copy Writers & Art Directors      **Present**
Chicago Portfolio School taking Creative Writing      **Present**

## COMMUNITY SERVICE/ACTIVITY

St. Louis Crisis Nursery      **1998–Present**
Chicago Marathon—ALS Foundation      **2002–2003**
San Diego Marathon—ALS Foundation      **2004**
Marketing Chair for National Vietnam Veterans Art Museum      **Present**

# Carrie Carmichael

1607 West Carolton ♦ Chicago, IL 60611
312.187.2258 ♦ CarrieCarmichael@aol.com

## EXPERIENCE

**NATIONAL VIETNAM VETERANS ART MUSEUM,** MARKETING CHAIR, Chicago, IL, 1/06–Present
- Presenting brand positioning for organization's first communications campaign
- Conducted qualitative and quantitative research to help guide new creative efforts
- Evaluate all potential sponsorship/partnership opportunities

**SZABO ADVERTISING,** SENIOR PLANNER, Chicago, IL, 4/04–10/05
*Kellogg's—Frosted Flakes, Corn Pops, Apple Jacks, new products, Philip Morris USA—Marlboro*
- Proposed, sold, and spearheaded Corn Pops's first-ever ethnography project exploring hip-hop, gaming and skater/BMX cultures in three US cities
    - Results inspired radically new Corn Pops positioning impacting packaging and creative, rejuvenating brand image, and increasing sales, share, and awareness
    - Conducted crib chats and environmental studies among hundreds of tweens
    - Visited graffiti parks, sneaker stores, and skate parks to immerse in tween culture
- Worked closely with consultant to conduct archetypal study for Frosted Flakes, cementing Tony the Tiger's personality as inspirational coach
    - Repositioning helped increase sales +10% during air times
- Researched multi-channel marketing efforts of five key advertisers to prepare comprehensive report on how to target baby boomer women for agency-wide project
- Explored multicultural trends and developed volumetric sales analysis to convince Kellogg's to address diverse "nontraditional" audiences across all 17 kid-targeted brands
- Partnered with nationally recognized Teens Research Unlimited (TRU) presenting leading research studies to entire 50-person Kellogg's kid brand and agency teams
- Crafted positioning for winning Tiger Power concept–mom targeted Cheerio fighting cereal
- Wrote more than 20 Kellogg's creative briefs on brands targeting moms and kids
- Created a Marlboro-first brand personality chart spanning family of 10 varieties fundamentally altering new creative executions, and segmenting mailings to millions of adult smokers
- Helped launch Marlboro 72's, developing creative brief for "club-themed" new product
- Developed, sold, moderated, and interpreted results for more than 100 qualitative focus groups and one-on-one sessions for Marlboro
- Led several key internal brand team ideation sessions across new products, promotions, and Marlboro racing school, preparing holistic planning platforms and guiding brand personality studies

**BUILD A BEAR WORKSHOP,** STRATEGIC MARKETING ANALYST, St. Louis, MO, 3/02–3/04
- Introduced planning discipline and mass advertising techniques to entertainment retailer with more than $250MM in sales
- Turned 17% sales decline into 20% increase in two years by overhauling entire marketing effort and launching company's first-ever national advertising campaign
- Introduced new psychographic target and launched television, radio, magazine, billboard, theater, sponsorship, partnership and licensing plan helping stores grow from $100MM to $250MM in sales
- Conducted company's first-ever foray into qualitative research inspiring creative executions for nationwide campaign launch
- Developed emotional laddering perspective based on store intercepts and customer observations
- Helped source and secure company's first advertising agency
- Created a comprehensive brand equity tool spanning usage of characters, personality, symbols, and functional/emotional offerings guiding all marketing communications

**DARCY/MEDIAVEST,** ACCOUNT PLANNER/MEDIA SUPERVISOR, St. Louis, MO, 3/98–3/02
*Masterfoods (M&M's/Mars)—Skittles, Uncle Ben's, Seeds of Change*
- Researched and reviewed sales and volumetric data throughout Europe for a global new product launch combining Milky Way/Mars brands internationally
- Championed a host of strategic planning tools helping differentiate/anchor key M&M's/Mars brands within the context of multiple product lines
- Extended Masterfood's Kid's Point of View (KPOV) qualitative research program to include 75 inner city schools providing a more diverse constituent perspective
- Developed agency competitive analysis standards and processes correlating media activity to sales
- Designed and conducted proprietary nationwide research study on inner city teens used by agency for all M&M's brands

**MOTTERT, KRIEGER & ASSOCIATES,** MEDIA PLANNER/BUYER, St. Louis, MO, 1996–1998
*The Brown Shoe Company—Life Stride, Naturalizer, Natural Spot, Buster Brown*

**THE UNITED STATES ARMY,** COMPUTER LOGISTIC SPECIALIST, 1992–2000
*Served for two years of active duty and six years as reservist*

## EDUCATION/TRAINING/RESEARCH TOOLS

**CHICAGO PORTFOLIO SCHOOL**—CHICAGO, IL, 2005–PRESENT
- Creative Writing

**KANSAS STATE UNIVERSITY**—MANHATTAN, KS, 1996
- Bachelor of Science in Business Administration

**BURKE INSTITUTE TRAINING**—CINCINNATI, OH, 2002–2004
- Moderating, Brand Positioning, Specialized Qualitative with Children, One-on-One Interviewing

**ACCOUNT PLANNERS CONFERENCE**—ATLANTA, GA, 2002–2005

## COMMUNITY SERVICE/TEACHING

**CHICAGO PORTFOLIO SCHOOL,** 2006–PRESENT
- Teach weekly "Planning 101" course to Copywriters and Art Directors

**ST. LOUIS CRISIS NURSERY,** VOLUNTEER, 1998–PRESENT
**SAN DIEGO MARATHON RUNNER** ALS FOUNDATION FUNDRAISER, 2004
**CHICAGO MARATHON RUNNER** ALS FOUNDATION FUNDRAISER, 2002–2003

# Laid Off

Our next client found himself in a difficult situation. He was a great employee, and he was valued by the company. He enjoyed his job, and he excelled in his position. Unfortunately, the organization was forced to restructure, and Joseph's position was eliminated. Joseph suddenly found himself without a job. Especially because he was so passionate about his work and the organization, Joseph was deflated and a little discouraged. If you hated your old job, then it's easier to embrace the job search when you lose it, but if you loved your job, then it's more difficult to focus your energies on moving forward.

Many people find themselves in the latter position. Through little to no fault of their own, many employees find themselves jobless. Maybe the company is experiencing tough economic times, so it conducts mass layoffs, or maybe they have to restructure to cut costs. Fortunately, in these cases, the company is more likely to help its people transition into another job. In addition to providing severance packages, many companies connect employees with outplacement firms and recruiters. If you are laid off for reasons other than personal or behavior problems, then you should leverage your company and its network in your job search.

You can ask your boss if he or she knows of other companies in the industry that are hiring. Don't be afraid to ask for names or contacts. Your boss probably feels horrible about having to let you go, and will most likely jump at the opportunity to help you transition smoothly. Simarly you should "network" with anyone you can in the organization. They know you and your work. Typically, they will be delighted to help you land the next job.

Luckily, Joseph was an exemplary employee, and his organization wanted to assist him with the next step. Joseph's company actually hired JobBound to write his resume so he could be as marketable as he could be.

As you will see, Joseph wasn't planning on the job search, so his resume was not up-to-date. The first thing we did was add Joseph's most senior position and his accomplishments at B&D, Inc. We also removed his old job as a waiter, which made him appear more junior.

We then advised Joseph to give his resume to his boss at the company that he was leaving. That way his boss could forward it along to any contacts that he had, and he would also have the resume on file in case another opening came up at B&D, Inc.

# Joseph Templin

621 Quads Drive
Jackson, MS 60233

833.222.1211
joseph@gmail.com

## *WORK EXPERIENCE*

LEADERSHIP CONSULTANT                                            *June 2004 to Present*
*B&D, Inc*

- Traveled extensively throughout the United States and Canada visiting chapter officers advice and counsel
- Received an extensive three-month training
- Coordinated and **facilitated leadership and team building retreats**
- Published Summaries and letters reviewing each chapter and region visit
- Conducted **strategic planning** at each chapter
- **Facilitated discussion groups** on topics including recruitment, marketing, risk management, organizational and personal values, and member education
- Consulted chapters on recruitment and its effects on chapter operations
- Assisted middle management in **reviewing, revising, and creating programs and services** offered to the members of the organization
- Established credibility and carry out responsibilities in a variety of situations and circumstances at more than 30 locations each year

BARTENDER AND SERVER              *August 2000 to June 2004*
*Chili's Bar and Grill, Jackson, MS*

- **Trained new employees** and Managers in Training
- Designed and implemented sales incentive programs

HEAD BOOKKEEPER              *June 2003 to August 2003*
*Dante Payroll, Jackson, MS*

- Entered all company transactions and client data into QuickBooks database
- Tracked productivity and growth using various information systems
- **Designed information systems** and trained employees to use them

## HONORS AND ACTIVITIES

- Past President and member of Order of Omega
- **First Associated Students Director of Public Relations**
- **2002 & 2003 New Student Orientation Leader**
- 2002 Most Valuable Orientation Leader

## EXPERIENCED ON ALL COMPUTER SKILL

Excel—Windows—Precision Tree—Access—PowerPoint—Project—Word—Outlook—Outlook Express—Mind Manager—QuickBooks—Quicken

## VOLUNTEER WORK

- Multiple Sclerosis Walk 2005, Chicago, IL
- Martin Luther King Jr. Annual Celebration, Speaker
- P.A.L.S. (police activity league supporters), City of Jackson
- AIDS Walk 2003

# JOSEPH TEMPLIN

621 Quads Drive ♦ Jackson, MS 60233
833.222.1211 ♦ joseph@gmail.com

## *EXPERIENCE*

**DIRECTOR OF BUSINESS DEVELOPMENT**, B&D, INC., JACKSON, MS, 2005–Present
- Oversee a staff of two managing year-long process establishing new chapters at two state universities
- Convinced Dean of Students and VP/Student Affairs to create new campus chapters
- Competed and won in two out of two new initiative presentations, leading team in competition with as many as four other national fraternities
  - Wrote presentation and delivered pitch to audience of more than a dozen university officials
- Manage a budget of more than $100,000, creating budget plan from scratch and securing approval from Strategic Budget Committee
- Developed targeted marketing campaign and met with more than 40 student organizations and faculty advisors to recruit members
  - Exceeded annual recruitment goals by 15%
- Trained a staff of 20 serving as functional specialists and advisors for all executive board positions
- Wrote and delivered quarterly presentations to Board of Directors

**LEADERSHIP CONSULTANT,** B&D, INC., JACKSON, MS, 2004–2005
- Traveled more than 40,000 miles, meeting with university officials, organization representatives, and undergraduate members overseeing operations at 32 college campuses
- Partnered with collegiate administrators including University Presidents, Deans of Students, and VP Student Affairs
- Delivered more than 50 presentations to a total audience of 9,000 on topics spanning overall operations, financial accountability, and academics
- Prepared more than 30 strategic summaries based on SWOT analyses
- Consulted with 12 chapters that received awards for overall excellence

**HEAD BOOKKEEPER,** DANTE PAYROLL, JACKSON, MS, Summer 2003
- Managed entire bookkeeping process for business with 45 corporate clients
- Entered more than 1,000 company transactions weekly across a dozen job categories
- Handled semimonthly and independent contractor payroll for 16 employees
- Developed company's first-ever sales tracking tools dramatically increasing efficiency and productivity
- Oversaw Accounts Receivables enhancing collections process for dozens of outstanding accounts

## *EDUCATION*

**MISSISSIPPI STATE UNIVERSITY**—May 2004
- Bachelor of Science in Accounting; School of Business and Economics
- Major GPA 3.7/4.0; Dean's List Spring 2004

## *ACTIVITIES*

- Featured Speaker, Martin Luthur King Jr. Annual Celebration, 2003
  - Spoke to 450 religious leaders about Dr. King
- President, Order of Omega, 2003
  - Selected out of more than 600 men on campus
- New Student Orientation Leader, 2002–2003
- President/Treasurer/Member, Student Government Association, 2000–2004

# Laid Off

As a result of a merger, Bradley was laid off after almost ten years with his company. Basically, Bradley's entire department was absorbed by the new company, so his team and his bosses were all jobless.

Bradley had excelled at Apex, and he was concerned that his age and salary history would discourage companies from considering him. Bradley wasn't ready to retire, but he didn't want to take a big salary cut and minimize his standard of living.

First, we wrote a succinct summary and emphasized his accomplishments. We downplayed his age by not including his school graduation years, and we made the most out of Bradley's extensive network and professional organizations.

Through the years, Bradley had been involved with numerous companies, symposiums, conferences, and associations. Since people in Bradley's line of work need a large network, we really highlighted his multifaceted connections on his resume. Any recruiting director would want an employee who brings a wide scope of possible new clients.

In addition, we prepped Bradley on ways to answer interview questions about the layoff since most people in his industry were aware of the merger. First, we advised Bradley to be honest and positive.

Even though it may be difficult, you don't want to speak negatively about your past employer. You want to state the reason for the layoff and then focus on the experience you gained:

*Due to the company merger, my entire department was laid off, but while I was at Apex, I was able to accomplish . . .*

*Although it was an unfortunate situation for many people at the company, I am really looking at this as an opportunity to meet new challenges . . .*

With his new resume and a positive perspective, Bradley was able to gain a great position after being laid off.

# Bradley Aldrich

61782 Peace Drive, Freedom, LA, 59494
321.322.232
bradley.aldrich@gmail.com

## Skills Summary

- Heavy financial-services background (sales, marketing, research, corporate finance)
- Extensive knowledge of Wall Street standards and practices
- Broad writing and editing experience, including press releases, annual reports, quarterly reports, marketing campaigns, advertisements, and topical publications of all lengths
- Crisis-management experience (1987 market crash and 2000 market top)
- Corporate speechwriter (Dow, Paine Webber, Kemper, and Transamerica)
- Media-relationship manager (regional and national print and broadcast outlets)
- Production manager for time-sensitive sales, marketing, and research content
- Extensive new-product development/strategic marketing experience
- Corporate communications trainer (Dow, Louisiana Society of CPAs, University of Houston)
- Degrees in both science and humanities

## Professional Experience

**APEX EQUITY SERVICES,** Freedom, LA, June 1999–October 2008

### *Principal, Market Strategy Consulting*

- Develop and market time-sensitive investment strategies for institutional investment managers
- Produce and sell custom market-strategy white papers
- Conduct custom research to dovetail with proprietary efforts
- Evaluate portfolios for managers of all valuation disciplines
- Provide ad hoc services to financial-services firms on a contract basis
- Emphasize value-added sales skills, effective needs analysis, and accurate market analysis using full complement of analytical tools

**MILO + CO.,** Freedom, LA, March 1990–May 1999

### Institutional Sales, National Accounts

- Sold proprietary research, proprietary computer software, and custom consulting services to premier institutional money managers of all valuation disciplines
- Heavy emphasis on very large consultative sales of proprietary computer software
- Wrote and marketed time-sensitive commentary for performance-driven managers
- Recognized as top salesperson during 1999 (% increase 6X salesforce average)
- Won only sales contest (both % and absolute increase) completed during tenure with firm
- Achieved consistently high client-retention rates
- Cut travel expenses by implementing self-designed client care telephone support system
- Initiated and produced comprehensive price-point analysis of all competitors
- Developed new products to expand market share
- Worked closely with design teams to introduce new products effectively

**Relevant Background**

**BOYLAND & KINYETTA INC.**, Freedom, LA

**Vice President, Equity Research.** National equity-marketing manager, institutional sales, senior writer, equity analyst, market strategist.

- Doubled firm's research output in 8 months with no staff increase.
- Managed all media contact for 1987 market crash (TV, radio, and print)

**DAN NEWMAN, LLC**, Freedom, LA

**Vice President, Equity Research.** National equity-marketing manager, institutional sales, senior writer, equity analyst, market strategist.

- Increased firm's research output fivefold in 6 months with no increase in staff

**CLOUT EQUITY**, Freedom, LA

**Vice President, Equity Research.** National equity-marketing manager, institutional sales, senior writer.

- Managed research output for most productive Wall Street firm in history (Greenwich poll)
- Increased firm's research output by 50% in less than 12 months with no increase in staff

**KOBUSSEN RESEARCH COMPANY**, Freedom, LA

*Speechwriter, Editor*

- Wrote time- and content-sensitive speeches for top corporate management. Wrote, edited, designed, and produced complex, large-scale research reports (with exceptionally heavy graphic content) on a wide range of energy-related subjects for worldwide think tank.

# Education

MA—Thesis Program, English Literature, University of Louisiana
BA—Chemistry/English Literature (double major), Indiana University. James A. Workman prize
   nominee for Outstanding Senior English Student.

### Speaking Engagements

- Featured speaker (national events): University of Louisiana Annual Technical and Professional Writing Symposium, Environmental Hazards Convention and Exposition
- Featured speaker (regional events): International Association of Financial Planners (MS, LA, and CA), Texas Society of Certified Public Accountants (Houston and Dallas), National Association of Investors (LA, NY), Southwest Communications Association

# Certifications

- NASD Series 7 and 63; Louisiana Life Insurance license

**Awards and Personal Development**

- National Endowment for the Humanities creative writing award
- Bronze medalist, 2004 California State Master's Track Cycling Championships
- Volunteer—Cedars-Sinai Medical Center POOCH program (my Labrador and I visit AIDS and cardiac-care patients as part of a comprehensive-care initiative)

# Bradley Aldrich

61782 Peace Drive ♦ Freedom, LA, 59494
321.322.2322 ♦ bradley.aldrich@gmail.com

## *SUMMARY*

- Seasoned research professional with 10+ years leading and enhancing quality and quantity of output of equity research teams at companies including American Securities and Paine Webber
- Strong project manager balancing multiple roles in research, sales, marketing, and crisis management for some of the largest companies, funds, and institutional investors in the county
- Exceptional writing and presenting skills–National Endowment for the Humanities Writing Award winner, and frequent keynote speaking engagements at national conferences and meetings with audiences as large as 3,000
- Dedicated financial research expert with a documented track record of accurate predictions leading up to and through the bear market

## *EXPERIENCE*

**APEX EQUITY SERVICES, PRINCIPAL, MARKET STRATEGY CONSULTING,** FREEDOM, LA, 1999–2008
- Worked with more than 35 mutual fund and hedge fund managers developing investment strategies for institutional equity investors
- Recommended internal investment strategies for a several billion dollar family of 20 mutual funds across 12 portfolio managers
- Provided pairs trading recommendations for 200 industry groups for one of the largest hedge funds in the country
- Executed custom research on mutual funds, hedge funds, foundations, and institutional family trusts providing buys, sells, and shorts for thousands of individual stocks
- Performed asset class reviews using an enhanced suite of fundamental, qualitative, quantitative, and technical skills for institutional investors of all types
- Published newsletter in March 2000 accurately predicting the top of NASDAQ, SOX, and BTK, and issuing strong sell recommendations on DOW and S&P 500

**MILO & CO., INSTITUTIONAL SALES, NATIONAL ACCOUNTS,** FREEDOM, LA 1990–1999
- Sold proprietary research, computer software, and custom consulting services to more than 50 of the premier institutional money managers across all valuation disciplines
- Worked closely with key clients to recommend and sell several million dollars annually of proprietary computer software and value-added aftermarket support
- Recognized as top salesperson out of 16 by increasing sell percentage more than six times sales average in 1999
- Won only company sales contest in both percentage and absolute increase in first year on job
- Increased sales dramatically, and cut travel expenses by launching client care telephone support system
- Created comprehensive price-point matrix tracking strengths, weaknesses, and pricing of 70 competitors
- Developed new entry level product line expanding market share without impacting margin
- Assisted client with tools and recommendations helping company win "US Investing Championship" in 1998
- Achieved firm's highest client retention rates by focusing on dedicated consultative sales
- Wrote weekly 2–10 page newsletter tracking individual stocks, strategic market issues, and industry group developments distributed to entire clientele
- Advised top mutual fund growth fund of 1999

**BOYLAND & KINYETTA, VICE PRESIDENT, EQUITY RESEARCH,** FREEDOM, LA, 1986–1990
- Doubled firm's research output by 20% in eight months with no increase in eight member staff
- Helped transition Lovett's specialty firm energy expertise into Kemper as part of takeover
- Managed all media contact across television, radio, and print for 1987 market crash

**DAN NEWMAN, LLC, VICE PRESIDENT, EQUITY RESEARCH,** FREEDOM, LA, 1983–1986
- Increased firm's research output fivefold with no increase in staff

**CLOUT EQUITY, VICE PRESIDENT, EQUITY RESEARCH,** FREEDOM, LA, 1981–1983
- Managed research output for most productive Wall Street firm in history (Greenwich poll)
- Increased firm's research output 50% in less than 12 months

**KOBUSSEN PRODUCTION RESEARCH COMPANY, SPEECHWRITER, EDITOR,** FREEDOM, LA, 1979–1981
- Wrote dozens of speeches for top corporate management including CEO as part of Exxon's worldwide think tank

## EDUCATION

**UNIVERSITY OF LOUISIANA**
- Master of Arts—Thesis Program, English Literature

**UNIVERSITY OF INDIANA**
- Bachelor of Arts—Chemistry/English Double Major

## SPEAKING ENGAGEMENTS

- National Association of Investors, International Association of Financial Planners, Louisiana Computer Investor's Association, Society of Certified Public Accountants, Southwest Communications Association, University of Louisiana Annual Technical and Professional Writing Symposium, Environmental Hazards Convention and Exposition, Women in Health

## SKILLS/AWARDS/INVOLVEMENT

- NASD Series 7 and 63
- Louisiana Life Insurance license
- National Endowment for the Humanities creative writing award
- Bronze medallist, 2004 Louisiana State Master's Track Cycling Championships
- Volunteer, Cedars-Sinai Medical Center POOCH program, visit AIDS and cardiac care patients with Labrador

# MOVING UP IN AN INDUSTRY

You've put in the time. You've paid your dues. Now you're ready to move out and up.

There are countless career-driven people who always want to be the best, earn the most money, and keep climbing the ladder to the top. They are constantly seeking promotions, better experiences, and more responsibilities. Hey, there's nothing wrong with that.

Sometimes, one company simply cannot provide this type of growth and opportunity. Often, it requires a change in companies to get the salary you think you deserve, the title that you want, or the new challenges that you crave. If you decide to begin looking for a new job in your industry, there are a few things you want to keep in mind:

## 1. Do not tell your boss or your colleagues you are job-searching

If the company knows they will have to replace you, they may do that before you expect it.

## 2. Act with professionalism in all that you do

The way you conduct your job search is a reflection on you. We've heard (and seen) far too many instances of resumes sitting on the copy machine, Yahoo! HotJobs left on the computer screen, or multiple instances of a grandmother dying unexpectedly on Wednesdays from 1:00–2:30. Not only does this give you a bad reputation, but it can also cost you your current job.

## 3. Don't put your work email address on your resume

And list your cell phone number, not your work number.

## 4. Try to squeeze in interviews during lunch breaks or take a vacation day

"Calling in sick" is not a good idea.

## 5. Keep your interview suit hidden

If you normally dress casually for work, you will raise some eyebrows with your three-piece suit.

## 6. Don't be too quick to get into bed with your new company

Don't betray company or client confidences, don't bad-mouth your current company, and don't give less than the industry-standard two weeks' notice if you do quit.

Why should you care about any of these things for a company you are leaving? If you'd do them to your current company, recruiting directors will think you'd do them to their company as well down the road. Plus, it's a small world out there. People talk and people move jobs quite a bit. You don't want to burn bridges or be known around the industry as unethical.

• • •

The following candidates came to JobBound because they were ready for more challenges and a different company environment. They loved their industry, but for various reasons, they wanted to move to another company in the same industry. They were accomplished individuals who were basically seeking a promotion through a job change, so they needed an amazing resume to help them do just that.

# Moving Up in an Industry

Margaret was a senior executive who had great experience, but her resume was not compelling to read. Her *before* resume definitely wasn't doing her justice.

First, from a formatting perspective, she had three subheadings underneath each job listing: Responsibilities, Additional Responsibilities, Achievements. I don't understand that. What is the difference between a responsibility and an additional responsibility? It reminds me of people (especially students) who have a section on their resume called "Relevant Experience." What is the other experience—irrelevant?!

In any event, we certainly cleaned up Margaret's formatting, and then changed the content. We filled her resume with dozens of meaningful and impressive accomplishments. If Margaret wants to move up in advertising, she has to show why she deserves it.

Margaret had also worked with a couple of world-renowned companies, so we stated the company names first on her resume. To have worked at two of the top USA agencies speaks volumes for Margaret's experience and exposure.

You will also notice that her *before* resume did not include her current job. Clearly, this was just a case of Margaret not updating her resume. That's a great lesson for you. You should update your resume *at least* every six months.

That doesn't mean you have to be looking for a job then. The problem is that many folks forget what they've accomplished as the years go by. Countless times we work with candidates who cannot remember any of their accomplishments. Your results and the scope of your work are critical to making you sound as good as possible. Don't let them drift away as distant memories!

# Margaret Baptiste
782 E. Marberry, Unit 47.
McHenry, Illinois 60682
Mobile–773-842-7227
Home–341-722-8482
mbaptiste@msn.com

---

**Key Assets**

---

Strong Strategic Skills
Leadership and Personnel Development Skills
Extensive Financial Management Skills

Entrepreneurial Business Experience
Client and Agency Experience
Blue Chip Packaged Goods Clients

---

**Business Experience**

---

May 2000–September 2001    **Fallon Advertising Worldwide**
Minneapolis, Minnesota      Account Director

**Responsibilities:**
- Led team management of Holiday Inn Hotels, the agency's most profitable account.
- Management of resource allocation including Strategic Planning, Creative Services and Media.
- Personnel management of 3 Account Managers.

**Additional Responsibilities:**
- Account Director–Fallon Global Expansion working on South American and Asian offices.
- Account Director–Caux Round Table–A global business ethics organization.

**Achievements**
- Holiday Inn's "Mark" campaign won Gold Effie in 2000.
- Co-Author of successful new business pitch and RFP response for integrated marketing pitch with Fallon Interactive for Bass Hotels' account.
- Developed new Brand blueprint for Holiday Inn and proposed Brand Architecture for Bass Hotels.

1997–April 2000     **J. Walter Thompson Advertising**
Toronto, Canada         Group Account Director: Kraft Foods Canada

**Responsibilities:**
- Led team management of 10 active brands including Kraft Dinner, Philadelphia, Nabob, Miracle Whip and Singles.
- Financial responsibility for profitability and resource allocation on account.
- Personnel management of 3 Account Managers and 2 support staff.

**Additional Responsibilities:**
- Active Role in New Business Pitches including wins on Shell Oil and Kraft Direct Marketing.
- New Business Development Director–Retail Segment.

**Achievements:**
- Developed over 20 television spots and multiple print and radio campaigns for Kraft Foods.
- JWT received incremental financial bonus of 3% of revenue based on Account Service rating in 1999.
Developed strategic positioning and managed creation of Kraft Dinner copy that won Gold -London International Advertising Award–Best TV/Cinema Food

---

| February–November 1999 | **Millennium Eyewear** |
| Toronto, Canada | Co-Owner |

An entrepreneurial venture developing and marketing novelty items for the Millennium. Specific responsibility included the creation of product and management of a branded product program for Holt Renfrew stores. This included product development, marketing support, procurement and delivery management.

| 1990-1996 | **Vandalay Industries** |
| Toronto, Canada | Director of Product Development |

This senior management position, reporting directly to the President, encompassed development, execution and strategic marketing of the complete product line for this multi-million dollar international company.

**Responsibilities:**
- Conceptualized and created all products and packaging for Bath, Beauty, and Candle categories as leader of the product management team.
- Negotiated and supervised development and execution of product and packaging through a variety of contract vendors. Vendors included chemists, manufacturers, and artistic, print and component sources both domestic and overseas.
- Managed all integrated marketing efforts including a yearly full color catalogue and numerous trade shows throughout North America.
- Researched current industry style trends through travel in Europe, Asia and N. America.

**Achievements:**
- Strategic marketing direction implemented by company resulted in double-digit annual sales growth with company volume increasing 200% during my tenure.
- Created 11 product lines including the two most successful in the company's 26-year history.
- Company's product voted #1 personal care line in 1994 by retailers in Giftbeat, the leading industry trade publication.

| 1987–1989 | **The Hudson's Bay Company** |
| Toronto, Canada | Senior Planning Manager—Cosmetics |

Responsible for financial and inventory management of Corporation's largest retail purchasing budget in excess of $ 160 million.
**Responsibilities:**
- Developed and negotiated purchase parameters with entire divisional supplier base for 87 Bay stores.
- Target market and demographic analysis using company and industry research to redesign distribution.

**Achievements:**
- Financial management in cosmetics accomplished a 14% sales increase and $ 2.4 million profit improvement.
- Co-chair of Corporate Distribution Task Force. Recommendation implemented reduced distribution expenditures by $2 million in one fiscal year.
- Chosen as only management trainee for promotion and re-location to Corporate Head Office in Toronto.

---

**Educational History**

Bachelor of Commerce (Honors), Marketing Major, **University of Manitoba**

Certification Retail Marketing and Merchandising—**Hudson's Bay Company**—management training

# Margaret Baptiste

782 E. Marberry, Unit 47 ♦ McHenry, IL 60682
773.824.7227 ♦ mbaptiste@msn.com

## EXPERIENCE

**MARC USA,** VP, GROUP ACCOUNT DIRECTOR, Chicago, IL/Pittsburgh, PA, 2002–Present
*True Value, New Business Development, Moen, WMS Gaming, Mohawk Carpets*

- Orchestrated two-year strategic brand overhaul for True Value, fundamentally recasting brand as destination for do-it-yourself enthusiasts
  - Developed a comprehensive consumer and retailer program spanning qualitative and quantitative research incorporating segmentation study
  - Created a communications plan covering all touch points within organization including store owners, corporate employees and consumers
  - Sold and executed entire multi-media integrated communications platform including TV, print, radio, in-store, local templates, Internet, apparel, and more
- Rebranded and developed strategy for new paint business brand creating positioning for "Color Made Simple" integrated program in 2,000 True Value stores nationwide
- Seamlessly transitioned agency's second largest account from Pittsburgh to Chicago in 2005
  - Hired staff, developed all infrastructure, and managed entire cross functional transition
- Oversaw all aspects of fast-paced $20MM retail account with 5,000 national outlets serving in many instances as client's de facto marketing department developing everything from crew uniforms, shopping bags, and trade show materials, to national advertising campaigns
- Manage two accounts and all agency new business working with an integrated staff of more than 20 across account management, strategic planning, creative, media, interactive, PR, and direct
- Worked on 12 new business pitches leading team in seven efforts and securing five new clients representing $5.5MM in revenue
- Prepared dozens of RFPs and worked on several pitches in categories including OneValue, Radiance, and Milford Notes.
- Launched entirely new North American campaign for Moen Faucets following successful new business win–airing new campaign just 12 weeks after winning assignment
  - Campaign's second month represented highest monthly sales in company history (+$10MM)
  - Intent to purchase jumped more than four points vs. year ago–representing 8% market share increase
  - Unaided brand awareness rose 5.4 points compared to year ago figures
- Won several national creative awards for Mohawk Carpets including National ADDY, and Creative Arts Honorable Mention

**FALLON ADVERTISING WORLDWIDE,** ACCOUNT DIRECTOR, Minneapolis, MN, 2000–2001
*Holiday Inn*

- Created brand architecture for interactive assignment in winning Bass Hotels (Holiday Inn parent) digital pitch
- Worked with ethnographer/psychologist developing innovative research approach to uncover a new competitive brand positioning within the family of Holiday Inn brands
- Led repositioning of historically leisure brand, recasting Holiday Inn as the preferred destination for business travelers
  - Increased mid week occupancy 5%
  - Drove RevPar (revenue per average room) up 9% as a result of new positioning
- Negotiated exclusive sponsorship of NCAA men's Final Four, creating an integrated promotional/creative campaign targeted to business travelers

- Shepherded highly successful continuation of award-winning "Mark" campaign developing a series of new, fresh executions and negotiating talent payments for lead actor

**J. WALTER THOMPSON,** GROUP ACCOUNT DIRECTOR, Toronto, Canada, 1997–2000
*Kraft Foods, New Business Development*
- Managed 10 active brands including Kraft Dinner, Philadelphia Cream Cheese, Miracle Whip, and Kraft Singles for agency's largest account
- Responsible for JWT receiving incremental financial bonus of 3% of revenue based on superior account service rating in 1999
- Developed strategic positioning and managed creation of Kraft Dinner advertising that won Gold at the London International Advertising Awards, and a Cassie Silver (Canadian EFFIE)
  - New campaign doubled non-promoted sales to 60% of brand's volume
  - Increased market share 2.6% in 1999 following decline in 1998
  - Exceeded planned annual shipments by 8% in 1999
  - Key creative execution received highest Millward Brown AI score in North America, exceeding norm by 550%
- Won Shell Oil new business pitch—only country in the world where business was retained during global alignment to Ogilvy & Mather

**VANDALAY INDUSTRIES,** DIRECTOR OF PRODUCT DEVELOPMENT, Toronto, Canada, 1990–1996
- Helped company sales increase from $9MM to $30MM in six years
- Established company's first-ever marketing department, growing group to 15 employees from 0
- Marketing efforts resulted in six years of double digit annual sales growth
- Created 11 new product lines including the two most successful in company's 26-year history
- Developed entirely new line of products selling to a wide variety of US retailers–representing first efforts in US market
- Managed all aspects of development and launch of more than 500 SKUs spanning body lotion, candles, soap products, ceramics, novelty items, and more
- Conceptualized and created all products and packaging for bath, beauty, and candle categories
- Company's product voted #1 personal care line in 1994 by leading trade publication

**THE HUDSON'S BAY COMPANY,** SENIOR PLANNING MANAGER, Toronto, Canada, 1987–1989
*Cosmetics*
- Responsible for financial and inventory management of corporation's largest purchasing budget in excess of $160MM for Canada's largest retailer
- Overhauled departmental financial management, resulting in 14% sales increase and $2.4MM profit growth
- Reduced distribution expenditures $2MM as Co-chair of Corporate Distribution Task Force
- Negotiated purchase parameters with entire divisional supplier base for 87 national Bay stores

## EDUCATION

**UNIVERSITY OF MANITOBA**—WINNIPEG
- Bachelor of Commerce with Honors; Marketing Major

**RETAIL MARKETING AND MERCHANDISING CERTIFICATION**—HUDSON'S BAY COMPANY
- Management Training

# Moving Up in an Industry

When Milo came to JobBound, he felt as though his career was stalled. Milo had a very clear-cut career path in cabinetry sales. He had sold cabinets for over fifteen years for a few different companies. His expertise and breadth of experience were significant. Milo wanted to use his background to secure a VP position in the industry that he knew and loved. To do that, Milo really had to capitalize on his industry know-how.

Unfortunately, Milo's *before* resume is a classic example of a job description resume. There's nothing on it that indicates how much he had accomplished. Just by reading the *before* version, you would think he was your typical salesman as opposed to a great asset to any company.

Let's look at his summary, for instance. Milo has loaded his *before* version with what I call "self-ascribed" attributes. According to Milo, Milo is results-oriented, has great customer service skills, and has a track record of success. In actuality, anyone can write that on a resume. If Milo weren't results-oriented, do you think he'd write: "Moderately results-oriented, but usually I don't get it done."

Of course not. That's why in the *after* version we support each summary point with a fact. Recruiting directors are a skeptical lot. If they don't see a number, they probably assume you are making something up!

We also began each entry with the name of Milo's company. Milo wanted to stay in cabinetry, so we highlighted the company names to showcase Milo's clear dedication to the field.

# Milo Jay

831 Sacramento Street
Southshore, NJ 87315
(843-481-9870)
milo@yahoo.com

## *Summary*

Twenty-two years of award winning Sales and Sales Management experience. A self-motivated leader who is results-oriented with proven ability to manage multiple tasks at one time, work independently, and contribute to a team effort. Excels at assessing customer needs and providing products/services to meet those needs. Works well in a fast-paced, high pressure environment and provides input to enhance company operations. Areas of expertise include:

- Sales Team Management
- Customer Service
- Marketing

- Territory Development
- Budgeting and Forecasting
- Communication

## *Professional Experience*

**Kensington Sales, LLC**  Kensington, CT.
**Manufacturer's Sales Representative**            2003-2005
- Establishing and maintaining new product lines in Northern New Jersey, New York, and New England territories.
- Developing and maintaining accounts in these territories.

**Schieber Sales, Inc.**  Doylestown, PA.
**Outside Sales Representative**            2002-2003
- Managed some existing sales in Northern New Jersey territory.
- Developed and opened up new accounts in the New England market.
- Increased sales over 50% in first year.

**Ward's Cabinetry**  Clanton, Alabama
**Vice-President of Sales & Marketing**            2001-2002
*Directed inside sales force of five and outside sales force of nine covering 14 states. Developed sales budget. Responsible for hiring and training of sales staff.*
- Increased outside sales force to expand territory and establish a broader customer base.
- Instituted new marketing and sales aids including creation of promotional materials and advertising products.
- Developed start-up kits for sales representatives and new dealers.
- Initiated updating of website to broaden the appeal to a more sophisticated customer base.
- Involved in revamping of product pricing structure and product development.

**Kraftmaid Cabinetry, Inc.**  Middlefield, Ohio
**Regional Sales & Marketing Manager**            1991-2001
*Directed northeast sales activities to dealers in nine states and three Canadian Provinces ($35 mm annual sales). Managed a staff of five Sales/Marketing Representatives. Formulated budgets and sales projections. Called on key accounts and traveled with sales staff. Provided comprehensive product presentations and product training to customers.*
- Increased territory sales revenues from $13mm to over $30mm for the period (1996-1999).

- Consistently met/exceeded sales and budget objectives.
- Generated largest regional sales increase in 1998.
- #1 Regional Sales Manager in company each year for 1992-1996.
- Successfully developed Sales/Marketing Representatives who have assumed company management responsibilities.
- Hired as a Sales Representative and promoted to Regional Sales Manager after only one year based on outstanding sales performance.
- Previous Sales Management responsibilities included calling on large retail home centers such as Home Depot.

**Riviera Cabinets, Inc.** Pompano Beach, Florida
**Sales Representative**                       1991
- Managed sales in New York, New Jersey and Connecticut territory.
- Met/exceeded monthly sales objectives.
- Retained a major account (Grossmans) utilizing effective sales and customer service skills.

**Rogers Sash & Door** Newington, Connecticut
**Kitchen Cabinet Showroom Manager**           1988-1991
- Opened a 3K square foot showroom in Newington, Connecticut.
- Hired, trained and managed Sales personnel (both on the road and in the showroom).
- Developed sales revenues within the new showroom. Implemented inventory control procedures to effectively service the customer base including coordination of deliveries.
- President of Southern New England Chapter of N.K.B.A. (National Kitchen & Bath Association)

**Independent Manufacturer's Representative**         1987-1988
- Represented lock lines and material handling equipment throughout the Northeast territory.

**Merillat Industries** Adrian, Michigan
**Sales Representative**                      1986-1987
- Managed sales activities for the #1 company account.

**Sales Representative for Lock Manufacturers**       1983-1986
- Received Key Club Award for Outstanding Sales.

**Managed Retail Hardware and Convenience Store Operations**    1977-1983
- Responsible for over 14 stores and up to 200 personnel.

## Education
**Western New England College** Springfield, Massachusetts
Bachelor of Arts in History

# Milo Jay

831 Sacramento Street ♦ Southshore, NJ 87315

843.481.9870 ♦ milo@yahoo.com

## SUMMARY

- Seasoned sales professional with more than 17 years of experience representing a wide variety of kitchen cabinetry lines across New England and New York/New Jersey
- Proven track record of success having successfully launched several new lines through network of strong, established industry relationships
- Dedicated manager with background leading teams as large as 14 and overseeing more than $45MM in sales annually
- Recognized industry leader with experience at some of the most prominent manufacturers in the nation and having served as President of regional trade association

## EXPERIENCE

**KEN CABINETS,** MANUFACTURER'S SALES REPRESENTATIVE, Kensin, CT, 2002–Present
- Grew business to more than $2MM in sales from nothing in less than three years representing four distinct product lines across New England and Northern New Jersey/New York
- Developed 25 account relationships with both new and existing retailers including Consumer's Warehouse, Nuway, and Kitchen Expo
- Established significant recognition for previously unknown product lines for both custom and stock brands including Elmwood Kitchens, Helmstown Vanities, and Haas Cabinets
- Generated positive cash flow in first four months while registering $545,000 in sales in year one
- Launched new high-end cabinetry line in Northern New Jersey and New England opening 12 new accounts in first year

**WARD'S CABINETRY,** VP OF SALES AND MARKETING, Clanton, AL, 2001–2002
- Managed, hired, and trained inside/outside sales force of 14 covering 14 states throughout the Southeast
- Oversaw budgeting, operations, and logistics for unit generating $10MM in sales annually
- Dramatically increased customer base by revamping outside sales force relationships, trimming existing roster and adding six new agencies
- Developed organization's first-ever start up sales kits for sales representatives and new dealers
- Launched fully integrated marketing and sales program distributed to more than 100 retailers, and overhauled company website
- Substantially increased profitability and sales by spearheading major revision of product pricing structure across more than 200 individual items

**KRAFTMAID CABINETRY,** REGIONAL SALES MANAGER, Middlefield, OH, 1991–2001
- Directed team of five Sales/Marketing Representatives generating $42MM in annual sales across nine Northeastern states and three Canadian provinces
- Increased sales 130% from 1996–1999 by revamping training and overhauling sales goals
- Exceeded/met sales goals every single year
- Ranked first in sales out of seven regional sales managers for five consecutive years
- Drove territory sales from two stores and $1MM to more than 86 stores and $47MM, necessitating territory split

- Saved company more than $500,000 in 2001 by successfully managing sales force budget
- Trained and managed more than seven Sales Representatives who later were promoted to Regional Sales Managers
- Responsible for company's largest regional sales increase in the nation in 1998
- Called on large retail home centers including Home Depot, Sears, and Lowe's
- Promoted from Sales Rep to Regional Manager in only one year

**ROGERS SASH & DOOR,** KITCHEN CABINET MANAGER, Newington, CT, 1988–1991
- Managed all operations for opening of 3,000 square foot state-of-the-art showroom
- Hired, trained, and managed a staff of four sales professionals
- Generated more than $2MM in sales revenue for new showroom location
- Elected President of Southern New England chapter of the National Kitchen & Bath Association (NKBA)

**MERILLAT INDUSTRIES,** SALES REPRESENTATIVE, Adrian, MI, 1986–1987
- Managed sales for the company's number one account

**LOCK MANUFACTURERS,** SALES REPRESENTATIVE, Rockford, IL, 1983–1986

**MANAGER,** RETAIL HARDWARE STORES, Springfield, MA, 1977–1983

# EDUCATION

**WESTERN NEW ENGLAND COLLEGE**—SPRINGFIELD, MA, 1977
- Bachelor of Arts in History

# Moving Up in an Industry

Adam was steadily progressing in the field of communications. He had worked at a couple boutique agencies, and he was ready to parlay his experience at an international full-service agency.

The first thing you notice about Adam's *before* resume is that it is very difficult to read. Content is certainly more important than format, but if the recruiting director can't read your resume, you are not going to get hired. Obviously, the *after* version is easier on the eye, and therefore, much more likely to be considered.

For the content, Adam did a decent job trying to highlight his accomplishments, but the *after* version is even better. We see a very clear picture of what he did and how he was able to save his company a lot of money. Who wouldn't want to hire a person who could save the company $650,000 a year?

# Adam Arlington

971 Antioch Ave. #54–Azure Plains, AZ 52910
879.458.2261 / email: AdamArlington@msn.com

## SUMMARY

Experienced marketing communications professional and account manager conceives, plans and implements advertising campaigns and sales promotions for packaged goods marketers. Collaborates with creative staff, directs junior account executives and manages vendors in fast turnaround environments. Skilled in financial and project management. Extensive print production experience.

## EXPERIENCE

**2000–2002: Account Manager        Art Directors' Service, Inc. Azure Plains, Arizona**
**Managed agency's relationship with Kraft Foods North America east coast packaging division, which generated $2.4 million in billings per year. Implemented efficiencies that reduced production costs by 4%, minimized mechanical production time and helped client achieve "speed to market" objectives.**

- Worked with team of client-side design managers and several design firms to plan and prepare generic and promotional packages according to Kraft official guidelines.
- Provided key internal and external communications and technical expertise concerning the yearly production of digital mechanical files for 5,500 SKU designs.
- Supervised assistant account executives and production artists completing design file projects and related tasks.

**1998–2000: Account Supervisor        Carrafiello-Diehl & Associates, Irvington, New York**
**Managed advertising and promotions agency's relationship with Paragon Trade Brands, the world's leading supplier of private label diapers. Trade and account specific promotions produced a 12% gain in product sales, expanded relationships with Wal-Mart and SAM'S Club, and resulted in client's designation as the sole supplier of Target's *Show-Offs*, Toys R' Us *Adorables*, Costco's *Signature* and Albertson's *Baby Basics* brands.**

- Assisted in development of strategic marketing plan and account specific marketing proposals
- Created video and print presentations for sales force use in communicating with the trade.
- Developed trade advertisements and trade show marketing materials.

**1995–1998: Account Executive        The Guild Group, White Plains, New York**
**Worked with client brand managers and sales promotion agency staff to develop consumer and trade promotion concepts, programs and collateral materials. Prepared creative briefs. Managed day-to-day agency activities including project estimates and invoices, creative and production timelines and budgets, status reports and legal approvals for all promotion materials prior to release for production. Consistently achieved agency profitability targets.**

- Clients included **Kraft Foods, Unilever, Pepperidge Farm** and **Nabisco.** These accounts contributed $2.5 million in annual agency revenue.
- Originated value-added promotion programs within client guidelines.
- Executed national consumer promotions including sweepstakes, contests and games, FSIs and coupons, in-store media and direct mailers.

## PROFESSIONAL DEVELOPMENT

**2004: New York University, School of Professional and Continuing Studies**. Marketing Management Certificate. Coursework included advertising and sales promotions, strategic marketing, brand management, and account service management.
**2003: New York University, School of Professional and Continuing Studies**, Certificate from Integrated Marketing Communications Institute
**1999:** Certificate from APMA, Promotion Planning for Professionals program

## EDUCATION

Graduated **Hofstra University**, New York, with Bachelors Business Administration

---

# Adam Arlington

971 Antioch Ave. #54 ♦ Azure Plains, AZ 52910
879.458.2261 ♦ AdamArlington@msn.com

## EXPERIENCE

**Account Manager,** <u>Art Directors' Service</u>, Azure Plains, AZ                    **2000–2002**
*Kraft Foods North America*

- Key liaison between 16 client-side project managers and 10 design firms in the development of packaging for brands such as Jell-O, Breyers, Life Savers, POST cereals, Maxwell House, and Tang
- Eliminated procedural redundancies and reduced production costs by 4% saving Kraft Foods $650,000 in one year.
- Trained client staff and agency personnel in the use of E-Works, Kraft's proprietary and internal electronic project management system.
- Supervised six assistant account executives and five production artists
- Created project budgets and timelines, job estimates and final invoices for Client generating $2.4 million in agency billings per year.

**Account Supervisor,** <u>Carrafiello-Diehl Associates</u>, Irvington, NY                    **1998–2000**
*Paragon Trade Brands—world's leading supplier of private label baby diapers*

- Helped increase client sales 12% annually by creating and executing first–ever account specific advertising and sales promotions campaigns.
- Oversaw the development and execution of fully integrated promotions for private label brands such as Albertson's *Baby Basics*, Toys R' Us *Adorables*, and Costco's *Signature* brands.
- Assisted in developing strategic marketing plan used by the client to solicit new accounts and expand relationships with retailers including Wal-Mart, Target, Kroger, Rite Aid and CVS.
- Created and produced sales presentation video and other materials used by 100 salespersons nationwide to solicit new business.
- Planned and produced client's annual Private Label Manufacturers Association trade show booth and collateral materials
- Directed daily routine of an account executive, three art directors and two copywriters.
- Created budgets, estimates and invoices for Client generating $1.6 million in annual agency revenue.

**Account Executive,** <u>The Guild Group</u>, White Plains, NY                    **1995–1998**
*Pepperidge Farm, Unilever, Nabisco and Kraft Foods North America*

- Collaborated with brand managers and sales promotion agency staff to develop multiple consumer and trade promotion concepts, programs and collateral materials annually
- Wrote creative briefs, oversaw creative development process and executed national consumer and trade promotions including the "Treasure is Meant to be Discovered" sweepstakes and field event for Pepperidge Farm's Milano brand and the NCAA March Madness in-store cross-sell promotion for Nabisco's Planters Peanuts.
- Conceived and executed national, semiannual direct mailers of laundry tips and coupons for Unilever's Snuggle and All brands as well as assorted FSIs, and point-of-purchase materials for Kraft Foods dessert brands.
- Prepared project estimates and invoices, creative and production timelines and budgets, status reports and obtained legal approvals for promotion materials.
- Helped agency exceed all revenue and profitability targets.

## EDUCATION/PROFESSIONAL DEVELOPMENT

**New York University**, School of Professional and Continuing Studies                    **2003–2004**

- Marketing Management Certificate
- Integrated Marketing Communications Certificate
- **Promotion Marketing Association**, Promotion Planning for Professionals Certificate

**Hofstra University**, NY, Bachelors Business Administration

---

# STUCK IN A RUT

Our next few clients found themselves in a situation familiar to many. They simply were stuck in a rut. Some were job-searching for a few months with no results. Some felt like they'd hit a dead end in their job. Some of them were not even getting a chance to sell themselves in the interview because their resume was not getting their foot in the door.

We hear the same scenario and story from many of our clients:

You call but hear no answer. You leave a message but get no reply. You email but receive nothing. You send a letter or even call again but you never hear back. You know they're interested—you can see all over that they want someone. You know you'd make a great match. So why don't you ever hear back?

If I've heard one common lament from anyone looking for a job, it's this— the person rarely hears back on time or at all for the jobs he or she applies for. Senior executive, junior employee, new grad—it doesn't matter, there's virtually never a timely response from a company.

So why does it happen? Why do you get the cold shoulder and why do they play hard to get? Here are three reasons:

## 1. Sheer volume

Most companies, and especially the large ones, get flooded with resumes. When I worked at Leo Burnett, it was not uncommon to get upward of five to six hundred resumes for one job opening. The sheer boundaries of space and time do not allow the typical recruiting director to personally get in touch with each and every candidate. To make matters worse, you've all been told to send your resume and then follow up in a week. Don't expect a call back if you do contact a company. There just simply isn't time.

## 2. There is no job

Could this be true? Yes, it is. Companies often post jobs when they don't necessarily have an opening. Here's why:

- They want to collect resumes, so that when they do have an opening, they have people to consider.
- They have to post the job for governmental or legal reasons.
- They forgot to take the posting down from the last opening they had (happens more than you'd think).

In these instances, you will likely never hear back from a recruiting director.

## 3. Bad business

At some companies, recruiting becomes one of the last priorities. There are client demands, meetings, emails, coworker issues, and so on. Companies then relegate recruiting to the bottom of the list. Recruiting should be the top priority since we all run on brain power, but not every company thinks that way. As a result, you send the resume, you even interview, but you never receive a response.

So given that most recruiting directors are not that into you, how do you deal? How do you get out of the rut?

## 1. Don't take it personally

It's going to happen. Assume no one will get back to you, and then you can be pleasantly surprised when someone does. Don't get discouraged; rejection is just part of the game.

## 2. Let your friends do the dirty work

If you have a friend or acquaintance working at the company, don't be afraid to have them check in for you. It will seem like less of a nuisance to a recruiting director if his own employee checks in.

## 3. Be persistent, not a stalker

If you're applying for a job by sending your resume online or in person, make the call after a week to check in to see if they received it and to see if they want to talk. Don't expect a response, and don't follow up again.

If you've actually interviewed for a job, you can be more persistent. After every interview, ask when you can expect a reply, and then feel free to follow up if you have not heard back. Call, then email, then call again. Feel free to contact them every three or four days, but switch up how you reach out.

## 4. Know when to take a hint

Just like the guy or gal who never calls, there is a time for you to move on. You need to think to yourself, "Do I want to work for a company that doesn't have the common decency to even call me back to tell me if I have the job?" You may wonder how they treat their current employees if this is how they treat their recruits.

The truth is the job search is a lot like dating. You may have to deal with a lot of rejection before you find the right match.

Our next clients needed some help getting out of the rut and finding the right match. They needed a resume that would take them from average to great. The *before* resumes were mostly job description resumes. We constantly reinforce that you must focus on your accomplishments to get noticed. This is the key component of a great resume that most people don't realize. But now that you're reading the book, say good-bye to being stuck in a rut!

# Stuck in a Rut

Two things should instantly strike you as very bad about the following *before* resume:

1. It is six pages long. I repeat, six pages long!
2. What's up with the third person?

It is one thing when LeBron James says, "LeBron had a great game last night." But Cameron Calapas does not sound quite as effective referring to himself when he writes his resume. Remember, there is a big name at the top of the resume that says it all. When we see Cameron Calapas at the top of the page, we assume everything else on the resume is going to be about Cameron!

Instead of saying:

Cameron has over nine years of business and technical experience

We say:

Over nine years of business and technical experience

It takes too long for a recruiting director to read full sentences. Write using bullet points. Try to start every bullet point with a powerful action verb (and try not to repeat them). For tasks that you have already completed, use the past tense, and for ongoing tasks or projects, use the present tense. We have included a list of powerful action verbs in the appendix if you need a few ideas.

As for the length of Cameron's resume, there certainly wasn't the need for all the detail. While it may be important to you, the reader is not interested in what you did ten years ago. Especially with technology jobs, where the fact that you installed several Commodore 64's in 1985 is not particularly relevant. You definitely want to focus more of your resume and more of the recruiter's time on what you did most recently.

# Cameron Calapas
## Senior Principal Consultant

Cameron has over nine years of business and technical experience in project management, software consulting, process analysis, systems analysis, software development, and training. He has expertise in several PeopleSoft Enterprise modules, specializing in Human Resources, Recruiting, and HCM Collaborative Applications. Cameron has over six years of PeopleSoft Enterprise HCM consulting experience with all major versions of the product from 7.5 to 8.9. He has been involved in all phases of system implementation, including assessment, design, construction, testing, and post-implementation support, utilizing proven system methodologies.

Cameron client base has covered a wide variety of industries, including retail, healthcare, information technology, financial services, and government. Prior to joining PeopleSoft Enterprise, Cameron worked as a Consultant for a "Big 5" consulting firm.

## Professional Experience

**PeopleSoft Enterprise HCM 8.8 Global Recruiting Solutions Implementation**
Information Technology Industry
Fortune 500

**Recruiting Solutions:** Cameron served as the Functional Lead on a HCM Global Recruiting Solutions Implementation effort for an Information Technology Fortune 500 company.

- The objective was to replace the existing Recruiting systems with PeopleSoft's Recruiting Solution r8.8.
- Applications included Recruit Workforce, eRecruit, eRecruit Manager Desktop, and Resume Processing.
- Managed team through design, testing and go live.
- Assisted in standardizing recruitment to new hire "end-to-end" business process and supporting values (codes) to create frameworks that are usable across locations.
- Managed the customization design and build effort.
- Managed the Functional and UAT testing efforts. Coordinated the testing efforts and managed the client and consulting team through completion.
- Provided post-production support.

**PeopleSoft Enterprise HCM 8.9 Setup Manager & Candidate Gateway**
Internal Development Support

**Setup Manager:** Cameron served as the Project Manager on a HCM r8.9 Setup Manager testing effort.

- Managed a team of resources in the overall testing of the new tools available for Setup Manager r8.9 prior to release.
- Worked very closely with PeopleSoft's r8.9 development team to understand the changes in HCM r.8.9.
- Worked with resources closely to setup all HR, Payroll, Benefits, and Recruiting data for Setup Manager validation and testing.
- Worked with the development team in resolving issues encountered during testing.
- Developed reference and training materials for PeopleSoft's consulting organization.
- Continues to serve as a contact for the consulting organization with questions or issues.

**Candidate Gateway:** Cameron served as a valuable resource and contact for the testing effort of the Candidate Gateway r8.9 prior to release.

- Served as a liaison between the development team and PeopleSoft's consulting organization.
- Assisted in actual testing and review of products.
- Worked with the development team to understand all the r8.9 changes.
- Worked with the development team in resolving issues encountered during testing.
- Continues to serve as a contact for the consulting organization with questions or issues.

**PeopleSoft Enterprise HCM 8.8 Global Recruiting Solutions Implementation**

**Recruiting Solutions:** Cameron served as the Functional Lead on a HCM Global Recruiting Solutions Implementation effort for an Information Technology Fortune 500 company.

- The objective was to replace the existing Recruiting systems with PeopleSoft's Recruiting Solution. Applications included Recruit Workforce, eRecruit, eRecruit Manager Desktop, and Resume Processing.

| | |
|---|---|
| Information Technology Industry Fortune 500 | • Provided boardroom presentations to the executive team.<br>• Worked with the management team during the strategy and planning phases. Identified best approach for confirming requirements and identifying any gaps.<br>• Lead 3 months of global design workshops for the US, Canada, and Latin American countries.<br>• Provided functional expertise to the client on how to best use the system to meet their business needs and evaluate gaps for modifications/customizations.<br>• Provided alternative resolutions to disposition items (gaps) and documented/presented proposals.<br>• Managed a team responsible for<br>  1. Identifying and documenting "As-Is" and "To-Be" processes.<br>  2. Requirements gathering and documenting configuration needs.<br>  3. Writing functional and technical specifications for customizations.<br>  4. Data mapping and interface requirements. |
| **PeopleSoft Enterprise HCM 8.8 Global HR and Recruiting Solutions Upgrade Optimization** Oil and Gas Industry | **Human Resources:** Cameron served as the Functional Lead on a HCM HR and Recruiting Solutions Upgrade Optimization effort for an Offshore Drilling company.<br><br>• The objective was to review PeopleSoft's 8.8 SP1 HR and Recruiting functionality and identify where new functionality would resolve current issues and customizations. Applications included Administer Workforce, Recruit Workforce, eRecruit, eRecruit Manager Desktop, and Resume Processing.<br>• Discussed the new HCM 8.8 SP1 functionality that would impact Recruit Workforce, current recruiting issues (to determine if HCM 8.8 SP1 might address the issues) and current HCM 8.0 functionality that could benefit Recruiting.<br>  1. Discussed the new HCM 8.8 SP1 functionality that would impact Human Resources, current Human Resource issues (to determine if HCM 8.8 SP1 might address the issues) and current HCM 8.0 functionality that could benefit Human Resources.<br>  2. Delivered and overview demonstration of PeopleSoft's 8.8 SP1 HR and Recruiting functionality. Provided answers to specific functionality questions.<br>  3. Provided functional expertise to client on how to best use the system to meet their business needs and evaluate gaps for modifications/customizations.<br>  4. Identified areas where functionality that is currently not being utilized can best be used moving forward. |
| **PeopleSoft Enterprise HCM 8.3 Recruiting Solutions Implementation** Financial Services Industry Fortune 500 | **Recruiting Solutions:** Cameron served as the Functional Lead on a HCM Recruiting Solutions implementation for a Fortune 500 Financial Services company.<br><br>  1. The objective was to replace the existing Recruiting system with PeopleSoft's Recruiting Solution. Applications included Recruit Workforce, eRecruit, eRecruit Manager Desktop, and Resume Processing.<br>  1. Delivered an overview and demonstration of Recruiting 8.3 functionality. Provided answers to specific functionality questions.<br>  2. Conducted requirements gathering sessions.<br>  3. Conducted Fit/Gap sessions and delivered a Fit Gap Analysis.<br>  4. Provided functional expertise to client on how to best use the system to meet their business needs and evaluate gaps for modifications/customizations.<br>  5. Provided alternative solutions to gaps and evaluated level of effort.<br>  6. Identified and documented "As-Is" and "To-Be" processes.<br>  7. Developed a global solution for Recruiting and limited HR transaction processing that follows industry standard.<br>  8. Recommended flexible and robust business transaction process to accommodate changing needs while remaining "vanilla" as possible.<br>  9. Assisted in standardizing recruitment to new hire "end-to-end" business process and supporting values (codes) to create frameworks that are usable across locations.<br>  10. Managed the customization design and build effort.<br>  11. Managed the Functional and UAT testing efforts. Coordinated the testing efforts |

and managed the client and consulting team through completion.

12. Provided post-production support.

**PeopleSoft Enterprise HCM 8.3 Global (French) HR, Recruiting Solutions, and Collaborative Applications Implementation**
Information Technology Industry
Fortune 500

**Human Resources, Recruiting Solutions, and Collaborative Applications:** Cameron served as the Functional Lead on a Global (French) HCM HR, Recruiting Solutions, and Collaborative Applications implementation for a Fortune 500 Information Technology company.

- The objective was to replace the existing Human Resources, Recruiting, and Self Service systems and establish one source for integrated global human resources information using a single database worldwide. Applications included Administer Workforce, Recruit Workforce, eRecruit, eRecruit Manager Desktop, eProfile, eProfile Manager Desktop, and ePay.

2. Delivered an overview and demonstration of Administer Workforce, Recruiting, and Self-Service 8.3 functionality.
3. Conducted requirements gathering sessions.
4. Conducted Fit/Gap sessions and delivered a Fit Gap Analysis.
5. Provided functional expertise to client on how to best use the system to meet their business needs and evaluate gaps for modifications/customizations.
6. Provided alternative resolutions to disposition items (gaps) and documented/presented proposals.
7. Identified and documented "As-Is" and "To-Be" processes.
8. Developed a global solution for HR, Recruiting, and Self Service transaction processing that follows industry standard.
9. Recommended flexible and robust business transaction process to accommodate changing needs while remaining "vanilla".
10. Assisted in standardizing recruitment to termination "end-to-end" business process and supporting values (codes) to create frameworks that are usable across countries.
11. Provided suggestions on new functionality in 8.3 that could streamline existing business processes.
12. Managed project team through the Construct Phase.
13. Managed the customization design and build effort.

**PeopleSoft Enterprise HCM 8.3 Recruiting Solutions Proof of Concept**
Public Sector

**Recruiting Solutions:** Cameron served as the Functional Lead on a PeopleSoft Recruiting Solutions Needs Assessment and Proof of Concept effort for a Fortune 500 company.

- The object was to determine that PeopleSoft's Recruiting Solution would meet the requirements and would be an acceptable solution to replace the existing Recruiting system. Applications included Recruit Workforce, eRecruit, and eRecruit Manager Desktop.

1. Delivered an overview and demonstration of the Recruiting 8.3 functionality. Provided answers to specific functionality questions from the audience.
2. Conducted requirements gathering sessions.
3. Delivered documents ranging from To-Be Process documentation, Conversion Approach, Workflow Approach, Gap Assessment for PeopleSoft's 8.8, Risk Watch List, Rollout Approach and Workplan.

**PeopleSoft Enterprise HCM 8.3 HR and Recruiting Solutions Upgrade**
Government Sector

**Human Resources and Recruiting Solutions Upgrade:** Cameron served as the Functional Lead on a PeopleSoft HR and Recruiting Solutions Upgrade for a University.

- The objective was to upgrade PeopleSoft's HCM 7.5 to PeopleSoft HCM 8.3 and to implement additional Recruiting Solutions functionality.
- Applications included Administer Workforce, Position Management, Recruit Workforce, eRecruit, eRecruit Manager Desktop, and Resume Processing.
- Delivered an overview and demonstration of HR and Recruiting 8.3 functionality.
- Conducted requirements gathering sessions for HR and Recruiting.
- Conducted Fit Gap sessions and delivered a Fit Gap Analysis for HR and Recruiting.

- Provided functional expertise to client on how to best use the system to meet their business needs and evaluate gaps for modifications/customizations.
- Provided alternative solutions to gaps and evaluated level of effort.

**PeopleSoft Enterprise HCM 8.3 Recruiting Solutions Proof of Concept**
Healthcare Industry

**Recruiting Solutions:** Cameron served as the Functional Lead for a Proof of Concept for PeopleSoft's Recruiting Solution.

- The object was to determine that PeopleSoft's Recruiting Solution would meet the requirements and would be a viable solution to replace the existing Recruiting system.
- Applications included Recruit Workforce, eRecruit, and eRecruit Manager Desktop.
- Conducted Fit Gap sessions and delivered a High Level Fit Gap Analysis for Recruit Workforce, eRecruit, and eRecruit Manager Desktop.
- Delivered the final presentation for the proposed business processes and provided a high-level workplan for implementation and resource requirements.

**PeopleSoft Enterprise HCM 8.4 Recruiting Solutions and Collaborative Applications Implementation**
Retail Industry
Fortune 500

**Recruiting Solutions and Collaborative Applications:** Cameron worked on the assessment and design phases of a strategic HCM Recruiting and Collaborative Application global implementation for a Fortune 500 Retail company.

- The objective was to replace the existing Recruiting and Self Service systems and establish one source for integrated global human resources information using a single database worldwide.
- Applications included Recruit Workforce, eRecruit, eRecruit Manager Desktop, eProfile, eProfile Manager Desktop, eCompensation, eCompensation Manager Desktop, eDevelopment, eDevelopment Manager Desktop, and ePay.
  1. Delivered an overview and demonstration of Self-Service 8.4 functionality. Provided answers to specific functionality questions from the audience.
  2. Conducted requirements gathering sessions.
  3. Conducted Fit/Gap sessions and delivered a Fit Gap Analysis.
  4. Provided functional expertise to client on how to best use the system to meet their business needs and evaluate gaps for modifications/customizations.
  5. Provided alternative solutions to gaps and evaluated level of effort.
  6. Identified and documented "As-Is" and "To-Be" processes.
  7. Developed a global solution for Self Service and HR transaction processing that follows industry standard.
  8. Recommended flexible and robust business transaction process to accommodate changing needs while remaining "vanilla".
  9. Assisted in standardizing recruitment to new hire "end-to-end" business process and supporting values (codes) to create frameworks that are usable across countries.
  10. Provided suggestions on new functionality in 8.4 that could streamline existing business processes.

**PeopleSoft Enterprise HCM 8.4 Global HR Implementation**
Retail Industry
Fortune 500

**Global Human Resources:** Cameron worked on the Fit/Gap phase for a strategic HCM Global HR implementation for a Fortune 500 Retail company.

- The objective was to establish one source for integrated global human resources information using a single database worldwide.
  1. Scoped client's business requirements.
  2. Conducted Fit/Gap analysis on the following products: Administer Workforce and Recruit Workforce.
  3. Provided functional expertise to client on how to best use the system to meet their business needs and evaluate gaps for modifications/customizations.
  4. Developed a global solution for HR transaction processing that follows industry standard.
  5. Recommended flexible and robust business transaction process to accommodate changing needs while remaining "vanilla".
  6. Assisted in standardizing new hire to termination "end-to-end" business process

and supporting values (codes) to create frameworks that are usable across countries.

7. Provided alternative resolutions to disposition items (gaps), documented/presented proposals, and evaluated level of effort.
8. Recommended alternatives to customizations to best meet the client's business processes requirements.
9. Prepared functional design documentation for proposed customizations and collaborated with Technical Developers to develop the customizations.

**PeopleSoft Enterprise HCM 8.1 Global HR Implementation**
Healthcare Industry
Fortune 500

**Global Human Resources:** Cameron led the User Acceptance Testing (UAT) effort for 8 countries moving to PeopleSoft HCM 8.1 at a Fortune 500 Healthcare company.

- Delivered an overall UAT strategy, testing standards and benchmarks for this effort.
- Developed and translated all the required documentation for UAT.
- Coordinated the UAT efforts within each site and managed the client and consulting team through completion.

**PeopleSoft Enterprise HCM 7.5 Global HR Implementation**
Healthcare Industry
Fortune 500

**Global Human Resources:** Cameron provided functional support through the assessment and design phases for a PeopleSoft HCM 7.5 implementation effort at a Fortune 500 Healthcare company.

- This effort consisted of merging the HR functions of two companies into one and producing a Fit/Gap analysis for PeopleSoft's ability to meet the requirements for all U.S. and U.K. employees.

1. Assisted in requirements gathering sessions and documented requirements.
2. Identified and documented 'As-Is' and 'To-Be' process flows.
3. Assisted in the Fit/Gap analysis for Administer Workforce and completed the Fit/Gap documentation.
4. Provided alternative solutions to gaps identified and evaluated level of effort.

**PeopleSoft Enterprise HCM 7.5 Global HR Implementation**
Information Technology Industry
Fortune 500

**Global Human Resources:** Cameron served as the Functional HR Implementation Lead for the PeopleSoft HCM 7.5 implementation at a Fortune 500 Information Technology company.

- He led, coordinated, and provided support during the design, implementation and support phases for the following Asia Pacific country implementations: People's Republic of China, Hong Kong, Taiwan, Japan, Singapore, Australia, New Zealand, and Fiji.

1. Maintained the project plans and managed the client/consulting team throughout implementation.
2. Managed the implementation and conversion efforts for the Pay Adjustment and Global Benefit modules throughout 50 countries.
3. Managed all country interface development.
4. Managed all efforts for a customization in Australia, New Zealand, and Fiji for Total Remuneration.
5. Assumed the responsibilities associated with the development, implementation, and testing of a position creation program.
6. Worked with both the functional and technical staff consultants to convert the data, determine the database structures and migration, and to ensure the functionality met the original defined scope.

**Pricewaterhouse Coopers**

- **Senior Consultant:** Worked for PwC as a Senior Consultant in the PeopleSoft practice. Lead several large engagements in implementing PeopleSoft's Human Resource products globally.

**Equifax**

- **Senior Consultant:** Cameron was a key player in Equifax's system implementation of GEAC SMARTStream, Human Resource and Payroll modules (formerly Dun &

| Financial Industry | Bradstreet Software). Specialized in the Human Resource module and Human Resource process improvements. |
| --- | --- |
| **TRW Systems**<br>Integration Group | • **Consultant:** Worked for TRW on a government contract with the Centers for Disease Control and Prevention managing software development and support to the agency's Internet information resources. |

## Skills Summary

**PeopleSoft Enterprise Human Capital Management Applications**

- Human Resources
- Administer Workforce
- Recruit Workforce
- Base Benefits
- Training Administration
- Manage Competencies
- Setup Manager

- eProfile
- eProfile Manager Desktop
- eRecruit
- eRecruit Manager Desktop
- Resume Processing
- eDevelopment
- eDevelopment Manager Desktop
- eCompensation
- eCompensation Manager Desktop

*Hardware & Operating Systems*

- Windows NT
- Windows 2000

**Programming Languages**

- PeopleCode
- UNIX
- HTML

**Engagement Experience**

- Applications Development
- Project Management
- Strategy/Planning
- Compass Methodology
- Fit/Gap Analysis
- Testing

- Business & Technical Process Reengineering
- Data Conversion
- Conversion
- Configuration

## Other Accomplishments

**Education**

- Bachelors of Science, Business Administration, Embry Riddle University

**Training**

- PeopleSoft Enterprise PeopleTools (I & II)
- PeopleSoft Enterprise Recruiting Solutions (eRecruit-eRecruit Manager, Resume Processing)
- PeopleSoft Enterprise HCM
- PMI Certification in progress

**Certifications & Associations**

- Human Capital Management, PeopleSoft Enterprise

**Presentations & Publications**

- Global HCM Presentation, PeopleSoft Enterprise Connect Conference, 2003
- Fit/Gap Analysis Presentation, Midwest Region Conference, 2001

**Recognition & Awards**

- PeopleSoft Outstanding Contributor Award, 2003

# Cameron Calapas

4423 North Columbus Drive ♦ Clear Creek, MN 327891
807.598.5731 ♦ ccalapas@aol.com

## SUMMARY

- Dedicated Project Manager responsible for planning, designing, implementing, enhancing, and supporting enterprise Human Resource, Benefits, Recruiting, and Payroll solutions for some of the world's largest companies
- Extensive experience identifying ways to optimize use of human capital management applications to reduce financial risk and improve operating efficiencies across multiple offices globally
- Seasoned manager overseeing national and global teams as large as 30 consultants
- Trusted team member and leader singled out by peers and by management as top performer and HCM subject area expert
- Track record of delivering on-time and on-budget project work for several multimillion-dollar Human Resources projects

## EXPERIENCE

**ORACLE|PEOPLESOFT INC.**, SENIOR PRINCIPAL CONSULTANT, Atlanta, GA, 2002–Present
- Managed 13 separate engagements implementing end-to-end HR solutions across payroll, benefits, recruiting, training and development for some of the world's largest companies
    - Served as project lead implementing more than $40MM in HR software tools ultimately accessed by thousands of end-users worldwide
- Selected as prestigious product lead out of hundreds of HR consultants for both Recruiting Solutions and Set-up Manager
    - Serve as liaison between development team and entire worldwide HR consultancy determining best practices
    - Conduct monthly conference call with all HR consultants worldwide, serving as subject matter expert for both products
- Advising Verizon Wireless executive team including HR director and EVPs daily on program management for recruiting implementation
- Built $25MM Recruiting Solutions system for IBM
    - Managed a team of 30 consultants creating system for 100 recruiters nationwide generating more than 1MM hits and processing 100,000 resumes monthly
- Led on-site French implementation of Lexmark full-service global HR solution for benefits, training, recruiting, payroll and compensation team
    - Completed highly complex bilingual project both on-time and under budget
    - New product ultimately eliminated multiple, duplicative systems across several countries
- Developed integrated global human resources tool utilizing a single worldwide database for a Fortune 500 retail company with offices in throughout the world
- Key member of business development team, working on 10–20 new business engagements annually
- Chosen as one out of 250 consultants for Outstanding Contributor Award in 2003
- Selected to present on Global HCM solutions at PeopleSoft Enterprise Connect Conference

**PricewaterhouseCoopers,** Senior Consultant, Atlanta, GA, 1998–2002
- Led eight large engagements implementing PeopleSoft's Human Resources products globally for companies including Office Depot, Compaq, and GlaxoSmithKline
- Spearheaded Asia/Pacific efforts introducing HR solutions for Compaq in eight separate countries
- Introduced PeopleSoft single platform following Glaxo Welcome and SmithKline Beecham merger impacting several hundred users globally
- Team member on US and UK 10-month installation of HR product representing Office Depot's first-ever global HR harmonization
- Oversaw system and user acceptance testing for major Baxter global implementation spanning 10 different countries
- Led all internal college recruiting efforts for the state of Georgia

**Equifax Inc.,** Senior Business Systems Analyst, Atlanta, GA, 1997–1998
- Key player in implementation of GEAC SMARTStream Human Resource and Payroll modules to company with 14,000 employees
- Selected to work with entire executive team, educating them on new HR program

**TRW,** Consultant—Systems Integration Group, Atlanta, GA, 1993–1997
- Managed software development on a government contract for the Center of Disease Control and Prevention

# EDUCATION

**Embry-Riddle University**–Daytona, FL, 1992
- Bachelor of Science in Business Administration

# Stuck in a Rut

Olivia is a very interesting person, but she let a little too much of her eclectic personality show on her resume. She was a qualified candidate, but her resume wasn't getting any hits.

Fortunately, we were able to help her out of the rut.

First, you will notice the resume is three pages long. That is a no-no. We never go more than two pages (unless we are writing an academic resume or CV). Perhaps more troubling is that it is incredibly disjointed. She starts with a section called "Engagement History." What does that mean? Was she recounting her past marriage proposals?

Now, in fairness to Olivia, some of the terminology and jargon that she used would be familiar to someone working in her field. Here is a key point for you to heed: Even though a recruiting director may work for a particular company, that does not mean he or she has a strong grip on the hard skills of the company's jobs.

It is important for you to strip out some of the overly technical jargon since the first person looking at your resume is likely to be an HR professional and not a "line" person. Recruiting directors may work at a bank one day and at an engineering firm for their next job. They become familiar with the terms and expressions of the business, but they would not know nearly as much as a loan officer or a mechanical engineer would about his or her specific job.

You will notice we cleaned up Olivia's resume, and we also did a few nontraditional things as well. Olivia wanted to work in planning, which is a field that embraces eclectic backgrounds. For that reason, we included things like the fact that she is a chef, she enjoys belly dancing, and she worked in London. Normally, those items would be removed.

Olivia O' Brien
8835 North Ontario Street, Chicago, IL 60604. 312-729-7211. oliviaobrien@earthlink.net

| Engagement History | |
|---|---|

2001–Present

## Plan B Inc.
Account planning for small advertising agency

- Wrote creative briefs based on information from client, competitors and category research, to give direction to creative concepts for new business pitches

- Wrote marketing plans, including brand personality, image & positioning, as well as tactical concepts for direct and promotional campaigns.

- Presented marketing strategy in new business pitches to tie in strategic, creative, and media plans

- Brand positioning strategy for a Mutual Fund client's internal, direct marketing campaign to increase Financial Advisor's awareness of and enthusiasm toward top performing products in order to improve sales

## Draft Worldwide
Field research for R. J. Reynolds, Kelloggs and new business pitches

- Ethnographic research on dietary regimes and regimens to gain strategic insights into target consumer, resulting in a successful bid to win a substantial new client.

- In-depth one-on-one concept testing interviews in bars to gain insight on current and potential branding, promotions and event campaigns

- On-camera interviews of children and adults on camera to test attitude towards mascot at specific events and venues to gauge potential success of promotional and direct marketing concepts

## Accenture
Competitive research and analysis

- Analyzed how major competitors position themselves through marketing messages to identify core business strengths/weaknesses. Industries include financial services, telecom, travel/transportation, human resources, pharmaceutical, automotive and consumer packaged goods

- Recommended specific marketing tactics to differentiate Accenture's message which will defend Accenture's core business strengths and proactively build a sustainable market position through increased sales

**LLW Group**
Research analysis

- Observed and analyzed qualitative research to gain insight on consumer behavior and attitudes towards IT service providers

**Consumer Connections, Inc.**
Research analysis

- Observed and analyzed qualitative research for Sassy Toys to gain insight on consumer reactions towards new toy and packaging concepts

- Observed and analyzed qualitative research for Illinois Bureau of Tourism to determine future design and brand strategy for website

**Strategex**
Qualitative research and project management

- In-depth one-on-one interviews on business-to-business topics including brand awareness, competitive marketplace, and new product development

- Qualified and recruited respondents for participation in qualitative research

**Employment History**

2000
marchFIRST

*Strategic Branding Consultant*

Strategic planning and research for branding group of internet consulting company, for healthcare, high-tech, travel, business-to-business financial services, consumer packaged goods, retail, and manufacturing clients

- Corporate brand strategy for Cybrant, a business-to-business technology company

- Competitive SWOT analysis for clients including 3Com, Allstate, OAG, John Nuveen Co., and Unilever

- In-depth one-on-one interviews and client reports for Ralin Medical to gain insight on brand, website usability and relevance of product to target market

*1999–2000*

*The Geneva Companies, Chicago, IL*

*Marketing Assistant*

Research and account management for the mergers & acquisitions group of an investment banking company

Va Pensiero, Evanston, IL
1998–1999
**Cook/Pastry Chef**

University of Minnesota, Minneapolis, MN
1996-1998

*Teaching Assistant*

Gorman & Company
1994–1996

**Executive Assistant**

Standards Institute, London, England
1994

**Public Relations Coordinator**

Quaker Oats Company, Northbrook, IL
1993
**Gatorade Sales and Marketing Assistant**

**Education**

M.A. in English literature, University of Minnesota, 1998
B.A. in English literature, University of Wisconsin—Madison, 1993

# Olivia O'Brien

8835 North Ontario Street ♦ Chicago, IL 60604
312.729.7211 ♦ oliviaobrien@earthlink.net

## EXPERIENCE

**STRATEGIC PLANNER,** AMBROSI, Chicago, IL, April 2004–Present
*Sears, Home Depot, Best Buy, Sunbeam, Ulta Cosmetics, Mervyn's, The Great Indoors*

- Managed several benchmark and quantitative research studies, wrote more than 10 creative briefs, and oversaw numerous online surveys for some of the country's largest brands
- Led project overhauling and rebranding all marketing efforts for Wahl Clippers
  - Conducted company' first-ever customer segmentation study, fundamentally redefining target market
  - Wrote creative briefs tailored to new target, inspiring entirely new advertising efforts
  - Significantly increased unaided brand awareness more than 25%
- Redefined customer segments for Great Indoors into unique lifestyle groups
  - Increased both store traffic and overall sales
  - Segmentation resulted in development of proprietary new Great Indoors private label packaging rolled out to all stores nationwide
- Agency expert on consumer trend forecasting, having published white paper, "Coolest Dad Ever" presented at annual Retail Marketing Institute conference
- Managed agency planning efforts on seven winning new business/existing client pitches, including Fannie May Candy, FAO Schwarz, and Mervyn's

**PRESIDENT,** JEN○B RESEARCH AND PLANNING, Chicago, IL, January 2001–April 2004
*Draft Worldwide, Accenture, Plan B Inc., LLW Group*

- Conducted dozens of quantitative and qualitative research studies and marketing/strategy development projects for brands including Kellogg's, R.J. Reynolds, and the Illinois Bureau of Tourism
- Performed extensive in-market research for highly successful Camel flavored cigarette launch, gauging consumer reaction to product concept, and potential marketing programs
- Led ethnographic research project for new business pitch, documenting all life activity surrounding food, used for successful Milk Board pitch for Draft
- Managed off-site, on-camera mascot study, tracking perceptions of Tony the Tiger among more than 100 consumers
  - Video presented to client at meeting to promote new promotional marketing campaign
- Developed comprehensive competitive business analysis, tracking marketing efforts, sales techniques, and overall strategy for five major technology companies including Microsoft, Oracle, and IBM
  - Personally interviewed 12 business decision makers over the course of four months who selected products and services other than Accenture
  - Recommended fundamental changes to marketing programs to help address consumer needs

**STRATEGIC BRANDING CONSULTANT,** MARCHFIRST, Chicago, IL, 2000
*Unilever, 3Com, Allstate, OAG, John Nuveen*

- Developed corporate brand strategy platform for Cybrant, including creation of "complexity made simple" tagline

- Managed several "brand blueprint" projects for some of companies largest clients comprising upfront consumer and secondary research, SWOT analyses, and concept development
- Spearheaded project to redesign and relaunch John Nuveen Co. website
- Conducted comprehensive website usability study on Ralin Medical insuring content delivered to consumers via both design and function

**MARKETING ASSISTANT,** THE GENEVA COMPANIES, Chicago, IL, 1999–2000
- Performed research and account management for investment banking company

**PASTRY CHEF/COOK,** VA PENSIERO, Evanston, IL, 1998–1999

**TEACHING ASSISTANT,** ENGLISH LITERATURE, University of Minnesota, 1996–1998

**EXECUTIVE ASSISTANT,** GORMAN & COMPANY, Chicago, IL, 1994–1996

**PUBLIC RELATIONS COORDINATOR,** STANDARDS INSTITUTE, London, England, 1994

**GATORADE SALES/MARKETING ASSISTANT,** QUAKER OATS, Northbrook, IL, 1993

## EDUCATION

**UNIVERSITY OF MINNESOTA**–Minneapolis 1998
- M.A. English Literature

**UNIVERSITY OF WISCONSIN**–Madison 1993
- B.A. English Literature

## ACTIVITIES/INTERESTS

- Chicago Canine Rescue Volunteer, 2004–Present
- Belly dancer, avid reader, accomplished cook, pop culture consumer, cultural trend forecasting guru, and obsessed with human/computer interaction

# Stuck in a Rut

Nathan was a very qualified, senior candidate who had some wonderful experience. He just needed a way to make it easily digestible and quantifiable. That is where JobBound helped.

As you already know, we dislike summary statements that list self-ascribed attributes. That's what Nathan had, and we changed it. Notice how much better the *after* version looks.

Then we needed to ensure his vast accomplishments were recorded accurately and were easy to understand in a quick scan. One of the techniques we use with senior candidates is to ask, "What did you do, and what happened?"

Look at a few entries to see how this works. Here is a great example:

- Increased sales among teens more than 10%—reversing negative sales in past seven of eight years—by orchestrating company's first-ever, teen-targeted, back-to-school promotion
- Reached teens via Internet, radio, sweepstakes, TV, and teen musical festival sponsorships
- Efforts have continued at double digit growth rates

We listed the bullet point with his accomplishments, but then included a few "sub-bullets" to help bring more texture and description to the point. Just by reading this one entry, you learn so much about what Nathan has done.

Now look at his entire *after* resume, and tell me you aren't impressed with him!

# Nathan P. Efferson

8733 North Napelton, Newberry, TX. 77833   (281) 551-0097   email: efferson@aol.com

**Highly accomplished executive with significant experience in all facets of marketing and advertising arenas.** Proven record of success in conceptualizing, brand development and orchestrating internal and external advertising agencies to support top producing, highly profitable sales organizations. Demonstrated ability to lead and develop large advertising departments to maximize advertising efficiencies that have generated significant revenue and profit improvements. Core competencies include:

- Strategic Market Planning
- Sponsorships
- Loyalty Marketing
- Interactive Marketing
- Agency Management & Selection
- Database Management
- Print Buying and Negotiations
- Media Buying and Negotiations
- Broadcast Production
- Research & Development
- Direct Mail Campaigns
- Event Planning / Coordination

| 3/2004–08/2005 | Value City Dept. Stores | Columbus, Ohio |
|---|---|---|

**Sr. Vice President of Marketing**

Responsible for directing and implementing the advertising and marketing strategies, for Value City Department Stores. This includes developing and executing brand development, broadcast production, radio, tv, agency management, weekly pre-print, newspaper, direct mail, interactive marketing, Value City credit card, loyalty marketing, creating internal and external communication strategies, budgeting and forecasting results. Annual budget approximately $68 million.

Value City is an off price department store chain with 114 stores throughout the Midwest and northeast states. Owned and operated by Retail Ventures Inc. Value City has annual sales of $1.4 billion dollars. Retail Ventures also owns and operates DSW Shoe Warehouse and Filene's Basement Dept. Stores.

**Accomplishments:**
Implemented circular version strategy to maximize market demographics. This strategy allowed us to target underperforming markets with special marketing promotion offers. Revised preprint strategy in select markets to focus distribution within a 10 mile radius of stores. Increased stores performance on average 1.5%–6.9%.

Implemented new marketing strategy for back to school that increased sales over 10% by scheduling electronic advertising to launch at peak selling opportunities and broadening our target to include teens and young adults via internet, radio, sweepstakes giveaways, & teen music festival sponsorships.

Revised fall electronic target from 18–49 to 25–54 to attract more of Value City's core shopper. This change also resulted in 3 million in annual savings.

Developed Loyalty Marketing Program called V Rewards. Designed to create loyalty and increase frequency with existing customer base, and to provide platform to drive new customer trial.

Developed in-house photo studio that provided internal process improvements including an increased flexibility in printing schedule resulting in company savings of $1 million dollars annually.

| 1/2001–3/2004 | Eckerd Drugs Inc. | Clearwater, Florida |
|---|---|---|

**Vice President of Marketing & Advertising**

Responsible for managing the advertising and marketing programs utilizing a team of 54 professionals. Eckerd Drugs Inc. was a 2700 store pharmacy chain with sales of $14 billion dollars annually, located throughout the Northeast and South.  Annual Advertising Budget was approximately $275 million dollars.

**Accomplishments:**
Developed and implemented many new and successful key business strategies, including… "Get More at Eckerd" positioning strategy; Beauty positioning strategy "Feeling Beautiful Starts at Eckerd"; Photo positioning strategy "Photo Quality Assurance Guarantee" ; Private Label "Tested, Retested Guaranteed" program; New "Pharmacy First" positioning campaign; Developed several targeted loyalty programs including, "Senior Rewards"; "The Eckerd Baby Care Club"; Other accomplishments include developing a "Competitive Action" program; and "A New Market Entry" strategy for Arizona and Colorado markets.

**11/1994–9/2000**                    **Randalls Food Markets Inc.**           **Houston, Texas**
**Director of Advertising**

Responsible for managing and directing a marketing and advertising team in the design, development and implementation of all marketing and new business development activities for this $2.7 billion supermarket chain with 115 locations. Full responsibility for a $49 million budget that includes print, direct mail, radio, TV and billboard advertising, and database and consumer research.

**Accomplishments:**
Developed and launched several highly successful campaigns, including the Frequent Shopper Loyalty Card Program (the Remarkable card), Home Meal Replacement (Busy Chef), Continental and American Air miles Loyalty Program. Drove EBITA to over 68%, private label business from 12% to 16.34%, and increased store sales by 6.9% (industry average 3.3%).

Cultivated and built strategic business alliances within the vendor market, and launched several vendor-sponsored marketing programs, including The Million Dollar Millennium Sweepstakes, Haul Away the Savings, Randall's Senior Expo and Stork Club.

Appointed to the Board of Directors of the Advertising Food Marketing Institute and served as a featured speaker at their 1999 conference.

**1/1978–11/1994**                    **Kroger Co.**                    **Columbus , Ohio**
**Assistant Advertising Manager**

Assistant Advertising Manager
Began career working part-time while attending college. Rotated through a series of increasingly responsible administrative and marketing assignments to Assistant Advertising Manager, co-directing all advertising and marketing initiatives for this $1.6 billion, 94-store supermarket chain.

**Accomplishments:**
Developed and launched over 200 marketing and community promotions. Managed a $25 million operating budget.

Secured $12 million in co-op vendor funds developed and rolled out sales campaigns with local celebrities such as Jack Hanna, Archie Griffin, and Bobby Rahal.

Received National Award from the National Frozen Food Association for best sales campaign and results.

**Education**
Ohio University
Columbus, Ohio
BBA, Management/ Minor Psychology

# Nathan Efferson

8733 North Napelton ♦ Newberry, TX 77833
281.551.0097 ♦ efferson@aol.com

## SUMMARY OF QUALIFICATIONS

- Seasoned marketing, advertising, and sales professional with more than 25 years experience leading some of the nation's largest retailers including Eckerd, Kroger, and Value City
- Results-driven marketing leader with a track record of increased sales, profit, and fiscal responsibility managing budgets in excess of $250MM for billion-dollar-plus brands
- Innovative agent-of-change having launched dozens of business building initiatives spanning new targets, engaging promotions, and customer retention programs
- Dedicated manager, mentor, and instructor having led teams of more than 50 professionals
- Experienced leader with a diverse background spanning all aspects of marketing from consumer to trade, from traditional to interactive, and from mass to individual

## EXPERIENCE

**SENIOR VICE-PRESIDENT OF MARKETING,** VALUE CITY DEPT. STORES, Columbus, OH, 3/04–8/05
- Managed all aspects of $68MM marketing budget developing and executing brand development, traditional media, agency management, interactive, credit card, loyalty program, and more
- Responsible for a staff of 25 marketing professionals representing 114 stores generating $1.4 billion in annual sales
- Increased sales among teens more than 10%—reversing negative sales in past seven of eight years—by orchestrating company's first-ever teen-targeted back-to-school promotion
    - Reached teens via Internet, radio, sweepstakes, TV, and teen musical festival sponsorships
    - Efforts have continued at double digit growth rates
- Raised same-store performance 1.5%–6.9% by instituting a new targeted circular distribution strategy
    - Introduced special marketing promotions in underperforming markets
    - Overhauled circular distribution to align geography with local demographics
- Successfully spent to $68MM annual budget despite additional $12MM in mandatory budget additions
    - Realized millions in efficiencies by altering electronic target to better reflect key audiences
    - Brought ad agency in-house saving more than $3MM annually
    - Created in-house photo studio increasing print efficiency for more than 50 shoots weekly, and generating $1MM in annual savings
- Launched Value City's "Makeover" marketing concept, communicating "Great look at a great price" message, researching at 97% brand recall
- Developed V Rewards loyalty marketing program that ultimately secured 350,000 initial new members
    - Unique, targeted program rewards top customers and increased store visits
    - Program included quarterly mailings, monthly emails, substantial sweepstakes, personal "thank yous" and recognition to top 100 customers nationwide
    - V Rewards slated to hit 1,000,000 members by end of 2005

**VICE-PRESIDENT OF MARKETING/ADVERTISING,** ECKERD DRUGS, INC., Clearwater, FL, 1/01–3/04
- Oversaw a team of 54 professionals managing an advertising budget of $275MM for 2700 stores representing $14 billion in annual sales
- One of three individuals brought in specifically to revamp all operations to reverse annual net sales deficit
    - Dramatically increased store sales to $340MM profit from $100MM deficit in three years

- Planned, launched, and executed fundamental rebranding effort comprising all internal and external marketing programs
  - Introduced "Get More" campaign, redesigned logo, and substantially improved in-store experience
  - Developed and ran fully integrated marketing communications plan comprising television, print, POS, direct marketing, outdoor, and loyalty programs
- Increased beauty sales 8% on an ongoing basis by overhauling all aspects of beauty segment
  - Launched "store within a store" at 2700 locations, and created "Feeling Beautiful at Eckerd" campaign spanning print, broadcast, and radio
- Dramatically improved photo sales by introducing attention-grabbing offer to correct photo processing mistakes made by competitors including Walgreen's, Target, and Wal-Mart
- Raised Eckerd's Baby Club membership from 35,000 to more than 1,000,000 by creating unique hospital alliance reaching moms at the earliest possible stages of pharmacy decision making
- Introduced company's first-ever Senior Rewards Program increasing sales among store's largest demographic group
  - Launched a series of 3 "senior expos" attended by 20,000 customers each
- Developed a "competitive action" program established nationwide to disrupt grand openings of major competitors
- Created a new market entry strategy for developing Arizona and Colorado areas, quickly establishing initial sales and awareness

**DIRECTOR OF ADVERTISING,** RANDALL'S FOOD MARKETS INC., Houston, TX, 11/94–9/00
- Led marketing and new business development for $2.7 billion supermarket chain with 115 locations
- Successfully managed a $49MM marketing budget spanning television, print, out-of-home, direct mail, radio, and database/consumer research
- Increased same store sales 6.9%, more than doubling industry average of 3.3%, by launching a series of innovative, targeted marketing programs
- Developed and launched highly successful frequent shopper loyalty card program–The Remarkable Card–resulting in 80% of store sales emanating from the card
  - Invested more than $8MM in marketing Remarkable Card without shrinking ad budget, by managing marketing efficiencies
- Drove private label business from 12% to more than 16% invigorating new store brand
- Introduced a series of highly successful, innovative programs all helping EBITA to peak at 68%
  - Continental/American Air Miles Loyalty Program, Home Meal Replacement (Busy Chef), The Million Dollar Millennium Sweepstakes, Haul Away the Savings, The Randall's Stork Club
- Appointed to the Board of Directors of the Advertising Food Marketing Institute, and selected as featured speaker at 1999 conference

**ASSISTANT ADVERTISING MANAGER,** KROGER CO., Columbus, OH, 1/78–11/94
- Co-directed all advertising and marketing initiatives for this $1.6 billion, 94-store chain supermarket
- Created and executed over 200 marketing and community promotions and managed a budget of $25MM
- Won a national award from the National Frozen Food Association for bringing the giant pandas from China to the United States
- Secured $12MM in co-op vendor funds and developed engaging, business-building promotions with local celebrities including Jack Hanna, Archie Griffin, and Bobby Rahal

# EDUCATION

**OHIO UNIVERSITY—ATHENS, OH, 1981**
- BBA in Management, Psychology Minor

# Stuck in a Rut

Have you heard of the phrase "too much information"? It typically has a different meaning. In the case of Chris's resume, it means he overloaded his resume with a lot of irrelevant things. Chris was not receiving any requests for job interviews.

First of all, the resume is three pages. It simply won't get read. He actually devoted an entire page to a job he held in the eighties and early nineties. That is a problem.

Now, he happened to work for a cool company on some great accounts, but at this point in his career, he needs to limit that information to a few bullet points.

Secondly, he has a summary of qualifications that is too long and too bland. Without substantiation, his statements mean nothing to a recruiting director. Instead we wrote summary points like this:

- Dedicated new business professional having pitched and won several new accounts representing more than 25% of agency billings

There is substance around the statement, represented by numbers and facts.

We continued this thread through Chris's entire resume. In his *before* version, Chris had about five numbers listed to frame his accomplishments. In the *after* version, we have about twenty, even though the resume is a page shorter!

Chris's *after* resume secured him a great new job almost instantaneously.

# Chris Wayne
57 Corvette Drive, Craigster, CA 71121
(884) 999-9298 chriswayne@yahoo.com

## Summary of Qualifications
- Skilled marketing professional with proven success in building businesses and growing client relationships across a range of disciplines: packaged goods, retail, toys and online
- Extensive experience in strategic analysis and segmentation, brand positioning and identity development, account planning, product/market/media research and performance measurement
- Expertise in all advertising media, integrated marketing, direct-to-consumer and experiential programs
- Accustomed to making proposals and negotiating at all levels of agency and client structure
- Record of success in building and managing results-oriented internal teams and delivering beyond client expectations
- Proven effective and frequently involved in new business strategy and pitches
- Excellent written, verbal and quantitative skills

## Work Experience

**Marsha Lane, Inc.**
1994 to Present
*Account Supervisor–V.P., Group Account Director*
Fisher-Price/Mattel, Vivendi Universal, The Learning Company, Ehealthinsurance.com, Lyons Restaurants, California Café, Blistex, State Compensation Insurance Fund, Delta Dental
*Fisher-Price*:
- Strategic team leader for 12 years. Managed brand and product communication, launched new products, implemented experiential programs, negotiated the current incentive-based compensation agreement
- Grew business and revenue through acquisition of new categories beyond initial agency assignment
- Continue to maintain strong client relations through several changes in management and client contact
*Vivendi Universal*:
- Supervised the Knowledge Adventure Kids Software business that included Jumpstart, Barbie, and other licensed titles. Assignments included consumer and trade advertising and package design
- Actively involved in the brand and product repositioning of Jumpstart to address sales and retail challenges
- Organized and participated in the development of a new vision and strategic platform for the Learn and Play divisions in the Kids Business Unit
*The Learning Company*:
- Lead member of pitch team that won account for the agency
- Formulated and executed brand and advertising strategy for Reader Rabbit Learning Software that elevated and repositioned the brand
*eHealthInsurance.com*:
- Led pitch and won account for the agency

- Successfully introduced eHealthInsurance.com as the premier provider of online health insurance
- Managed launch and on-going campaign that included TV, print and direct-to-consumer

*Lyon's Restaurants*:
- Led pitch and won account for the agency
- Repositioned a mature brand and increased same store sales via an aggressive campaign that included TV, print, in-store and community programs

*California Café*:
- Won business based on strong relationship and outstanding performance on the Lyon's account
- Proposed and implemented a strategic program that included an internal company audit, as well as competitive evaluation and consumer research that led to the development of a new brand identity platform
- Reintroduced concept to consumer with measurable success via a thought-provoking and acclaimed print campaign

*Blistex*:
- Managed Stridex, a leading teen acne treatment brand that includes pads, face washes, spot treatments and gels
- Involved in extensive exploration of the teen demographic and in on-going new product experimentation against this target. Integrated program included TV, print and online

*Other*:
- Member of senior management team. Involved in company positioning and strategy

**Channel Company, Chicago, IL**
**1987 to 1993**
Client Service Trainee—Account Executive
McDonalds Corporation, Procter & Gamble, Kraft General Foods

*McDonalds*:
*Nutrition and New Products Marketing:*
- Responsible for the development and recommendation of marketing objectives and strategies, positioning, pricing, packaging and tactics for key new product initiatives and programs
- Assisted McDonald's Marketing in gaining local market participation to test new products/programs; communicated directly with local Ad Managers/Agencies to coordinate advertising efforts; prepared marketing/media presentations for local Co-ops

*McDonalds—(Cont)*:
- Key initiatives included:
  - Introduction and national launch of McLean Deluxe, a low-fat burger
  - Strategic implementation of the "Dinner" strategy
  - Introduction of "Breakfast Buffets" in test market

*Procter & Gamble*:
*CheerFree Laundry Detergent*
- Introduced CheerFree with nation-wide direct marketing program
  - Pioneer program in packaged good industry
  - Consumer response (11.6%) highest ever in P&G history
  - Generated immense database of self-selected skin-sensitive target consumers

- Developed/managed on-going consumer loyalty building program for test market
- Broad-based marketing program for national introduction included general TV, Direct TV and print -$20MM

*Pepto-Bismol Stomach Remedy*
- Managed introduction of Maximum Strength Pepto-Bismol. National marketing program included TV, print, radio and outdoor—$22MM with $10MM allocated to the Maximum Strength line extension
- Doubled annual share objective in less than six months with minimum cannibalization of parent Pepto brand
- Explored/tested various flavor flankers to original Pepto-Bismol
- Analyzed the stomach remedy category and consumer to identify segment/target growth opportunities and positioning of the Pepto brand franchise

*Kraft General Foods*:
*100% Natural Cheese, Kraft Light Naturals, String Cheese:*
- Responsible for national TV campaign for 100% Natural cheese
- Started highly successful advertised introduction of Kraft Light Naturals in major lead markets
- Re-introduced String Cheese as fun food targeted to kids

**Jessica Grey, Inc.**
**1984 to 1986**
- Helped start small women's garment manufacturing firm
  - Responsible for financial planning, business and marketing plans, pricing/loan generation
  - Helped penetrate larger scale stores, i.e., Talbots, Nordstrom, etc.
  - Strong client and supplier contact

## EDUCATION
Master of Science in Advertising and Marketing, Northwestern University, Chicago
MBA, Keller Graduate School of Management
Master of Arts in English Literature, Panjab University, India

# Chris Wayne

57 Corvette Drive ♦ Craigster, CA 71121
884.999.9498 ♦ chriswayne@yahoo.com

## SUMMARY OF QUALIFICATIONS

- Seasoned executive with a proven track record of success working on some of the world's premier brands including McDonald's, Fisher-Price, Procter & Gamble, and Kraft
- Dedicated new business professional having pitched and won several new accounts representing more than 25% of agency billings
- Strong background in new product introductions having launched more than 15 highly successful new products and brand extensions for Kraft, Stridex, Mattel, and McDonald's
- Expert marketer with experience working across all new and traditional media in categories including consumer package goods, quick service restaurants, retail, and online

## EXPERIENCE

**VP/GROUP ACCOUNT DIRECTOR,** MARSHA LANE, San Francisco, CA, 1994–2006
*Fisher-Price/Mattel, Vivendi Universal, Blistex, eHealthInsurance.com, Agency New Business*
- Key member of executive team helping grow agency billings 70% and tripling head count in 12 years
- Strategic lead for four winning new business pitches representing 12% of agency's total revenue
- Responsible for managing agency's largest and most profitable businesses
- Established or overhauled most key account management and agency operations including agency/client procedures, systematic store checks, and account management protocol
- Promoted from Account Supervisor in less than three years

*Fisher-Price/Mattel*
- Helped grow "Power Wheels" battery operated ride-in car total sales tenfold to more than $250MM annually over the course of ten years
  - Partnered extremely closely with senior clients to develop overall business and marketing strategy
  - Overhauled target based on extensive strategic exploration expanding reach to parents, grandparents, and Hispanics
  - Launched a series of cutting-edge, traveling, experiential marketing programs for children at several major events nationwide dramatically increasing awareness and sales
- Won prestigious "Worldwide Excellence in Advertising" award from Mattel for first-ever adult targeted Power Wheels ads
  - Awarded to one creative effort among 175 brands in 45 countries
- Agency secured additional $6MM in incremental Fisher-Price brand ad spending annually based on Power Wheels successes
- Negotiated agency's first-ever incentive-based compensation agreement insuring profitable transition from commission-based plan

*Vivendi Universal*
- Managed the Knowledge Adventure Kids Software business spanning all communication from consumer, to trade, to packaging, and to in-store for *Jumpstart*, *Barbie*, and other licensed titles
- Restructured brand's entire kid's learning division changing product offerings, sales strategy, marketing support, and messaging insuring brand momentum in a severely declining category
- Helped brand dramatically exceed all sales, share, and revenue objectives by more than 35% across a three-year period

*eHealthInsurance.com*
- Successfully introduced brand as the nation's premier provider of online health insurance during the "dotcom" explosion
    - Brand still ranks as 4th largest online today
    - Helped brand go from 0 in sales to over $250MM

*California Café*
- Developed and rolled out an entirely new brand identity platform extending across every internal and consumer touch point from advertising to point-of-sale, to internal company collateral
    - Proposed, sold, and executed a communication overhaul including an internal company audit, a comprehensive competitive evaluation, and in-depth consumer research to determine messaging
    - Interviewed 10 key decision makers including company CEO helping understand brand essence and all internal operations

*Blistex*
- Convinced conservative client to launch a "teen savvy" integrated marketing campaign helping stem share decline in intensely competitive category
- Launched 10 new products in less than 5 years guiding all elements of new product life cycle including product brainstorming, naming, concept testing, strategy development, and consumer introduction

**ACCOUNT EXECUTIVE,** CHANNEL COMPANY, Chicago, IL, 1987–1993
*McDonald's, Procter & Gamble, Kraft*
- Helped introduce and launch McDonald's McLean Deluxe burger–largest "health-focused" effort in brand's history
- Introduced CheerFree nationally via direct marketing resulting in the highest ever consumer response rate in P&G history
- Extended Pepto-Bismol brand with fully integrated launch of Maximum Strength line extension doubling annual share objective in less than six months
- Managed creative development and execution for national TV campaign for Kraft 100% Natural cheese
- Promoted from Client Service Trainee and Assistant Account Executive

**MARKETING DIRECTOR,** JESSICA GRAY, INC., Chicago, IL, 1984–1986
- Helped start small women's garment manufacturing firm ultimately selling into more than 400 stores nationwide including Talbots, Nordstrom, and Neiman Marcus

## *EDUCATION*

**NORTHWESTERN UNIVERSITY**—Evanston, IL, 1987
- Master of Science in Advertising and Marketing

**KELLER GRADUATE SCHOOL OF MANAGEMENT**—Chicago, IL, 1984
- Master of Business Administration

**PANJAB UNIVERSITY**—Panjab, India, 1981
- Master of Arts in English Literature

# Stuck in a Rut

Michael was having a tough time securing an interview. Michael is another guy who is fond of the third person. Eleven consecutive bullet points begin with his name. There is no need for third (or first) person on a resume since you aren't writing full sentences. Each bullet point should begin with an action verb, not a subject or noun.

Michael's *after* resume reveals another insider secret that we use at Job-Bound. Michael had two jobs in the past twenty years. He listed each assignment for each job title separately on his *before* resume. However, when putting together his resume for the *after* version, we wanted to condense it to make it easier to read. In his case, we simply listed all of his titles right after his company and then went into all the details. It just makes it easier to read and digest.

This worked for Michael because he was fundamentally doing very similar things and on a linear career path. Also, for those with a lot of experience from one company, the most recent or more senior positions will be most relevant.

If you worked for a while at one company but moved to different departments or had dramatically different assignments, then you will want to list them as distinct entries as opposed to grouping them together.

Michael's *after* resume got him out of the rut and moving forward.

# Michael Sciola
*Conulting Project Senior Principal*

***Summary***

Mr. Michael Sciola is a project manager, and a functional leader for the implementation of Enterprise financial and Supply Chain applications. His experience includes managing projects using PeopleSoft's Compass project management methodologies. He has broad functional experience in SupplyChain (Order to Cash, Procure to Pay and Manufacturing) and Financials.

Michael has over fifteen years of consulting experience in the Information Technology Industry, involving software development, customization and implementation of ERP Systems. His Client base covers a wide variety of organizations including High Technology, Manufacturing, Distribution, Health Care and Financial Management; and diverse assignments like Supply Chain Management for High Tech and industrial manufacturing, Procure to Pay for Health Care and Fund Management, including EDI Integration. As the past Order Management Product Lead he was the conduit from Consulting to Product Strategy, he is recognized as the process expert.

Prior to joining PeopleSoft Michael was a Project Manager for Systems Integration group at a Global IT Corporation where he managed ERP Implementation Projects. He has led turnkey implementation of Mfg/Pro involving Inventory, Production Planning, Shop Floor Control, Purchasing and Financials for CPG industry customers.

## PROFESSIONAL EXPERIENCE

**PeopleSoft Supply Chain Management 8.8 Implementation**
Manufacturing Industry

- Michael is currently managing the Supply Chain implementation for a large industrial manufacturing company implementing financials and supply chain in a phased manner. He has to lead fit-gaps, recommend best business practice, identify potential areas for changing business processes and design the customizations if required.
- Managed Fixed Fee contract for building custom functionality for customer unique business needs.
- Also Managed Time & Material implementation of EDI, Order to Cash related customizations. As the Project advisor led the customer thru evaluation of Supply Chain Planning product vs. custom development.

**PeopleSoft Supply Chain Management 8.4, Order to Cash**
Manufacturing Industry (CPG)

- Michael led the Proof of Concept of Order to Cash implementation for a CPG Customer. He completed the needs assessment and defined a workable model to be implemented, configured and facilitated the Proof of concept validation process. He did the functional design and recommended customizations and also helped the technical team with data mapping, designing interface between PeopleSoft to 3rd party system.

**PeopleSoft SCM8.4, Order to Cash Implementation**
HealthCare Services Industry

- Michael lead the implementation of Order Management, Inventory and purchasing for a customer with very unique drop-ship and pricing requirements. He studied the customer's current Order to Cash business processes, and defined a workable model to be implemented. He did the functional design and recommended customizations related to drop ship processes. He also led the technical team with data mapping, designing interface between PeopleSoft to a 3rd Party Sales Quote processing system. Followed PeopleSoft Project Management (Compass) methodology from Initiation (Structure) thru Transition (Closure) process.

**PeopleSoft Supply Chain Management**
Distribution Industry

- Michael lead the Order to Cash implementation for customer in Distribution business, with multiple warehouses and 150+ salespersons using Remote Order Entry system. He led the customer from Fit-gap thru transition phase of

HOW TO SAY IT ON YOUR RESUME

implementing PeopleSoft. He did the functional design and recommended customizations related to pricing, commissions and Invoice processing. He has also taken the additional responsibility of supporting the Inventory and purchasing functions.

**PeopleSoft Supply Chain Management**
Partner Integration

- Michael provided consulting support to the Software Partner for designing interfaces to Peoplesoft Inventory and purchasing modules. This involved reviewing the delivered EIP's for Item Loader, PO dispatch; PO expected receipts for interfacing their software. Worked in co-ordination with Peoplesoft PIT crew on the integration architecture.

**PeopleSoft Supply Chain Management**
High-Tech Manufacturing

- Michael was the lead consultant to implement Order Fulfillment process and resolve issues with Inventory and Billing journals being posted to General Ledger. Helped the customer optimize the month end closing process by implementing changes to the system setup and business processes. Implemented customized Combo-edit functionality for Order to Cash and Procure to pay process and helped the customer to reduce the number of issues during period end closing.

**PeopleSoft Purchasing & Inventory**
Electronics Manufacturing

- Michael provided functional consulting support to the customer with Purchasing and Inventory implementation, developed End-user training and go-live preparation. Analyzed the Inventory and purchasing needs and developed the process flow for implementing Cycle counting, Replenishments, Requisitions and Procurement. Defined the process and developed end user training document and pre Go-live review, test and support.

**PeopleSoft Supply Chain Management**
Financial Services

- Michael led the Order Management implementation and helped the customer to develop interface to other in-house systems. Analyzed the business requirements and developed a functional design for customization related to Product Kit price rollups and interface to FedEx for recording tracking numbers. Prototyped customer business scenarios for doing Inter unit transfers and setting up Product Catalogs. Order Management and Inventory Integration testing and resolve go-live issues. Reviewed the implementation model and suggested changes with the Inventory setup to resolve the issues with Reorder quantities and inactive items.

**PeopleSoft Supply Chain Management**
Healthcare Industry

- Michael provided consulting support to implement EDI and Purchasing for a large Health Care provider. He performed technical and functional implementation of Peoplesoft EDI manager, and testing of Purchasing/Payables with EDI setup. Implemented 850 Outbound PO, 855 Inbound PO Acknowledgements and 810 Inbound Invoices.

**PeopleSoft Inventory & Cost Management**
Manufacturing Industry

- Michael provided functional and technical consulting support in resolving Inventory issues. Customer had enabled staged date tracking feature for Inventory unintentionally and was having data corruption with inventory balances. He analyzed the problem and developed solutions to turn-off staged date tracking and clean up the corrupt data. Resolved issues with Inventory balances with inputs from PeopleSoft Development, and updates/fixes to help resolve the software problems.

**PeopleSoft Supply Chain Management**
Manufacturing–CPG

- Michael was the lead Consultant for implementing Order Management, Billing and PeopleSoft EDI for a multi-division, Multi-location Company. Implemented 850 Outbound PO, 850 Inbound PO, 810 Outbound Invoice, 856 Outbound ASN and receive 855 Inbound PO acknowledgement. This included the PO's being used for intra-company orders also. He analyzed the functional model for OM, Inventory and Billing setup linked with EDI transaction. Reviewed and suggested changes to the ship-to, and bill-to customer definition. He developed the configuration reference model for master Data setup for EDI implementation.

| | | |
|---|---|---|
| ***Corporate Affiliations*** | • Oracle Corporation—Burlington, MA<br>• PeopleSoft Inc—Waltham, MA | • Digital Equipment Corporation—<br>  Maynard, MA<br>• Digital Equipment Corporation—<br>  Stow, MA<br>• Digital Equipment Corporation—<br>  Andover, MA<br>• Digital Equipment (India) Limited—<br>  Bangalore, India |

# CAPABILITIES

| | | |
|---|---|---|
| **Engagement Expertise** | • Project Management<br>• Applications Implementation | • Business & Technical Process<br>  Reengineering |
| **Applications** | • PeopleSoft Order Management<br>• PeopleSoft Inventory<br>• PeopleSoft Purchasing<br>• PeopleSoft Manufacturing (Production,<br>  Bills& Routing, Cost Management) | • PeopleSoft Billing<br>• PeopleSoft Integration Broker<br>• EDI<br>• Business Process Modeler |

# EDUCATION, CERTIFICATIONS & AWARDS

| | |
|---|---|
| **Education** | ▪ Bachelor of Engineering, Electronics–Bangalore University |
| ***Training*** | ▪ Project Management<br>▪ Business Process Modeler<br>▪ Integration Tools<br>▪ Scheduling and Cost control<br>▪ Risk Management<br>▪ Project Leadership and communications<br>▪ Compass |
| **Certifications &<br>Organizations** | ▪ PeopleSoft Supply Chain Management–PeopleSoft Inc.<br>▪ Business Process Modeler–Mastery—PeopleSoft Inc. |
| **Awards** | ▪ PeopleSoft Outstanding Contributor Award, Q2, 2003<br>▪ PeopleSoft Pride Award, December 2001<br>▪ Digital Equipment Corporation's "What ever it Takes" Award, 1995<br>▪ Digital Equipment Corporation's "Excellence" Award, 1996 |
| **Languages** | ▪ **Kannada**, Read, write, speak–High proficiency<br>▪ **Hindi,** Read, write, speak–Moderate proficiency |
| **Presentations &<br>Publications** | ▪ Developed and presented Order to Cash–Business Process; PeopleSoft Consulting<br>  internal Webinar. |

# Michael Sciola

611 Main Street ♦ Murrel Creek, MA 56273
385.563.7921 ♦ sciola@aol.com

## SUMMARY

- Dedicated functional leader and project manager with a track record of on-time, on-budget successes for implementations with revenue as large as $3.8MM
- Seasoned manager leading teams as large as 30 across enterprise financial and supply chain (order to cash, procure to pay and manufacturing) applications
- Trusted client partner selected to sit on customer implementation steering committee and recognized as providing honest, thoughtful, competent advice to key clients
- Versatile Senior Project Manager with 15 years experience across more than 10 client categories including Health Care, CPG, Manufacturing, Technology, and Finance

## EXPERIENCE

**ORACLE–PEOPLESOFT INC.,** Burlington, MA, January 1999–Present

| | |
|---|---|
| Senior Principal: | 2005–Present |
| Project Manager: | 2004–2005 |
| Process Specialist: | 2002–2004 |
| Senior Consultant: | 2001–2002 |
| Consultant: | 1999–2000 |

- Led Oracle/PeopleSoft portion of full lifecycle, 12-month, $3.5MM supply chain project for $2 billion manufacturing company
  - Managed a team of 22 implementing, customizing, and supporting six modules across Financial and Supply Chain product lines
  - Served as a liaison with customer and competitor/partner (Bearing Point) to implement system used by more than 200 at multiple offices across the United States
  - Successfully completed project on time and under budget avoiding pre-negotiated late fees built into the contract
  - Helped increase Oracle–PeopleSoft revenue more than $600,000 as a result of project successes
  - Requested by client to sit on prestigious Steering Committee alongside CEO and CFO helping oversee entire project from design to implementation
  - Advised client and sold recommendation on difficult decision on whether to integrate with existing business solution or to develop customized product
- Oversaw high-pressure Supply Chain proof of concept project helping secure $2MM license and consulting fee for $400MM consumer package goods company
  - Proposed methodology, presented solutions, and delivered proof of concept building trust with highly demanding client
- Strategically analyzed and lead Order Management implementation on comprehensive and unique order-to-cash process for health care services company

- Managed a team of eight customer resources partnering extremely closely with client to design functionality and customization
- Chosen by Project Strategy Manager as Product Lead serving as liaison between strategy and field—providing insight, direction, and support to more than 100 consultants
- Reduced from $1MM to $5,000 monthly unreconcilliations between corporate and division by repairing and implementing new Order Fulfillment process for high tech manufacturing client
- Launched Order Management, Billing and Electronic Date Interface system for inbound/outbound purchase orders and invoices helping client avoid more than $50,000 in invoice penalties daily from key customer
- Developed and presented "Order to Cash–Business Process" webinar available to entire PeopleSoft internal consulting practice
- One of 55 consultants out of more than 2,000 worldwide to capture PeopleSoft's "Outstanding Contributor" award for noteworthy achievement in Q2 2003

DIGITAL EQUIPMENT INDIA/USA, May, MA/Brin, India, August 1991–January 1999

| | |
|---|---|
| Project Manager: | 1996–1999 |
| Senior Software Specialist: | 1994–1996 |
| Software Specialist: | 1992–1994 |
| Software Engineer: | 1991–1992 |

- Managed a team of 30 running the pilot program ultimately used on more than 2,000 internal Y2K applications across the globe
- Awarded "Certificate of Excellence" for completing MFG/Pro customization and implementation on time and under budget
  - Lead application design and development of functionality for Distribution Resource planning
- Responsible for pre-sales and post-sales implementations of ERP products for more than five clients in categories including, Consumer Products, Manufacturing, and Distribution
- Recognized by management with "Whatever it Takes" award for service above and beyond expectations

CUSTOMER ENGINEER, Bangalore, India, September 1989–August 1991

## EDUCATION/AFFILIATIONS/APPLICATIONS

BANGALORE UNIVERSITY—BANGALORE, INDIA, 1989
- Bachelor of Engineering in Electronics

PROJECT MANAGEMENT INSTITUTE, MEMBER, 1987—PRESENT

APICS, MEMBER, 1987–PRESENT

PROFICIENT IN: MANMAN, MFG/PRO, BPCS, PEOPLESOFT

# Stuck in a Rut

The first thing you may notice about Carlos's resume is that he overdid it on the categories. He delineated ten different sections on his *before* version. He listed Profile, Objective, Professional, Civic, Charitable, Military, Languages, and the list goes on.

Remember, this is not a book with chapters but rather a resume to be scanned in about fifteen seconds.

This brings up a very important point. You can put a lot on your resume, but it doesn't make a difference if no one will read it. Remember my earlier comparison: When you see an advertisement for Tide detergent, they don't tell you everything in the world about Tide—just enough to get you to buy the product.

You have a limited amount of time and space in a resume. It is critical that you focus on what will get you hired.

In Carlos's case, we first condensed the sections from ten to four. That makes it easier for the recruiting director to digest. We also shortened the resume to two pages. Again, a business resume should not be more than two pages. To accomplish that, we focused more attention on what Carlos had done recently. Typically, you don't need four bullet points describing a job you did twenty-five years ago. Simply listing the job and a bullet point or two will suffice.

Finally, we highlighted an important past accomplishment. We placed his award—National Endowment for the Humanities Fellow—in his summary section in case the reader didn't make it all the way to page two.

# CARLOS CABALA

440 Clark Avenue
Carpenters Canyon, New York 044041
Office (441) 490-1914      Home (441) 119-0044
ccabala@iso.com

**PROFILE:**   Polished communications professional experienced in managing award-winning internal and external communications supporting growth strategies. Imaginative and decisive leader, strategic and tactical thinker, but known for hands-on ability and especially skill as a writer. Focused manager with reassuring manner and approach. Knows communications business and media well and is able to tackle most challenges immediately.

**OBJECTIVE:**   Senior communications position encompassing media relations, public relations, brand management, and executive communications functions in a dynamic organization.

**EXPERIENCE:**   **Insurance Services Office, Inc. (ISO), Jersey City, N.J. 1988-Present**

*Assistant Vice President*—Corporate Communications 2001-Present

ISO, a 2,700-employee global corporation headquartered in Jersey City, N.J., is a leading provider of products and services that help measure, manage and reduce risk. ISO serves professionals in insurance, finance and many other fields with data, analytics and decision-support solutions and sophisticated databases that accurately classifying risk and detect potential fraud. Visit the company's website at www.iso.com.

ISO's head of corporate communications:

- Is in charge of ISO's communications with the general public, the media, customers, shareholders and employee-owners.

- Has major responsibility for positioning ISO's products and services and the ISO brand through strategic media relations, advertising and marketing communications.

Accomplishments:

- Prominently positioned ISO's products and services and expanded ISO's brand image through strategic media relations in print, broadcast and on-line product publicity;

- Developed and executed key corporate publications, studies, corporate website and speeches for CEO's delivery to build ISO's corporate reputation and credibility;

- Developed a broad employee communications program that built ownership awareness, customer focus and teamwork among ISO's employees with quality employee print and on-line publications;

- Implemented crisis management and media relations expertise, including a broad network of contacts in the insurance trade and financial press to guide ISO through a major antitrust lawsuit;

---

- Effectively manage and direct professional staff of media-relations manager, writers, designers and project managers.

**The Prudential Insurance Company, Newark, NJ  1986-1988**
*Director, Public Relations*

Accomplishments:

- Directed public relations in a $2 million tort-reform campaign;

- Executed strategic media and grass-roots plan that won public and legislative support for civil-justice reform legislation;

- Launched **Prudential's** countrywide speakers' bureau.

**New Jersey General Assembly 1983-1986**
*Director of Communications*

Accomplishments:
- Planned and directed media coverage for Assembly speaker and majority members of the state legislature;
- Served as official spokesman for the speaker and legislative caucus;
- Wrote leadership members' speeches and edited caucus newsletter;
- Managed professional staff.

*The Home News-Tribune* daily and Sunday newspaper, New Brunswick, N.J. *City Editor* 1978-1983

Accomplishments:

- Directed 20-member award-winning staff.

*Editorial writer*

*Capital correspondent and chief political* writer

**The Associated Press,** Baltimore, Md.
*News reporter*

**EDUCATION**   Master of Arts degree, political science, Rutgers University, New Brunswick, NJ
Thesis: *Mass Media, Crisis and Political Change: A Cross National Approach*, in Communication Yearbook, Transaction Books.

Bachelor of Arts degree, communications, The American University, Washington, DC

The Wharton School, University of Pennsylvania's Aresty Institute of Executive Education, finance & accounting program for executives. 1996

**HONORS:**   The Fletcher School of Law and Diplomacy, Tufts and Harvard universities—National Endowment for the Humanities Fellow                     Accredited Public Relations (APR) Public Relations Society of America

Big Apple Award, PRSA-NY, best annual report, *A Challenge to Do More*—1997

Big Apple Award, PRSA-NY, <u>best annual report</u>, *Access To The Future*—1998
President's Award for Service to PRSA, New York–2004

**PROFESSIONAL:** Public Relations Society of America, N.Y. chapter president, 1998—board of directors

Sigma Delta Chi—Society of Professional Journalists

National Press Club, Washington, DC

**CIVIC:** Borough Council member, Highland Park, NJ 1984-1987 and Zoning Board of Adjustment, Highland Park, NJ

**CHARITABLE:** Trustee & former chairman of Lifeties, Inc., Trenton, N.J., a private, non-profit operator of long-term residential care facility for teenage AIDS victims and their babies.

**MILITARY:** U.S. Army–service Vietnam

**LANGUAGES:** Spanish, fluent

# Carlos Cabala

440 Clark Avenue ♦ Carpenters Canyon, NY 44041
441.490.1914 ♦ ccabala@gmail.com

## SUMMARY

- Seasoned public relations professional with more than 20 years experience producing award winning and results driven internal and external campaigns
- Dedicated agent of change having introduced, planned, and executed outreach campaigns covered by some of the world's biggest media outlets including the *New York Times*, *USA Today*, and *Time*
- National Endowment of the Humanities Fellow winner with exceptional writing skills honed as a reporter, editor, and published author
- Experienced manager having led diverse cross-functional work teams of more than 20 professionals

## EXPERIENCE

INSURANCE SERVICES OFFICE INC. (ISO), Jersey City, NJ, 1988–Present

Assistant Vice-President–Corporate Communications, 2001–Present
Director–Corporate Communications, 1988–2001

*ISO is a 2,700-employee global corporation providing products and services to help measure, manage, and reduce risk for professionals in insurance, finance, and many other fields*

- Revamped entire media relations outreach program establishing new strategic direction dramatically increasing company credibility and visibility
  - Generated more than 2 million impressions with over 1,000 placements featured in publications including the *New York Times*, *Wall Street Journal*, *USA Today*, *Time* magazine, and many others
  - Increased insurance trade press presence 20-fold via proactive media relations program establishing ISO as industry leading provider of content
- Overhauled all existing internal corporate communications creating strategic plan dramatically upgrading scope and quality of employee outreach.
  - Introduced new monthly employee magazine featuring 8–12 pages of content covering company's strategic direction, employee recognition/benefits, and new corporate initiatives
  - Launched "Inside ISO Online" weekly newsletter with corporate and employee news
  - Enhanced direct communication "Liaison" program featuring online updates for breaking corporate news and developments
- Planned, wrote, and produced company's annual report, winning Public Relations Society of America (PRSA) New York chapter recognition in 1997, 1998, and 2000
- Wrote more than 50 major speeches and keynotes for company CEO delivered at events including Independent Insurance Agents and Brokers of America Convention (7,000 attendees), Pacific Insurance Insurity Conference, and the Joint Industry Forum
- Deftly handled crisis communications for antitrust lawsuit filed by Attorney Generals from 19 different states spanning more than six years
  - Leveraged strong media relations fostered among insurance trade and financial press to avert negative backlash and win support in press for ISO's products and services as competitive
  - Managed internal communications helping keep ISO employees informed and positive
- Successfully managed media relations and internal communications for company transition from non-profit membership organization into a for-profit stock corporation

- Oversaw annual budgets in excess of $3MM and a staff as large as 24 across corporate communications, meetings and travel, project management, media relations, and design
- Navigated a corporate mandated downsizing effort significantly reducing staff, expenses, and payroll
- Leveraged industry and marketing contacts resulting in CEO being chosen as one of 100 Most Powerful People in Insurance for three years running
- Nominated company and prepared entry securing ISO as one of New Jersey's 25 Finest Corporations as chosen by New Jersey Business 2004
- Established company's first shareholder relationship function crafting quarterly publication distributed to more than 3,000 shareholders

**THE PRUDENTIAL INSURANCE COMPANY,** Director of Public Relations, Newark, NJ, 1986–1988
- Directed integrated, multi-layered PR campaign helping enact tort reform legislation in 12 states
- Launched company's countrywide speaker's bureau insinuating Prudential into local communities
- Wrote more than 10 speeches for Prudential CEO, EVP of Property and Casualty, and SVP/Corporate Secretary

**NEW JERSEY GENERAL ASSEMBLY,** Director of Communications, Trenton, NJ, 1983–1986
- Created organization's first-ever public communication function and staff informing public of General Assembly's accomplishments
- Drafted more than 100 press releases for a wide variety of legislative issues

**THE HOME NEWS-TRIBUNE,** City Editor, New Brunswick, NJ, 1978–1983
- Directed 20-member award-winning staff across investigative, sports, and consumer affairs writing

## EDUCATION

**THE WHARTON SCHOOL, UNIVERSITY OF PENNSYLVANIA ARESTY INSTITUTE OF EXECUTIVE EDUCATION**—Philadelphia, PA
- Finance and Accounting Program for Executives

**RUTGERS UNIVERSITY**—New Brunswick, NJ
- Master of Arts Degree; Political Science
- Thesis: *Mass Media, Crisis and Political Change: A Cross National Approach*
    - Published in Communication Yearbook, Transaction Books

**THE AMERICAN UNIVERSITY**—Washington, DC
- Bachelor of Arts Degree; Communications

## HONORS/AFFILIATIONS/SKILLS

- **National Endowment for the Humanities Fellow,** The Fletcher School of Law and Diplomacy, Tufts and Harvard Universities
    - Selected as one of 18 Fellows from more than 1,000 applicants
- **Chapter President/Board of Directors,** PRSA New York, 1990–Present
    - President's Award for Service to PRSA–2004
- **Sigma Delta Chi—Society of Professional Journalists,** 1980–Present
- **National Press Club,** 2003–Present
- **Trustee/Former Chairman,** Lifeties, Inc., 1983–Present
    - Private, nonprofit operator of long-term residential care facility for teenage AIDS victims and their babies
- **Fluent in Spanish**

# WONDERING WHAT ELSE IS OUT THERE

What else is out there? What is your dream job, and how do you make that dream a reality?

Sometimes, it's easy to get caught up in some of the work mantras—*Must have a great job. Must make a lot of money. Must be wildly successful.* Often, you can get so busy with the day-to-day, hectic tasks of your current job that you lose sight of where you are going and where you want to be.

Many professionals have this dream of landing the perfect job in the perfect city for the perfect amount of money, benefits, and self-fulfillment. So how do you get there? Well, you have to gain spectacular experience, write an amazing resume, craft a catchy cover letter, dazzle the interviewers, and network like crazy! Quite honestly, these thoughts are immobilizing. With that perspective, it's easy to cast your dream job off as just that—a dream.

Fortunately, we have some simple tips if you are wondering what else is out there. We all know that a journey of a thousand miles begins with one step, so take it!

## 1. Write down your goals

To start, write down a couple of your main career goals.

**GOAL: To be a travel writer for *National Geographic* magazine**

Then you want to break that down into manageable steps that you can track. Create a detailed, written description of each of your goals, using the SMART criteria as a guideline:

- *Specific.* You can describe the details—Who? What? Where? When? How?
- *Measurable.* You can measure the goal using either quantitative or qualitative assessments.
- *Achievable.* The goal is realistic given existing constraints, such as time and resources. "To be the National Geographic CEO on the cover of next month's issue" might be a little lofty.
- *Realistic.* You are willing and able to accomplish this goal. You believe in it.
- *Time bound.* Ground the goal with a specified time frame. "Before I retire" isn't specific enough.

Examples of SMART goals:

- To complete my resume and have it proofread and critiqued by three people by May 1.
- To start a personal travel blog by May 10 and post one story every week.
- To set up and complete three informational interviews with three members of my Outdoor Writers Association by May 30.
- To attend two networking events in Washington, DC, by June 1.

---

- To get two travel articles published in *Travel + Leisure* magazine by June 15.
- To have three mock interviews before my job interview with *National Geographic* on July 1.

## 2. Post your goals and tell someone

Put your goals on your refrigerator, put the dates on your calendar, or make little inspirational banners or Post-its. This makes your goals seem more real and permanent. Tell your friends and family. This holds you accountable, and it gives your goals life.

## 3. Reevaluate your career goals at key checkpoints

Things change. Every month, you should sit down to make sure you are taking strides in the right direction. You want to be focused, but some career opportunities can come along and surpass your dreams. You want to have the flexibility to seize new, great opportunities.

## 4. Celebrate your achievements

Although writing, posting, and reevaluating goals can seem like quite the chore, there are ways you can make it fun. Set up rewards for yourself when you reach goals and make positive steps. These celebrations will keep you energized and pushing forward.

## 5. Stop just wondering

Maybe you are not miserable at your current job, but you are curious about other companies, salaries, and work environments. You have career goals, and you're wondering if you should take a different step to get there.

Take the first step in your job search, with your career, and for your dream job by setting small goals. One of the first small steps will be to update and enhance your resume!

• • •

Our next clients wanted to test the water for other opportunities. They wanted to brush up their resume, send it out, and see what opportunities arose. Take a look at how you can stay up-to-date.

# Wondering What Else Is Out There

Gina was one of those people who wonder what else is out there. As a partner (VP) at a big advertising agency, she had a lot of great experience, but was struggling with how to make it stand out and sound impressive. That's where JobBound helped.

The first thing you may notice is that it is nearly impossible to read Gina's resume because the font size is so small. If a recruiting director can't read your resume, then you won't be considered for the job. Always print out your resume, and show it to a few people to make sure it's easy to read.

The second thing you'll observe is how much more specific we made Gina's jobs sound. Instead of merely listing her duties—

- Perform all generalist functions—heavy recruitment, staffing and employee relations

which every associate HR director ever in the history of the human resources field has done—we actually showed her accomplishments:

- Revamped company recruitment process dramatically streamlining requisition-to-hire time for office hiring 150 candidates annually

Which version sounds better to you?

We can't stress enough how important it is to write an accomplishment resume versus a job description resume. Think about it this way. If the person who held the job before you or who held it after you can write on his or her resume what you wrote on yours, rip up your resume and start over.

That screening worked well for Gina. Obviously, the person before her and after her performed all generalist functions. I am guessing the person before or after her did not revamp the company recruitment process.

This kind of writing is what will make your resume stand out.

Gina Gleason _____

163 Gunnison Street—Apt. #6G ▪ Atlanta ▪ GA ▪ 56992 ▪ (836) 266-1238 ▪ggleason@yahoo.com

## QUALIFICATIONS

Seasoned Human Resources Professional with a record of consistent achievements throughout work history. Proven track record of developing and implementing human resource initiatives that are in line with the organizational needs of the company as well as the overall goals of senior management. Responds positively to demanding situations while providing and executing solutions. Dependable, trustworthy and highly resourceful.

## PROFESSIONAL EXPERIENCE

**WPP Group plc (6/97–Present)**
MindShare, Mediaedge:cia and Ogilvy sister agencies all wholly owned by WPP Group. WPP is one of the world's leading communication services groups which offers services to national, multinational and global clients.

**MINDSHARE, USA INC.**                                                                       New York, NY
**Partner, Assistant Director of Human Resources**
**(Employment Dates: 8/05–Present)**
*Report to Director of Human Resources, USA:*
- Formulate and implement recruitment diversity plan for the New York office
- Perform all generalist functions–heavy recruitment, staffing and employee relations
- Revamp recruitment processes in order to meet the growing needs of all departments and create career development programs
- Wrote HR process document to remain SOX compliant
- Supervise HR Assistant on daily work assignments and special projects

**MEDIAEDGE:CIA**                                                                             New York, NY
**Partner, Human Resources Manager**
**(Employment Dates: 9/02–8/05)**
*Reported to North American Director of Human Resources:*
- Main point of contact for Senior Management–coach, advise on all areas as it relates to staffing, compensation and employee relations for the entire agency and serve as an consultant for regional offices
- Manage Recruitment—source candidates for all departments within the New York Office and other field offices
- Spearhead and manage all facets of the Internship Program and On Campus/College Recruitment
- Manage Staffing–facilitate rotations and transfers between departments in order to foster career development
- Mentor, supervise and train Recruiter and HR Coordinator on daily work assignments and special projects
- Provide counsel to managers on employee development, career pathing, disciplinary action, and other issues
- Solely monitor and handle all Immigration/Visa issues to ensure they are handled appropriately with legal counsel
- Maintain and ensure integrity of employee data in coordination with the Payroll department in order to monitor the forecast for staffing
- Handle raise planning and compensation analysis for the New York office
- Develop and implement agency initiatives to help build employee morale and foster a positive corporate culture
- Revise policies and procedures to ensure they are legally compliant with Federal and State guidelines

**MINDSHARE, USA INC.**                                                                       New York, NY
**Partner, Human Resources Manager**
**(Employment Dates: 6/00–9/02)**
*Reported to North American Director of Human Resources:*
- Part of the original HR team that helped to start the company in 2000, through the merger of media departments of ad agencies Ogilvy & Mather and J. Walter Thompson
- Responsibilities included recruitment of exempt staff from junior to mid management level
- Worked closely with HR Director to set goals, build the HR department and develop company infrastructure
- Implemented and managed summer internship program by recruiting, interviewing all interns; also organized training workshops for interns as well as supported with guidance both interns and supervisors
- Supervised HR Coordinator on daily work assignments and special projects
- Handled staff reductions, severance agreements, exit interviews and other termination issues
- Created ad hoc reports for the Finance department and Regional offices
- Handled employee relations, counseled Senior Management
- Developed policies and procedures that are consistent with the company's goals and objectives
- Administered performance evaluation process–counseled management on effective performance writing techniques
- Developed the MindShare Foundation–acted as the spokesperson for industry-wide events and was featured on national television for the Children's Miracle Network program in 2002

**OGILVY & MATHER**                                                                                            New York, NY
**Human Resources Manager**
**(Employment Dates: 6/97–6/00)**
*Reported to Director of Development and Administration:*
- Recruited and managed all permanent and temporary administrative, entry-level account management and finance positions for all divisions of Ogilvy & Mather (Successfully recruited a monthly average of 15 available positions)
- Provided employee relations counseling, including but not limited to performance issues, sexual harassment, exit interviews, policy and procedure inquiries and career development
- Implemented and promoted the employee referral program resulting in reduced costs of recruitment fees by 30%
- Established strong relationships with various employment agencies and negotiate contracts to reduce placement fees
- Tracked turnover and work closely with senior management to increase retention rate
- Created and placed personnel ads in appropriate print media and internet sites
- Counseled Senior Management on the best utilization of applicants and current staff
- Developed and coordinated staffing plans with all departments for the entire administrative population

**Human Resources Coordinator**

*Reported to Manager of Information Systems:*
- Recruited permanent employees for various levels of finance and information technology
- Maintained the HRIS database for over 1,000 Ogilvy & Mather employees and provided support to six branch offices
- Conducted weekly orientation sessions for all new hires
- Developed, implemented and managed corporate-wide 1998 Take Our Daughters to Work Program
- Prepared Adverse Impact Analysis upon request due to staff reductions
- Prepared yearly Equal Employment Opportunity reports to show hiring trends throughout the agency

**MORGAN STANLEY, DEAN WITTER, DISCOVER & CO.**                                        New York, NY
**Equal Employment Opportunity Administrator**
**(Employment Dates: 8/95–6/97)**
*Reported to EEO Coordinator:*
- Prepared various statistical analysis to ensure compliance with federal, state, and local affirmative action and Equal Employment laws
- Prepared Adverse Impact Analysis quarterly to determine discriminatory trends with regard to hiring, promotion, and termination practices
- Prepared goal reports for Senior Management to monitor the achievement of females and minority goals
- Wrote queries and produced reports to support ad hoc data requests required by internal and external counsel
- Represented the company at job fairs; also coordinated and managed community outreach programs
- Educated employees on EEO policies

---

## EDUCATION

**Bernard Baruch College, City University of New York, January 1995**
B.B.A. Human Resource Management; Minor: Corporate Communications

**Professional Education:**
**Cornell University School of Industrial and Labor Relations**
Program included courses in: The Law of EEO, Conducting a Utilization Analysis, Preparing an Affirmative Action Plan

**American Management Association**
Program included courses in: Recruiting, Interviewing and Selecting Employees

**Padgett Thompson**
Program included courses in: HR and the Law Seminar

---

## PROFESSIONAL AFFILIATIONS

- American Association Of Advertising Agencies (AAAA) *Co-Chair, Diversity Committee*
- National Association Minorities in Communications (NAMIC)
- African Americans in Advertising (AAIA)
- Society of Human Resources Management (SHRM)

---

## *SKILLS*

- HRIS, People Soft, SAP, QMF-SQL, Microsoft Office, Access, Power Point and Lotus Notes

---

# Gina Gleason

16 Gunnison Street, Apt. #6G ♦ Atlanta, GA 56992
836.266.1238 ♦ ggleason@yahoo.com

## SUMMARY OF QUALIFICATIONS

- Strategic Human Resources professional with more than eight years of experience working for one of the world's largest advertising agency holding companies
- Seasoned manager having helped create an HR department post-merger for an organization with more than 700 employees
- Experienced generalist with substantial background in all aspects of HR including hiring, retention, staffing, benefits, HRIS, EEO, Affirmative Action, termination and more
- Dedicated agent-of-change with a background of launching several agency wide initiatives spanning Foundation partnerships, intern programs, employee benefits, and recruiting programs

## EXPERIENCE

WPP GROUP, PLC, June 1997–Present
*MindShare, Mediaedge, and Ogilvy & Mather are all sister agencies of WPP—one of the world's largest communication services groups with offices in 25 countries worldwide*

**PARTNER, ASSISTANT DIRECTOR OF HR,** MINDSHARE, USA INC., New York, NY, April 2005–Present
- Revamped company recruitment process dramatically streamlining requisition-to-hire time for office hiring 150 candidates annually
- Manage employee relations for workforce of 750 across New York headquarters and 11 regional offices
- Oversee 80 yearly employee moves and staffing changes for seven departments
- Developing company's first-ever comprehensive diversity plan, comprising recruitment and retention
- Overhauled agency's summer internship program launching "Battle of the Interns" competition culminating in Gillette case study presentation to CEO and senior management
- Wrote HR process document detailing all internal processes including recruiting, onboarding, staffing, promotions, transfers, and firing to insure Sarbanes-Oxley compliance
- Enhancing internal perception of HR department by focusing on strategic solutions and timely action

**PARTNER, HR MANAGER,** MEDIAEDGE:CIA, New York, NY, September 2002–April 2005
- Served as main liaison with senior management, advising and coaching on all aspects of human resources for office with 650 employees in New York and additional 200 across the country
- Wrote and delivered recruitment, staffing, and compensation presentation for senior management helping facilitate work process and improve relationships with HR
- Conceived, planned, and executed "Employee Appreciation" day featuring senior management serving breakfast to employees
- Managed recruitment for office hiring 200 annually, at all levels and throughout all departments
- Revived agency's volunteer day, spearheading efforts supporting local New York charity
- Developed course materials and presented workshop to management on effective and lawful interviewing
- Revised all policies and procedures, harmonizing efforts across branch offices and insuring federal and state compliance
- Handled all aspects of company's immigration/visa issues for five cases annually
- Relaunched agency's internship program and on campus/college recruiting efforts
- Forecast staffing, analyzed compensation, and managed raise planning for New York office
- Trained and supervised a staff of two

**PARTNER, HR MANAGER,** <u>MINDSHARE, USA, INC.</u>, New York, NY, June 2000–September 2002
- Key member of original HR team responsible for starting company in 2000 through the merger of the media departments of Ogilvy & Mather and J. Walter Thompson
- Worked closely with HR Director to fundamentally build an HR department from scratch, establishing policies and procedures to guide the new company
- Managed all aspects of 125-person staff reduction as a function of merger
- Developed the Mindshare Foundation and served as spokesperson at industry-wide events
  - Featured on national television for the Children's Miracle Network program in 2002
  - Forged Foundation relationships and raised more than $25,000 for charity
- Launched an extensive program of formal and informal events designed to develop a cohesive corporate culture and meld two distinct work groups post-merger
- Initiated company's summer internship program from recruitment, to program development, to training
- Converted entire HRIS system from Query 2000 to SAP

**HR MANAGER,** <u>OGILVY & MATHER</u>, New York, NY, June 1997–June 2000
- Reduced recruitment fees 30% by overhauling, promoting, and enhancing employee referral program
- Increased retention rates by working closely with senior management to identify and recognize star performers
- Successfully filled an average of 15 positions monthly across several different departments
- Maintained HRIS database with more than 1,000 Ogilvy employees across seven offices
- Oversaw all aspects of inaugural "Take Our Daughters to Work Program"
- Promoted from HR Coordinator to HR Manager in less than two years

**EEO ADMINISTRATOR,** <u>MORGAN STANLEY</u>, New York NY, August 1998–June 1997
- Managed day-to-day EEO tracking and compliance for 25,000 employees across seven regions

## EDUCATION

**BERNARD BARUCH COLLEGE, CITY UNIVERSITY OF NEW YORK** , 1995
- B.B.A., Human Resource Management—Minor, Corporate Communications

**PACE UNIVERSITY—NEW YORK, NY, 2004–Present**
- HR Certification preparatory course

**CORNELL UNIVERSITY SCHOOL OF INDUSTRIAL AND LABOR RELATIONS—NEW YORK, NY, 2002**
- Program courses in: Preparing an Affirmative Action Plan, and The Law of EEO

**AMERICAN MANAGEMENT ASSOCIATION—NEW YORK, NY, 2000**
- Program courses in: Recruiting, Interviewing, and Hiring

**PADGETT THOMPSON—NEW YORK, NY, 1997**
- Program courses in: HR and the Law

## ACTIVITIES/INTERESTS

- American Association of Advertising Agencies
- National Association of Minorities in Communication
- Society of Human Resources Management
- Interests include boating, cooking, and reading

# Wondering What Else Is Out There

We don't like sentences. There, we said it.

When it comes to writing resumes, you need to make your document as easy as possible for the recruiting director to read and scan.

As we have mentioned before, recruiting directors will spend about fifteen seconds looking at your resume during the first glance. They will not read every word, and they will not cover every point. If they like you after that first glance, then they may spend up to a minute on your resume.

With that in mind, a resume structured like Frank's simply will not get the attention it deserves. Long, flowing, prose statements on a resume are not read. Instead of learning about his job experiences, the recruiting director is likely to look at his titles and then pitch the resume.

Notice how in the *after* version we used bullet points which quickly and succinctly communicate the great things he has done. Start all of your bullet points with action verbs (try not to repeat them). Use past tense for jobs you have completed, and utilize present tense for current jobs or assignments. Of course, keep the points brief and focused on your accomplishments.

A strong resume was particularly important for Frank. He had been at his company for several years. He enjoyed the job, but his company was considering major layoffs. Frank wanted to update his resume, test the waters, and make sure he was ready for the next step if his job came into jeopardy.

Frank distributed his resume while his company was going through a transition. The resume gave him the confidence and reassurance he needed during a shaky time.

**Frank Freidman**

557 W. Fresco Drive (778) 985-5567 Farmington Fields, FL
65781 ffreidman@earthlink.net

## Summary

Project Manager, with over 16 years experience covering project management, client management, design and development of software. The range of projects varies from complex enterprise wide package applications implementation to simple departmental custom application development. Track record of delivering solutions on time and within budget and managing teams to achieve organizational and project goals. Possesses strong communication skills, analytical skills.
- ✓ Excelled in customer retention through high customer satisfaction by identifying and managing project risks.
- ✓ 5 years of client management
- ✓ 9+ years of project management coupled with deep knowledge of business processes in Supply Chain, CRM across several industries like Manufacturing, Insurance, Services and wholesale distribution.

**Experience    Oracle-PeopleSoft, Inc.**              Southfield, MI
07/98- Present
### Consultant

Responsibilities and achievements include leading several large Order-to-Cash projects in diverse industries. Significant participation in license sales and business development-assessing product fit to business needs of customers, identifying and addressing project risks such as change management, scope creep associated with retiring legacy systems, risks or re-implementing legacy systems, and product fit. Trusted advisor to customers. Mentored colleagues and consultants both on a formal and informal basis.
- ✓ Worked in 7 major PeopleSoft implementations to retire different homegrown legacy systems.
- ✓ Managed different internal and external project stakeholders successfully for critical situations. Managed large cross-functional teams.
- ✓ Worked for two years as conduit and facilitator for transfer of knowledge and best practices (Order Management) between the field Consulting team, and the product development organization. (Product Lead).
- ✓ Led the global implementation for a telecom gear manufacturer to retire five operational systems with packaged software. Managed cross-functional teams from five countries, and worked with stakeholders and partners.
- ✓ Provided decisive advice to a client to terminate a project based on all available options and constraints. Co developed the business case for the Board.

09/93–06/98 **Covansys, Inc–Manager** Farmington Hills, MI

Led development teams of programmers and analysts. Developed, and supported custom and packaged software for clients ranging from top automotive companies to internet start-up companies. Led and participated in multi-man year, multi-site development, and maintenance projects.

✓ Led the pilot project for an internet direct marketing company that formed the basis of a very successful **IPO.**

08/ 92–08/ 93 **Wipro Systems—Marketing** Bangalore, India

Responsible for support and marketing activities to sales team, from the offshore HQ. Direct report to the President and Executive Council of the organization. Successfully led and managed corporate vendor reviews, culminating in the launch of offshore software development partnerships for three global clients.

✓ Successfully sold and managed a data warehousing consulting engagement for the Asian subsidiary of global food products company.

02/ 89–07/92 **UBICS—Project Manager** Bangalore, India

Led the very first offshore and then onsite development team during the startup phase of the company. Served as the Regional Manager and managed 20 resources for a 30 man-year development project.

11/86–01/89 **Tata Services–Senior Analyst-** India

Achievements and roles include managing early adapter software projects, custom offshore development, and offsite support of mission critical applications.

✓ Led the offsite development of Executive Reporting systems for a major trading house in India. This was one of the earliest implementations of ORACLE in India.

✓ Developed custom software offsite and then provided implementation support offshore and onsite for an insurance company.

## Other Activities

- "Keys to Successful Order Management Implementations" session—Connect 2000.
- Product Lead for Order Management 2000–2002—PGS Global Services.

**Education**    M.S. in Physics from University of Hyderabad, India.

Certified Project Management Professional, PMI
PeopleSoft Certification—Supply Chain Management
Member, Great Lakes Chapter, PMI

# Frank Freidman
557 W. Fresco Drive ♦ Farmington Fields, FL 65781
788.985.5567 ♦ ffreidman@earthlink.net

## SUMMARY

- Dedicated Project Manager with more than 16 years experience across project management, client management, design, development and implementation of dozens of software systems for some of the world's largest companies
- Seasoned manager overseeing national and global teams as large as 85 consultants
- Trusted team member and leader consistently singled out by peers and by management as top performer and selected to tackle toughest internal and external issues
- Track record of delivering on-time and on-budget project work for several multimillion-dollar projects across Supply Chain Management and CRM

## EXPERIENCE

**ORACLE–PEOPLESOFT INC.,** CONSULTANT, Southfield, MI, July 1998–Present
- Lead 18 Order-to-Cash projects in diverse industries including electronics manufacturing, wholesale distribution, and insurance
- Key player in eight new business pitches helping secure $500,000 in incremental revenue
- Selected to lead global implementation for major telecom gear manufacturer
    - Managed a worldwide team of 85 consultants from the US, UK, Germany, Japan, and Australia implementing a new software system across 12 offices and plants with 300 users
    - Facilitated change management process of 5-year-old system for users ranging from CFO and controllers to data entry clerks and shippers
    - Dramatically minimized implementation costs by 23% by designing a fully-flexible system and fundamentally changing existing practices
- Convinced large property and casualty company to retain $2MM PeopleSoft license by single-handedly customizing new alternative CRM system
- Designed customization for educational testing service invoicing and settlement processes, minimizing changes to unique global implementation
- Personally chosen by PeopleSoft senior management to intervene in three crisis situations diffusing company's most difficult client problems
- Selected by peers to serve as knowledge expert on Order Management and liaison between Development, Project Management and Consulting for all 350 global consulting team members
- Presented "Keys to Successful Order Management Implementation" session at Connect 2000–worldwide PeopleSoft user conference in Los Angeles
- Co-developed business case for Board of Directors at large paper products company convincing client to terminate seven-month PeopleSoft project
- Successfully manage large cross-functional teams at all company levels including CFOs, CIOS, sales, customer retention, product management and more

**COVANSYS, INC.,** MANAGER, Farmington Hills, MI, September 1993–June 1998
- Led and participated in three multi-man year, multi-site global development and maintenance projects for some of the world's largest automotive, technology, and telecommunication companies

- Built custom order processing software for IBM resulting in $400,000 three-year project
- Developed unique data warehouse to analyze engine performance for large auto company
- Supported a call routing system for hearing impaired, handling more than 600 calls weekly

**WIPRO SYSTEMS,** MARKETING ANALYST, Bangalore, India, August 1992–August 1993
- Key member helping launch offshore software development partnerships for three global clients by leading and managing corporate vendor reviews
- Successfully sold and managed a data warehousing consulting engagement for the Asian subsidiary of a global food products company
- Reported directly to the President and Executive Council of organization with 80 employees

**UBICS,** PROJECT MANAGER, Bangalore, India, February 1989–July 1992
- Served as Regional Manager overseeing team of 20 for a 30 man-year development project
- Led company's first-ever offshore/onsite development team during startup phase

**TATA SERVICES,** SENIOR ANALYST, Mumbai, India, November 1986–January 1989
- One of the first analysts to implement ORACLE in India as part of offsite development of executive reporting system for a major trading house
- Managed early adapter software projects, custom offshore development, and offsite support of mission critical applications

## EDUCATION/AFFILIATIONS

**UNIVERSITY OF HYDERABAD—INDIA**
- Master of Science in Physics

**CERTIFIED PROJECT MANAGEMENT PROFESSIONAL—PMI**

**PEOPLESOFT CERTIFICATION—SUPPLY CHAIN MANAGEMENT**

**PMI GREAT LAKES CHAPTER—MEMBER**

# Wondering What Else Is Out There

Henrietta enjoyed her current company, but she was toying with the idea of moving to New York and getting a job there. She needed an amazing resume to see if she could secure a solid job with higher pay in New York City.

Henrietta was an amazing candidate. She grew up in Africa, graduated with honors from Harvard, and worked on some great brands at a large advertising agency.

Like many of our clients, she looked good on paper but not as good as she could have. So what did we do?

First of all, as with almost all resumes, we really drilled down her accomplishments, especially focusing on the scope of her projects and the results.

Second, you will notice that in her *before* resume she didn't have much on her most recent assignment, so we added more substance and bullet points there. Recruiting directors are usually most interested in what you did most recently.

Finally, we eliminated much of her college experiences. Nothing against Harvard, but we didn't need to delve into her clubs and activities now that she was several years out of school.

We took a good resume and made it incredible. See for yourself.

# Henrietta Hansel

992 N. Hoover, Apt. 402
Hartford, Illinois 60642

(416) 090-4331 (mobile)
hansel_h@hotmail.com

**EXPERIENCE:**   **Hearto Advertsing Inc.** Chicago, Illinois

**Hallmark, Senior Account Executive**                                        6/04-Present
- Responsible for all aspects of 2005 Gold Crown promotions creative development and production

**McDonald's Corporation, Account Executive**                              6/02-6/04
*National Kids Business*
- Launched advertising for Leo Burnett's first lead agency responsibilities on the adult calendar since 1997. Produced 5 TV spots, 2 radio spots and print, including a 3 page Hearst advertorial in support of the Go Active! Adult Happy Meal and the new premium Fiesta Salad. Led four other McDonald's agencies, Hearst publications, as well as internal teams in the development of the creative for these initiatives
- Led and managed cross-functional team to execute 5 Happy Meal programs over 6 month period; mitigated conflicting Client and promotional partner direction; preserved integrity of creative ideas throughout extensive comments from networks; shipped on time and on budget
- Presented multi-tier kid targeting agency recommendation to Marketing representatives and Owner/Operators at Kid and Family Committee Meeting
- Managed development and production of new Premium Salad communication
- Created plan for implementation of global kid nutrition initiative, including media implications, creative elements, talent/music and production costs

*Customer Experience Team—Pan-Agency Brand Consulting*
- Developed multiple service and event concepts based on consumer insights; tested concepts through an iterative process, making revisions and creating new concepts based on consumer learnings
- Managed the preliminary implementation stages of a Drive-Thru Packaging Operations Test working with a cross-functional team, bringing together various Client departments as well as other agencies and suppliers
- Analyzed various internal and external sources regarding the test market of the Speedpass technology

**Kellogg's All Family Brands, Assistant Account Executive**            8/00-6/02
- Developed Mr. Mini-Wheats Characters' story for innovative campaign; Tandemar TV Test results concluded that characters were instrumental in building brand presence and image
- Identified creative opportunity for highlighting new Mini-Wheats characters' personalities on packaging; resulted in Client awarding assignment to Burnett over another agency
- Confirmed validity of LB Brand Believers System to Client by utilizing data from Brand Shifting Analysis, a client Market Research tool, to identify brand volume losses and gains within the category
- Condensed MW consumer, product and category learnings into the key concept of an "illusion" and presented it as an integral part of the brand bond which client approved
- Sold agency recommended photographer to the Client despite the fact that his costs were significantly more than the Client had spent historically on similar print projects
- Convinced Client to produce two additional print executions than was reflected in original deliverables by generating recommendation that assessed media levels, creative messages and production implications for the campaign
- Implemented a more efficient process for Client approvals by providing comprehensive outlines that explained each stage of the 3D TV animation process and highlighted changes; outlines used in each Client review and aided in focusing Client comments and minimizing revisions
- Created and organized 3 one day agency orientations to expose various clients to the advertising process; template was used for all future new client orientations

**Agency**
- Served on Harvard recruiting team; responsible for on-campus presentations and selecting candidates
- Created Professional Development Seminar and presented to AAAA Minority Internship Program in New York

**EDUCATION:**   **HARVARD UNIVERSITY** Cambridge, Massachusetts
B.A. African History (with honors) ; Citation in French                    2000
- *Academic Honors*: Dean's List all semesters; Awarded John Harvard College Scholarship and Elizabeth Cary Agassiz Certificate of Merit for academic achievement of high distinction; Worked 8-12 hours per week to defray cost of education
- *Head Wine Steward*, Harvard Alumni Association. Responsible for a $100,000 liquor and labor budget. Hired and supervised staff of 53 bartenders, bar backs, and drivers. Scheduled multiple simultaneous bars for 3,600 alumni and allocated staff and stock based on analysis of size of event, age group, time and location. Coordinated transportation, arranged deliveries of stock items, and attended to concerns of employees, Alumni Association coordinators, alumni, security and caterers.
- *Publicity Chair,* Harvard African Students Association; *Intern*, Oxfam America; *Captain,* Harvard Student Porter Program; *Teacher*, Partnership for Empowering Neighborhoods; *Advisor*, Prefect Program; *Admissions and Information Office Liaison*, Crimson Key Society; *Actress*, Harvard Radcliffe Television; *Volunteer*, Peace Games.

**LANGUAGES:**   English, French, Ethiopian/Eritrean [Tigrinya and Amharic], Italian [reading]
**PERSONAL:**   Was born in Eritrea but also lived in Tanzania and Mali before coming to the USA
**INTERESTS:**   Theater, Reading, Belly Dancing, Running, Languages

# Henrietta Hansel

992 N. Hoover, Apt. 402 ♦ Hartford, IL 60642
416.090.4331 ♦ hansel_h@hotmail.com

## EXPERIENCE

**HEARTO ADVERTISING INC, USA,** Chicago, IL, August, 2000–Present

**HALLMARK,** ACCOUNT SUPERVISOR, June 2004–Present
- Manage all strategic and executional elements of $80MM Gold Crown business comprising seven annual promotions and a production budget of $2.5MM
- Developed strategic point-of-view fundamentally evolving Hallmark brand's creative direction resulting in some of the most memorable and likeable commercials in brand's history
  - Led team producing pool of four promotional spots ranked in the top 5% of more than 600 spots all-time
- Managed a series of music tie-in promotions with artists including James Taylor, Martina McBride, Michael McDonald, and Olivia Newton-John
  - Navigated highly complex last-minute production shoot with Martina McBride resulting in exclusive Hallmark-only CD selling more than 1MM copies
  - Managed multi-layered production process featuring RCA music label, Martina McBride's music managers, Hallmark, third-party promotional vendor and all internal departments
  - Achieved rare 100% sell through on all 1.5MM copies of James Taylor CD— first 100% sell through in 56 promotions
- Introduced concept used by creative team in execution of "Buzz" :30 TV spot that ranked as third most recalled and likeable spot in *Ad Age*
- Relaunching all marketing efforts for 4,200 Gold Crown stores, contemporizing brand and repositioning Hallmark's entire retail effort
- Promoted from Senior Account Executive in less than one year

**MCDONALD'S,** ACCOUNT EXECUTIVE, June 2002–June 2004
- Led production of 14 separate Happy Meal and Adult campaigns with a combined production budget in excess of $4MM, consistently producing work on time and on budget
- Launched advertising for Leo Burnett's first lead agency Adult calendar assignment since 1997
  - Managed more than $34MM in production across television, radio, and print
  - Developed all strategic direction for McDonald's first-ever print advertorial running in Hearst publication in support of Go Active! Adult Happy Meal
  - Served as team lead among four other McDonald's agencies, Hearst, and McDonald's
  - Campaign won McDonald's first EFFIE award for effective advertising since 2000, and first for McDonald's/Burnett campaign since 1996
- Selected to serve on prestigious pan-agency "consultancy" working with representatives from five other agencies to develop all-store promotional concepts and events
  - Created concept for "Winning Time" promotion replacing popular Monopoly game, executed across 13,000 stores in October 2001

- Presented comprehensive multi-tiered kid marketing agency recommendation to marketing representatives and 25 owner/operators at kid and family committee meeting
- Managed development and production launching new Premium Salad product—critical component of McDonald's brand turnaround
- Key liaison between McDonald's and licensing partners including Mattel, Miramax, and Mirage Inc.
- Created plan for implementation of global kid nutrition initiative, reclearing five spots featuring popular Willie Munchright character

**KELLOGG'S,** ASSISTANT ACCOUNT EXECUTIVE, August 2000–June 2002
- Developed extensive story outline to help sell Mr. Mini-Wheats Characters' story ultimately used by Kellogg's in 35 executions over two-year period
- Wrote story line used to convince client to award Burnett new packaging assignment traditionally assigned to other agency
- Introduced concept of "illusion" used to capture essence of Mini-Wheats brand—integral tool in creative development of new campaign
- Led development and execution of high-profile "Edible Art" campaign featuring Rice Krispie Treats in different everyday forms
- Managed highly complex promotional tie-ins with Monsters Inc., Spider-Man, and Disney, working closely with Pixar, Disney and Sony, and ten separate Kellogg's brands
- Created and organized three one-day agency orientations exposing dozens of clients to the advertising process—template used for all future new client orientations

## HARVARD ASSOCIATION, WINE STEWARD, Cambridge, MA, June 1999/2000
- Successfully managed a $100,000 liquor and labor budget
- Hired and supervised a staff of 53 bartenders, bar backs, and drivers
- Scheduled and staffed multiple simultaneous bars for 3,600 alumni
- Analyzed events, age groups, time and location to best deploy all product and staff

# EDUCATION

**HARVARD UNIVERSITY**—CAMBRIDGE, MA, 2000
- Bachelor of Arts in African History (with honors); French Citation
- Dean's List all semesters

# SKILLS/INTERESTS

- Fluent in French, Ethiopian/Eritrean (Tigrinya and Amharic), Italian (reading)
- Born in Eritrea—also lived in Tanzania and Mali
- Interests include: theater, reading, belly dancing, running, and languages

# Wondering What Else Is Out There

Jillian loved her current company, but she thought she deserved a pay raise. To prove that she deserved a significant raise, she wanted to see if she could receive higher offers from other companies. That way, she would have a solid justification for her new salary.

Our friend Jillian, however, had three of our most despised pet peeves on her resume:

## 1. Summary of qualifications

Jillian's summary is loaded with "self-ascribed attributes." According to Jillian, Jillian is a "proven leader," a "strong communicator," and has "diverse capacity in marketing and media in artistic, analysis, management, and purchasing roles."

Prove it! Never put anything in a summary without backing it up. If you are a great leader, write:

> proven leader with four years of experience leading teams as large as fifteen

Or:

> strong communicator having delivered more than 75 major presentations to audiences as large as 400 executives

Finally, Jillian doesn't even need a summary. She hasn't worked long enough to summarize a one-page resume.

## 2. References will be made available upon request

No duh! At the risk of being obvious, doesn't *everyone* have references that will be made available upon request? Can you imagine saying to a recruiting director, "I'm sorry, you can't have my references"? Trust me, if they want references, they will ask, and you better have some. There is no need to waste a line of your resume stating the obvious.

## 3. Job description

This resume is purely a job description resume. Jillian simply described what she has done—and what any other media associate has ever done in the entire history of the advertising business. Her accomplishments really come alive in the *after* version.

# Jillian Jozwick

*2945 East Juniper Street, Apt. 1J* ♦ *Jewel County, CA 20199* ♦ 416.395.2579 ♦ jillian.jozwick@aol.com

*Media associate with diverse experience in media, marketing, project management and artistry*

## Summary of Qualifications

- ♦ Diverse capacity in marketing and media in artistic, analysis, management, and purchasing roles
- ♦ Project management displaying leadership, market analysis and staff coordination capabilities
- ♦ Superior communicator based on vendor relationship management and staff direction
- ♦ Proven leader in the professional arena, as well as civic and educational environments

## Professional Experience

**Media Associate–*Starcom Worldwide*—Chicago, IL (Dec '03–present)**
*-Broadcast Investment Group: Collaborate with television sales venders to maintain multi-million dollar national television purchases. Clients: Allstate Insurance, Sun Microsystems, Applebee's.*
*-Media Planning Group: Form and execute multi-vehicle media plans for Hallmark Gold Crown including television, print, radio, and online.*

- ♦ Deal directly with national television sales vendors to ensure accuracy in advertisement placement and deal terms across all dayparts including sports
- ♦ Execute plans for launch of Allstate's Your Choice Auto
- ♦ Analyze marketing data for recommendations on Hallmark's targeting, geography, scheduling, support level and budget
- ♦ Graduate of SMGU training program in brand building and media skills

**Marketing Assistant–*General Growth Properties*—Northbrook, IL (Feb '03-Dec '03)**
*Managed center events for Northbrook Court Shopping Center to add revenues for center merchants*

- ♦ Managed fashion shows, art shows, car displays, and national tours
- ♦ Coordinated in-center signage, seasonal décor, and merchant advertising programs
- ♦ Analyzed monthly sales data and center traffic data
- ♦ Edited property website, updating content and composing articles

**Artistic Assistant–*Ravinia Festival*—Highland Park, IL (Summer 2002)**
*Diverse role as planner, administrator, and drafter of contracts for summer concert schedule*

- ♦ Drafted and issued contracts for young artist concert series
- ♦ Synchronized logistics for in-house production of Stephen Sondheim's *A Little Night Music*

**Production Assistant–*Ravinia Festival*—Highland Park, IL (Summer's '00 & '01)**
*Streamlined all aspects of performance production as part of a six-person team*

- ♦ Coordinated travel arrangements, housing, and catering for international artists and faculty
- ♦ Supported video production and stage management

## Education

**Miami University, Oxford, OH—GPA: 3.82 (Magna Cum Laude)**
Major: Music, Minor: Arts Management

## Leadership Roles and Civic Activities

**Section Leader–Chicago Chamber Choir—Chicago, IL**
**Founder/President/Musical Director–The Misfitz (a cappella chorus)—Miami University**

- ♦ *Created group, arranged music, directed rehearsals, selected members*

**Director of Marketing–Campus Activities Council—Miami University**

- ♦ *Designed and implemented marketing plans for the largest student organization on campus*

**References will be made available on request**

# Jillian Jozwick

2945 East Juniper Street, Apt. 1J ♦ Jewel County, CA 20199
416.395.2579 ♦ jillian.jozwick@aol.com

## EXPERIENCE

**MEDIA ASSOCIATE,** STARCOM WORLDWIDE, Chicago, IL, December 2003–Present
Media Planning Group/Broadcast Investment Group
*Hallmark, Allstate, Sun Microsystems, Applebee's*

- Developing strategic targets for all 2006 print-supported Hallmark products by analyzing psychographic and demographic data
- Work closely with Hallmark clients and media vendors managing ongoing value-added tie-ins for more than 120 shows
- Orchestrated complex sectional/cut-in plan for Allstate's "Your Choice Auto" campaign, dividing nation into groups as small as individual counties
  - Separated three creative messages, by state, across primetime, morning and sports programming
  - Effort represented one of the most complicated divided buys in network television history
- Managed relationships with 20 national sales vendors, directing make goods, audience deficiency units and schedule changes for $75MM in broadcast buys
- Quickly transitioned new client Applebee's into 04/05 upfront buying season, dramatically increasing quality and cost efficiency of $32MM national buy
- Optimized company-wide roll-out of "Media In Motion" proprietary cable loading and tracking software used to manage $60MM in inventory
- Manage $80MM in annual Hallmark budget and billing across all media vehicles
- Key liaison between Broadcast Group, Leo Burnett Account Management, and dozens of media vendors
- Graduate of Starcom University's intensive 13-week brand building and media skills training program

**MARKETING ASSISTANT,** GENERAL GROWTH PROPERTIES, Northbrook, IL, February 2003–December 2003

- Developed, planned, and executed all aspects of 15 mall events running throughout the year
  - Solicited and secured partnership agreements from mall merchants resulting in 10%–90% increases in individual Northbrook Court store sales
  - Created and produced a series of point-of-sale elements to promote event attendance
  - Served as liaison between all mall departments including vendors, security, and guest relations
- Designed messages and artwork for giant store "barricades" seen by thousands of customers
- Partnered with new ad agency to fundamentally rebrand Northbrook Court
- Created several key marketing pieces used to promote specific events and mall in general

**ARTISTIC/PRODUCTION ASSISTANT,** RAVINIA FESTIVAL, Highland Park, IL, Summers 2000–2002

- Worked closely with world-class musical talent including Yo Yo Ma, Journey, and Rodney Smithfield

## EDUCATION

**MIAMI UNIVERSITY**—OXFORD, OH, May 2002

- B.A. in Music; Arts Management Minor
- Magna Cum Laude Graduate; Overall GPA—3.8/4.0

## LEADERSHIP/ACTIVITES

- Section Leader, Chicago Chamber Choir—performance highlights include Ravinia and R. Kelly's home
- Founder/President/Musical Director, The Misfitz—Miami University a cappella chorus
- Director of Marketing, Campus Activities Council—Miami University

# FIFTEEN OR MORE
# YEARS OF EXPERIENCE

This section is for the more "seasoned" candidates.

After fifteen years of experience in the workforce, it becomes more difficult to streamline your resume. You've accomplished a lot, you've made a name for yourself, and you have a rich job history. While this may all be true, the recruiting director is not all that interested in your entire life story. Here are some suggestions:

## 1. List about ten to fifteen years' worth of job experiences

You've undoubtedly worked on a wide variety of projects, had numerous titles or companies, and handled a lot of different duties. If you listed all of your past experience in detail, your resume would be more like a novel. Plus, let's be honest, can you really remember what you did at that job in 1985?

## 2. Focus

When creating your resume, you have to sift through the all of the years of experience to pull out the most significant, relevant, and compelling accomplishments. The key is to streamline and to focus. As we've said before, you just need to tell the recruiting director enough information to get you hired.

## 3. Do not call attention to dates

There is no need to include your college graduation year, and of course, don't include a birth date.

## 4. Add any training courses or professional development workshops

If you fear that you will appear old-fashioned and out-of-touch, list any skills you have that show you are still in the game. Maybe you took an IT class or a digital media course. This reveals your willingness to adapt to the changing times.

## 5. Emphasize your know-how

Obviously, you have a wider scope of qualifications and achievements than younger workers. Play up your strengths and showcase your expertise.

Read on to find out other great tips and techniques.

# Fifteen or More Years of Experience

David had over twenty years of experience, and he'd worked his way up to the top of his company. He had been with the business several years, but headhunters were contacting him with exciting offers. He needed to put together his resume to satisfy his curiosity.

David really sold himself short. He had been working for years and listed just seven bullet points for all that work. Imagine that. He actually put more detail into the section about his volunteer soccer coaching than the one about his work experience!

His resume also brings up another good point. He wrote the *before* version as a "functional" resume. In essence, he lists some of his accomplishments in general—not related to a specific position. Then he simply lists all of his jobs.

As the resume reader, you do not know what accomplishments go with what job. For instance, David writes in the *before* version that he "Served as the Unit Publicist on several major Hollywood film productions." You don't know if he did that last week as a Partner at Jeross, Dempsey, and Scott, or if he did that in 1984 as a Unit Producer in New Orleans.

When we rewrote the resume, David really came to life. Since he was a PR guy, we made sure to drop a lot of names—both of the stars he booked and where he booked them. He got thirty different clients on *Oprah*; now, that's impressive!

We did not include bullet points for his earliest jobs since they were no longer relevant.

**David Dempsey**
**2611 West Dundee Road Decatur, IL 60413**
**630.789.4870**
**DavidDempsey@gmail.com**

| | |
|---|---|
| **Profile** | • Over 10 years experience as a Partner/Co-Manager of a Chicago based Entertainment Marketing agency |
| | • Nearly 20 years experience working in all aspects of Entertainment Marketing (Publicity, Promotion, Media Planning, Media Buying, pitching and developing new business, supervising I.T. system integration, Accounting) |
| | • Goal-oriented individual with strong leadership capabilities. |
| | • Organized, highly motivated, and detail-directed problem solver. |
| | • Extensive experience at successfully working on multiple projects simultaneously |
| | • Very comfortable as a team leader and/or as a role player |
| | • I am easy to work with and enjoy working with others. |
| **Education** | **B.A.,** Communications, University Of Michigan-Ann Arbor—1983 |
| | Graduated from the Players Workshop of Second City (1 year of improvisational comedy classes)-1986 |

**Relevant Experience & Accomplishments**

- Helped grow current agency from $10 million to over $30 million dollars in gross billings
- Oversaw creation, growth and operation of offices in Midwest markets-Kansas City, St. Louis and Minneapolis.
- Co-founded and assisted in the creation and business development of Dome, Newmark Wolf, an award-winning Consumer Product Publicity/Promotion agency (1997-2001-sold my interest in the company in 2001)
- Currently serve on the board of Chicago's Gene Siskel Film Center of the School of the Art Institute (also a member of the GSFC's marketing committee).
- Currently serve as an advisor to the board of the Chicago Film Critics Association
- Served as the Unit Publicist on several major Hollywood film productions.
- Successful game show contestant on Classic Concentration. Appeared on 3 consecutive episodes, followed by an additional appearance on the show's Tournament of Champions during its final year of production.

| | | |
|---|---|---|
| **Employment** | **Partner, Jeross, Dempsey, and Scott** | *1998-present* |
| | **Partner,** Dome Newmark Dempsey | *1997-2001* |
| | **Partner,** Sherman Wolf Advertising | *1992-1998* |
| | **Director of Publicity and Promotions Department**, Sherman Wolf Advertising | *1989-1992* |
| | **Media Planner/Buyer,** Sherman Wolf Advertising | *1985-1989* |
| | **Assistant News Producer,** WWL-TV (New Orleans) | *1984* |
| | **Student Teacher,** "Creativity, Mass Media & Society", University Of Michigan | *1982-1983* |
| | **Student Teacher,** Modern European History, Francis W. Parker High School (Chicago) | *1977-1978* |

**Community Involvement**

**Steppenwolf Theatre**–Personally provide pro bono publicity advice and support for many of their high profile fund-raising events.

**WOOGMS Parade**–For over 15 years have provided publicity advice and coordination for this popular Chicago neighborhood "do-it-yourself" parade group (now entering it's 44th year)

**Soccer Coach**–Coached both girls and boys park district soccer teams from Kindergarten to 3rd grade level.

# David Dempsey

2611 West Dundee Road ♦ Decatur, IL 60413
630.789.4870 ♦ DavidDempsey@gmail.com

## SUMMARY

- Seasoned entertainment publicity professional with 20 years of experience working with the biggest studios and talent in Hollywood including Miramax, Sony, Tom Cruise, Will Smith and many more
- Considerable local market PR expertise cultivating relationships with all major outlets including *The Oprah Winfrey Show*, the *Chicago Tribune*, and *Ebert and Roeper*
- Dedicated new business development expertise from winning dozens of major pieces of business across entertainment and consumer product segments
- Experienced manager and business leader growing billings and revenue to the multimillion-dollar level

## *EXPERIENCE*

**JEROSS, DEMPSEY, AND SCOTT,** CHICAGO, IL, 1985–Present

**PARTNER,** 1992–Present

- Co-manage entertainment marketing agency with four Midwest offices, $28MM in billings, and 36 full-time employees
- Helped grow agency threefold from $10MM to peak of $30MM in 12 years
- Oversaw creation, growth and operations of Kansas City, Minneapolis, and St. Louis offices, handling staffing, logistics, lease negotiation, and building client-base
- Manage company's entire accounting operation with four full-time employees, managing payroll, budgeting, billing, accounts payable/receivable, and banking relationship
- Key member of new business development team helping win more than 16 new business assignments representing $32MM in billings across categories including television networks, movie studios, and theater
- Secured Sony Pictures publicity and promotion business in seven markets nationwide—company's second largest account
- Cultivated and grew Lion's Gate Films business from one market and $110MM in billings in 1992 to six markets and $450MM in billings in 2005
- Negotiated and managed breakthrough promotional tie-in between McDonald's and Paramount Pictures promoting *Star Trek Generations* movie release on tray liners in all Chicagoland McDonald's restaurants representing first-ever market specific studio tie-in for McDonald's and generating 2MM impressions
- Worked as Unit Publicist on six major films for studios including Universal, Sony, and Miramax securing appropriate media coverage with dozens of outlets
  - Unit Publicist for Miramax's *Proof* starring Anthony Hopkins and Gwyneth Paltrow, managing both media coverage and insuring actor privacy—will be listed in film credits
  - Served as Unit Publicist for Chicago production of *Derailed* starring Jennifer Aniston and Academy Award nominee Clive Owen
- Placed more than 30 clients on *The Oprah Winfrey Show* from major stars including Halle Berry, Shirley McLaine, and Samuel Jackson, to compelling human interest stories

- Pitched, promoted, and marketed proprietary Chicago James Bond Film Festival at 3 Penny Cinema dramatically increasing theater attendance
- Promoted dozens of films within the Chicago market working with major studios, Hollywood's biggest stars, and ultimately generating millions of impressions across all major media outlets

**PARTNER,** DOME NEWMARK DEMPSEY, CHICAGO, IL, 1997–2001
- Co-founded successful consumer product publicity/promotion agency
- Assisted with key new business wins on Dean Foods, City of Chicago Department of Tourism, and Wrigley division Amurol
- Agency captured several prestigious awards including Gold Star for excellence in service

**DIRECTOR OF PR/PROMOTIONS,** SHERMAN WOLF ADVERTISING, CHICAGO, IL, 1989–1992

**MEDIA PLANNER/BUYER,** SHERMAN WOLF ADVERTISING, CHICAGO, IL, 1985–1989

**ASSISTANT NEWS PRODUCER,** WWL-TV, NEW ORLEANS, LA, 1984

## AFFILIATIONS/INVOLVEMENT

- Gene Siskel Film Center–School of the Art Institute, Advisory Board, 2001–Present
- Chicago Film Critics Association, Board Advisor, 1998–Present
- Steppenwolf Theater, Pro Bono Publicist, 1996–Present
- WOOGMS, Pro Bono Publicist for Chicago's oldest parade, 1989–Present
- Colombia College, Guest Lecturer, 1999–2001
- Milford College, Guest Lecturer, Sept. 2000
- *Classic Concentration Game Show*, Tournament of Champions and two-time winner, 1986
- Student Teacher, University of Michigan, "Creativity, Media & Society" 1982–1983
- Soccer coach, boys and girls kindergarten–third grade, 2003–Present
- Second City Players Workshop Improvisational Comedy Program Graduate, 1986

## EDUCATION

**UNIVERSITY OF MICHIGAN**—ANN ARBOR, 1983
- B.A. COMMUNICATIONS

# Fifteen or More Years of Experience

Marc had more than fifteen years of experience, and his resume was out-of-date and poorly formatted. Marc needed to utilize a cleaner, more contemporary design, and he needed to seriously work on the content.

When you work in finance, it is all about the money.

Obviously, for a financial job like Marc's, any future employer would want to know how he handled the cash.

- Did he save the company money?
- Did he balance the books?
- Did he ease the flow of capital throughout the organization?
- Did he make a financial difference?

When you read Marc's original resume, you really don't know. All he did was list his job descriptions. However, when you read the *after* version, it is bursting with his fiduciary accomplishments.

From the beginning, you realize that Marc handled an extraordinary amount of work and handled it quite well. He implemented some complicated new systems, he cleared up organizational issues, and he did nontraditional things above and beyond his normal job duties. That is what a recruiting director wants to see.

Furthermore, you will notice that we eliminated much of the detail about his jobs from more than fifteen years ago. Again, no one will care about the fact that he worked on the MSA Payroll System back in 1985 at Macy's. Of course, he can list the job, but it does not need any detail at this point.

One look at the new resume and you can see Marc is the man for the job.

**Marc Pelham**

123 King Drive

New York City, NY 22441

marcp@gmail.com
(212) 348-1293   Business
(973) 577-2846   Residence
(528) 993-9988   Cellular


## PROFESSIONAL EXPERIENCE

7/01 to   Present

**Mediaedge:cia** (Intercompany transfer from Mindshare–A Wrightwood Company) 1/03–Present
PAYROLL MANAGER
**Mindshare, Inc.** (A Wrightwood Company) 7/01–12/02
MANAGER, HR & FINANCIAL SERVICES
Manage payroll process for 750 employees using Peoplesoft through 2002 and SAP from 2003 through present.
Maintain detailed salary forecast ensuring that all open positions, salary changes and transfers are aligned with budgets and client approvals.
Prepare monthly payroll journal entry.
Maintain system and data integrity ensuring that all related GAAP and Sarbanes-Oxley requirements are being satisfied.
Reconcile payroll tax and liability accounts as well as assist in cash account reconciliation.
Conduct benefits open enrollment seminars as well as assist in resolving employee welfare and retirement account issues.
Prepare Salary Planning worksheets, EEO, Towers Perrin and Workman's Compensation reports.
Assist in preparing separation agreements and contracts as well as conduct exit interviews.
Prepare query reports used for staffing and compensation analysis as well as new business presentations.
Maintain client billing rates by position and assist with profitability analysis.
Co-plan and coordinate special event such as Take Our Children to Work day, Employee Appreciation day, and Administrative Assistants day.
Recruit Junior and Mid level Finance Staff.
Assist in managing employee relations issues and employee performance review process.
Assist with New Hire Orientation process.

6/89 to   6/01

**Allison Advertising, Inc.** (A Wrightwood Company)
PARTNER, PAYROLL & TAX MANAGER
Elected Partner (Vice President) 7/96
Diversified responsibilities include significant contributions in the Payroll, Tax, Finance, Human Resources, Benefits and Compensation areas.
Payroll, Tax Filing and Finance Responsibilities
Managed 2600 employee weekly and semi-monthly multi state payrolls for 8 companies using an in-house Infinium system.
Processed employee stock option and restricted stock payments.
Processed payments to expatriates and other foreign employees, applying appropriate taxation according to contract and VISA type.
Filed sales/use tax returns as well as various other miscellaneous tax returns.
Quarterly 941, state withholding/unemployment, annual 940 and Canadian tax returns.
Participated in payroll, sales and commercial rent tax audits. Negotiated with auditors and tax collectors to reduce tax liabilities.
Created payroll journal entries including cross charges/cross credits to various overseas and domestic offices.
Reconciled payroll tax, cash and balance sheet accounts as well as cash reporting.
System configuration for W-2 and 1099R processing.

HRIS and HR Generalist roles:
Established and maintained masterfile controls including income and deduction codes to ensure correct hierarchical and tax treatment.

---

Coordinated releases installation (system updates).

Conducted system training sessions for new HR, Benefits and Payroll employees.

Recruited for all payroll staff and assisted in the recruiting process of other HR staff members.

Wrote company policies. Overtime, Vacation and Sick pay policies were personally written, received legal review and ultimately adopted.

Primary contact for Workman's Compensation, EEO, DOL compliance and audits.

Principal coordinator of the Independent vs. employee issues of policy execution and compliance.

Benefits and Compensation Contributions:

Served on the Benefits Planning committee during plan design and carrier changes.

Conducting benefits orientation for new employees.

Assisted with stock option administration.

Assisted with administration of both qualified and non-qualified deferred compensation plans.

Assisted with the development and maintenance of the Executive compensation Database.

Assisted with the annual benefits open enrollment process.


8/88 to  6/89

**Garan, Inc.**

PAYROLL SUPERVISOR

Responsible for bi-weekly Control Data payroll including all aspects of payroll tax filing.

Administrator of three pension plans.

Prepared monthly journal entries, insurance reports and bank and tax account reconciliations.


10/85 to 8/88

**Automatic Data Processing Brokerage Services Div.**

PAYROLL SUPERVISOR

Processed weekly and monthly payrolls of 1400 employees in various states.

Prepared weekly Canadian payroll.

Prepared monthly journal entries and reconciled tax, benefit and other deduction accounts.


1/85 to  10/85

**Macy's Corporate**

PAYROLL ASSISTANT

Processed weekly and bi-weekly payrolls using MSA Payroll System.

Prepared various quarterly reports.


09/80 to 12/84

**Litwin Panamerican Corp.**

PAYROLL BOOKKEEPER

Processed weekly payrolls ranging from 400 to 1000 unionized employees.

Prepared weekly payroll invoices.

Full charge bookkeeper through trial balance.

Assisted in various Human Resources and Office management functions.


**Academic Background:**

Metropolitan College of NY.  New York, NY 1987—1990. Bachelors in Business Administration. Graduated Summa Cum Laude.

City University of NY (Baruch & Brooklyn College). Part time student 1985 and 1986.

College of the Virgin Islands. Part time student 1981–1984.

# Marc Pelham

123 King Drive ♦ New York, NY 22441
212.993.9988 ♦ marcp@gmail.com

## EXPERIENCE

**WRIGHTWOOD GROUP,** New York, NY, 1989–Present
*One of the world's largest advertising/communications holding companies*

**MEDIAEDGE:CIA,** PAYROLL MANAGER, 2002–Present
**MINDSHARE, INC.,** MANAGER, HR AND FINANCIAL SERVICES, 2001–2002

- Manage entire payroll process for company with more than 850 employees
- Project lead for intense, five-month conversion from PeopleSoft to SAP overseeing all aspects of total company transfer—process typically takes at least one year
    - Rectified and reconciled 400 employee records including salary history, transactional history, and hire dates to insure successful transition
    - Managed customization of several key fields and imported all payroll data
    - Saved company thousands of dollars in consultant fees by effectively managing all aspects of the conversion
- Establishing company's first-ever temporary worker payment process impacting roughly 150 workers annually
- Recommended and secured approval for management notification of all employee status changes
- Enhanced Sarbanes-Oxley process between HR and Finance insuring compliance and dramatically improving work flow
- Building a vacation database in SAP to help automate vacation accruals for complicated internal policy with many exceptions
- Maintain detailed salary forecast for up to 60 open positions, aligning budgets and client approvals with salary changes and internal transfers
- Launched company's first-ever payroll tax reconciliation process for $2MM in monthly payroll
- Prepare semiannual salary planning worksheets distributed to upper management outlining raise eligibility for all employees
- Assist with profitability analysis insuring appropriate employee position distribution for company increasing revenue 30% in the past four years
- Maintain client billing rates for 40 positions company-wide
- Compile annual EEO, Towers Perrin, and Workman's Compensation reports
- Contribute to several projects outside the traditional realm of Payroll and Finance including: preparing separation agreements, conducting exit interviews, managing employee relations issues, planning company-wide events, and assisting with the performance review process

**ALISON ADVERTISING, INC.,** PARTNER, PAYROLL AND TAX MANAGER, 1989–2001

- Managed weekly and semimonthly multistate payrolls for 2600 employees at eight companies
- Reduced tax liabilities from $4.5MM to $100,000 by negotiating with auditors and tax collectors

- Oversaw payments, tax allocation, and employee eligibility for Ogilvy's first-ever employee stock grant for 1800 employees
- Reconciled $75MM in payroll tax, cash and balance sheet accounts, and cash reporting
- Filed $5MM in sales/use tax returns
- Supervised eligibility of annual restricted stock payments for 50 of the company's senior-most executives
- Programmed system configuration for all W-2 and 1099R processing
- Established company's first-ever masterfile controls including more than 90 income and deduction codes to ensure correct hierarchical tax treatment for entire system
- Coordinated more than 50 system updates/releases for in-house Infinium system
- Crafted independent contractor vs. employee policy, and insured compliance for 150 temporary workers annually
- Created expatriate compensation packages for 20 employees in the UK and Asia covering salary, benefits, and additional compensation
- Personally wrote and had adopted company overtime, vacation, and sick pay policies
- Conducted system training sessions for 15 new HR employees
- Served on the benefits planning committee overseeing four plan design and carrier changes
- Primary contact for Workman's Compensation, EEO, and DOL audits

**GARAN INC.,** <u>PAYROLL SUPERVISOR</u>, New York, NY, 1988–1989

**ADP SERVICES,** <u>PAYROLL SUPERVISOR</u>, New York, NY, 1985–1988

**MACY'S CORPORATE,** <u>PAYROLL ASSISTANT</u>, New York, NY, 1985

**LITWIN PANAM CORP.,** <u>PAYROLL BOOKKEEPER</u>, New York, NY, 1980–1984

## EDUCATION

**METROPOLITAN COLLEGE OF NEW YORK**—NEW YORK, 1990
Bachelor of Science in Business Administration; Summa Cum Laude Graduate

# FIRST JOB AFTER SECOND DEGREE

In the old days, you went to school and then got a job. Even if you went to grad school, it was typically right after you completed your undergraduate degree. Those days are gone.

Many people receive their undergraduate degree, work for a few years, and then return to school to get an advanced degree. Some go back so that they can move up in their industry, while others return to make a career change.

Nonetheless, after gaining an additional degree or two (or three), many people come to JobBound to help them take the next step. They just spent tens of thousands of dollars going back to school, so they cannot afford to have anything but an amazing resume.

Here are some surefire tips to make sure you get the biggest bang for your new degree buck:

## 1. Put your education first

Your new degree is now your most relevant and compelling piece of information. Your new credentials qualify you for higher positions and bigger salaries, so you want to make sure that jumps out at the recruiting director.

## 2. Include any awards, scholarships, or honors that fall under your second degree

Most professionals strip their resume of all the school details. However, since you returned to school, you want to show that you were not only a student, you were an involved and accomplished student. If you had a GPA over a 3.0, include it in the education section. Note any scholarships or distinctions you received, with a short, one-line description after the name of the award.

You do not have to go into as much detail for your undergraduate degree since it is not as relevant. You can simply list the school and the degree.

## 3. List any relevant class projects

For some graduate programs, there are classes where the students do work for real companies. Often the work you did on that class project gives you more hands-on skills in the field than your past jobs. Just because it wasn't a "job" doesn't mean you can't add it in your experience section.

• • •

Let's take a look at how to craft the perfect resume for some postgraduate candidates.

# First Job After Second Degree

Taylor wanted to parlay her MBA, which she received while working, into a new job. In the *before* version, she starts with a long, unclear summary section that does nothing for her candidacy. First of all, it is incredibly vague.

Secondly, she speaks with a lot of industry jargon that those outside of her industry might not understand. She uses words like "spot," "network," and "clearance staff."

Her education was very important to her next job, so we moved that to the top. Also, we removed her associate's degree from the resume altogether. Since she went on to get a BA and an MBA, it was not relevant that she started with an associate's degree.

The same philosophy holds true for anyone who transferred schools as an undergraduate. You only need to include the school where you received your degree.

In the *after* version, you can see a much cleaner, more compelling resume that presents Taylor as marketable to a potential employer. By starting with her MBA, she paints herself as a high achiever ready for major responsibilities.

Taylor Allen
3610 Ontario Ave.
Oakbrook, IL 59156
567-186-8870
taylor@msn.com

**OBJECTIVE**: to obtain a position in accounting utilizing strong academic background along with excellent problem solving and customer service skills.

**Summary:**
- Assist with client/product set up for spot and network.
- Assist with billing profile maintenance
- Request spot and network billing requests.
- Partner with clearance staff to ensure timely client billing.
- Partner with local office billing coordinator to ensure timely client billing.
- Detailed oriented
- Audit and Reconciliation
- Thrive on challenges and new opportunities for accomplishment and success in helping the Billing department meet their objectives.
- FileNet System
- Donovan System
- AS400
- Cash handling experience.

**Education**: **Master of Business Administration/ Emphasis in Accounting**, Bellevue University, Bellevue, NE In-Progress
**Bachelor of Business Administration/Technical Studies**, Bellevue University January 2001 GPA: **3.75/4.00**
**Associate in Applied Science in Accounting**, Nebraska college of Business, 1999

**EXPERIENCE**:
- Accounting Internship, March 1999 to June 1999, Boystown,
- Interim supervisor for Records Department. Supervised an train volunteers on various tasks in the department.
- Files invoices after they were paid.
- Coordinates and cover employee positions in five location.
- Developed and maintained effective working relationship with client's management and staff at all levels.
- Established a high level of confidentiality while working with clients and their records.
- Working on the FileNet system-entering invoices for the new indexing system that was implemented.
- Currently working for Dillard's part-time in the men's department.

**ACTIVITIES:** Church, singing in choir, walking, reading books
**Computer Skills**: Word, PowerPoint, and Excel
**Committees**: Starfish Committee, Safety Committee

# Taylor Allen

3610 Ontario Ave. • Oakbrook, IL 59156
567.186.8870 • taylor@msn.com

## Education

**Bellevue University**—Bellevue, NE, January 2008
- **Master of Business Administration**
- Accounting Emphasis
- Relevant Coursework: Marketing Strategy, Internet Marketing, Operation of Markets

**Bellevue University**—Bellevue, NE, January 2001
- **Bachelor of Business Administration**
- Technical Studies
- Overall GPA: 3.8/4.0

## Experience

**Interpublic Group (IPG),** <u>Client Biller</u>, Omaha, NE, October 2001–Present
- Helped establish billing information for more than 50 clients including Home Depot, Bally Total Fitness, and Albertsons across spot and network, TV and radio
- Coordinate accurate and timely billing of more than 100 bills monthly
- Selected by management to handle shared services volume of billing across IPG network
- Reconcile actual commercial activity with billing across more than 50 individual executions on a monthly basis
- Developing procedures manual used to facilitate invoicing and indexing process
- Liaison with a variety of internal departments, helping source dozens of historical invoices
- Work closely with IPG offices across the country coordinating invoicing information
- Requested more than $10MM in spot and network billing from more than 50 clients
- Established centralized filing system compiling more than 2,000 records from five offices nationwide

**Boys Town Executive Office,** <u>Office Assistant</u>, Omaha, NE, May 1994–May 2001
- Interim supervisor for youth records department, managing more than 500 individual files
- Supervised and trained agency volunteers in departmental operations
- Communicated with dozens of vendors and internal departments resolving order and payment billing discrepancies
- Served as "jack-of-all-trades" filling in for several employees in seven office locations

**Dillard's Department Store,** <u>Sales Associate</u>, Omaha, NE, August 2004–Present
- Work 18–20 hours per week in addition to full-time job

## Computer Skills

- Filenet, AS400, Donovan System, Microsoft Office, IOS System

# First Job After Second Degree

We had an interesting challenge with Brittany. She had just completed her MBA, and she wanted to take a different career direction. Many of her past jobs had been clerical—secretary, reservations agent, and so on. When you read her *before* resume, you get the impression that she would not be ready for a managerial position.

The *after* version is quite a bit stronger. First of all, we kick off with her MBA. That says she is ready to take on new challenges. Then, we dramatically shortened and de-emphasized many of her early jobs. We simply listed them as opposed to going into detail. Let's be honest, a recruiting director is not going to be impressed with what she accomplished as an airline reservation agent more than ten years ago.

We also did some small things like remove how many words per minute she can type. Again, that screams administrative assistant job and not management job.

# BRITTANY LYNN

925 N. Bronx #31
Boskville, IL 60412
(419) 573-7919
brittany@yahoo.com

## PROFESSIONAL EXPERIENCE

**CHICAGO BEAMS INSURANCE COMPANY**, Chicago, IL.                    2/05-6/06

*Coordinator / Construction Escrowee*

- Responsible for inputting title orders and scheduling office closings.
- Assists Title Closing Officers with coordination of documents, customer title issues and various closing functions
- Liaison between Attorneys, Lenders and/or Mortgage Brokers
- Handles office management duties; customer service inquiries; office bookkeeping.
- Cross trained as Construction Escrowee
- Managed conduction of construction escrow services; opened several new construction accounts; maintained existing construction escrow accounts
- Developed and fostered new and existing business relationships with Lenders, General Contractors and Owners of various construction projects

**CLEAR CHANNEL COMMUNICATIONS**, Chicago, IL                    7/04-1/05

*Account Executive*

- Responsible for prospecting new business and building existing client business for WNUA Radio
- Develop customized presentations for new and existing clients
- Successfully achieve sales goals as defined by management
- Maintain call volume conducive to generation of high number of fact to fact client meetings per week
- Conduct weekly maintenance of sales logs and progress reports
- Involved with sales management in continuous development of business plans which include financial and non-financial goals

**CHICAGO TRIBUNE / TRIBUNE COMPANY**, Chicago, IL                    7/01-2/04

*Advertising Sales Coordinator (2/03-2/04)*

- Provided organizational, administrative and secretarial support to Director of Advertising, Manager of Chicago Tribune Magazine and a team of sales representatives
- Acted as liaison between sales representatives and clients
- Coordinated in-paper and free standing insert ads
- Responsible for ad order entry, client schedules and processing copy changes & facilitating general client requests
- Handled distribution and maintenance of sales materials

**TRIBUNE COMPANY**

*Executive Assistant (7/01-2/03)*

- Provided executive administrative support to CEO, Vice President, President of Publishing and team of Executive Assistants
- Greeted guests and handled conference room schedules and events for executive floor
- Responsible for coordinating travel itineraries for executives, handled scheduling of corporate jet and interacted with Chief Pilot of aircraft
- Performed daily office administrative tasks and assisted with general bookkeeping
- Orchestrated special projects for executives and executed daily office management responsibilities

**UNITED AIRLINES**, Chicago, IL                                        11/98-7/01
*Reservations Sales Agent*
- Responsible for development and issuance of domestic and international airline tickets
- Coordinated changes and updates to travel itineraries and upgraded mileage credit
- Assisted customers with airport and flight operations information
- Handled high traffic customer inquiries
- Provided customer assistance to unit

**CITIBANK**, Oak Brook, IL                                             9/97-11/98
*Customer Service Representative*
- Assisted management, personal bankers and tellers with daily administrative support
- Provided assistance to customers with transactions and updated bank accounts
- Assisted Vice President of Customer Relations with coordinating company meetings and special events
- Handled general accounting functions, assisted with bookkeeping
- Created various organizational computerized documents

**SOFTWARE ARCHITECTS**, Westchester, IL                               12/96-9/97
*Administrative Assistant*
- Responsible for greeting and accommodating clients
- Answered a 15-line busy switchboard and directed calls to appropriate individuals
- Coordinated company meetings and planned special events
- Created Excel spreadsheets, PowerPoint presentations and MS Word documents on a daily basis
- Handled general accounting and light bookkeeping duties

**THE WASHINGTONIAN MAGAZINE**, Washington, DC             10/95-5/96
*Advertising Sales Assistant / Intern*
- Provided overall administrative support to sales team, including planning and implementing sales proposals
- Assisted with generating ideas for creative advertising sales campaigns
- Developed PowerPoint presentations and coordinated several graphics projects

# EDUCATION

**HOWARD UNIVERSITY**, Washington, DC
*Bachelor of Arts in Journalism*, Advertising emphasis, May 1996

**KELLER GRADUATE SCHOOL OF MANAGEMENT**, **MBA Program,** Chicago, IL
*Masters in Business Administration*, Marketing concentration, June 2008

# SKILLS

Adept at Microsoft Word, Excel, PowerPoint, Word for Macintosh, 75 wpm

# Brittany Lynn

925 N. Bronx #31 ♦ Boskville, IL 60412

419.573.7919 ♦ brittany@yahoo.com

## Education

**Keller Graduate School of Business**—Chicago, IL, June 2008

- Master's in Business Administration—Marketing concentration
- Minority MBA club member
- Earned MBA in two years while working full-time

**Howard University**—Washington, DC, May 1996

- Bachelor of Arts in Journalism—Advertising emphasis

## Experience

**Chicago Beams Insurance Company,** Coordinator, Chicago, IL, 2005–2006

- Worked with Attorneys, Lenders, Mortgage Brokers, and Title Insurance Escrow Officers facilitating $10MM in real estate transactions weekly
- Opened 25 new construction accounts monthly, helping secure $14MM in new home financing
- Branch ranked second out of eight Chicagoland offices in monthly revenue in April 2006

**Clear Channel Communications,** Account Executive, Chicago, IL, 2004–2005

- Made more than 50 new business prospecting calls daily helping secure new advertising clients for WNUA
- Successfully sold advertising packages to a variety of new companies including Nationwide Insurance, 5M Company, and CargoShipping Inc.
- Consistently exceeded all business meeting goals setting up in excess of seven sales appointments weekly

**Chicago Tribune,** Advertising Sales Coordinator/Assistant, Chicago, IL, 2001–2004

- Responsible for overseeing editing and final production of dozens of monthly fashion ads for clients including Marshall Field's, Nordstrom, and Carson Pirie Scott
- Worked as a liaison between clients and newspaper facilitating production of more than $1MM in monthly print advertising
- Confirmed production and distribution of more than 50 multipage free-standing inserts for paper's premiere fashion advertisers

**United Airlines,** Reservations Sales Agent, Chicago, IL, 1998–2001

**Citibank,** Customer Service Representative, Oak Brook, IL, 1997–1998

**Washingtonian Magazine,** Advertising Sales Assistant, Washington, DC, 1995–1996

# First Job After Second Degree

As I have mentioned before, every resume is going to be different. There are a few hard-and-fast rules, but you want to think about your resume as a unique document. How you craft your resume is based not only on what you've done, but also on what you want to do next. That's a very important question you must ask yourself: What is the next step?

We see a great example of this in Benson's resume. In virtually every resume we put together at JobBound, we list experience first and education second for professionals. However, Benson had worked for a while and then went back to get his master's in Integrated Communication at Northwestern—a great school and a nationally recognized program. Also, Benson's most recent job was as owner of a small decorating business. Since he was looking to go into marketing upon completion of the program, we decided that his education trumped his experience.

We overhauled the resume to really highlight his education. He worked on a number of client-sponsored marketing projects—real assignments from paying customers—so we expanded that section immensely. We also highlighted his summer internship since it was in the marketing field.

If you return to school to make a career change, then this is a good technique to employ. Since you are gaining relevant skills through class projects and internships, these experiences are the most important and trump your official full-time job.

This is the approach virtually every advanced degree student should take. If what you did in school is relevant—be it a class project or an internship—then list it prominently on your resume. In the rare instance where your previous job is more relevant, you can simply play that up and minimize your school experiences.

We still included Benson's most recent full-time job, but notice that it made its way onto the second page. We pulled the best of what he had done out of the experience but lessened its focus on the resume. I think you will agree that the *after* resume looks dramatically better.

Benson Bryers

5921 East Bridalwood
Brooklyn, NY. 86423
Phone: 664.654.1257
Email: bensonbryers@yahoo.com

**Summary**

- Recently completed Professional Residency for U.S. Cellular as a member of The Product Group where I developed an original internal & external communications program designed to increase revenue and loyalty from existing customers while also working with the Sales Force to deliver enhanced product value at the point of purchase
- Experienced marketing professional with a track record of successfully developing and implementing original marketing and advertising programs from budgets through creative and ROI measurement
- Advanced skill set in the following areas
  - Leadership
  - Strategic vision
  - Audience segmentation, targeting and positioning
  - Marketing mix and ROI analysis
  - Customer segmentation
  - Utilization of advertising, sales promotion, and direct marketing vehicles
  - Cross-functional team building
  - Business Case Development
  - Creative Communication Strategies

## Education

**Northwestern University, Evanston, IL**
Master of Science Candidate, Integrated Marketing Communications (IMC) December, 2006

- *Team Consulting Projects*
  - Advertising Age
  - Alamo
  - City of Evanston
  - General Mills
- Anheuser-Busch–Presented marketing plan to senior management and selected as winning team

**University of Kansas, Kansas City, MO,** 1992-1997

- Undergraduate National Honor Student
- Additional graduate level coursework completed at University of Chicago's School of Business while employed full-time

## Employment History

**Windy City Decorating, Inc., Buffalo Grove IL          7/02-7/05**
**Co-Owner**

- Increased revenue by 300% upon implementing direct marketing, online marketing, and trade co-op advertising
- Managed sub-contractor and company employees, as well as relationships with customers and vendors
- Determined client needs, estimated project costs, and ensured satisfactory delivery of services
- Fulfilled commercial and residential decorating and remodeling contracts

---

- Responsible for financial management; including escrow accounts, S-Corporation accounting, payroll, accounts receivable and payable

**Nephrology News & Issues, Tucson AZ**          **7/02-5/03**
Advertising Sales Representative (As an Independent Contractor)

- Generated advertising revenue from pharmaceutical & medical device clients for the leading medical journal serving Nephrologists and Renal Care Professionals
- Average monthly sales: 31 pages (P4C & P5C)
- Managed relationships with clients
- Assisted in facilitating production process

**Abelson-Taylor, Inc., Chicago IL**          **11/00-7/02**
**Interactive Media Manager / Media Planner**
**Clients: Abbott, Amgen, Biogen, Eli-Lilly, Genentech, Solvay, Takeda and TAP**

- Responsible for the planning, implementation, and ROI measurement of media campaigns
- Developed and implemented online surveys to gain target audience insight for pitches
- Developed HIPPA compliant database for product website in conjunction with IT
Assisted Product Management in the development of advertising budgets
- Supervised Media Coordinator and Buyer
- Regularly presented Product Management with Media proposals and competitive analysis
- Knowledgeable regarding the regulatory measures affecting healthcare marketing

**Classified Ventures, Inc., Chicago IL**          **10/99-11/00**
**(Now Tribune Interactive)**
**Apartments.com**
**Marketing & E-Commerce Analyst**

- Consistently ranked #1 real estate website according to Nielsen and Media Metrix
- Managed multimillion-dollar marketing budgets
- Developed, implemented and evaluated marketing plans in team environment
- Used various communication vehicles to reach both business & consumer customers
- Aided in the development of sales promotion communication for trade show and other sales force distribution
- Negotiated opportunistic marketing and business development agreements with Yahoo, AOL and other online brands
- Tracked and presented competitive information, capital budgeting and performance reports to chief corporate officers
- Participated in the design, implementation and interpretation of focus groups
- Coordinated affiliate marketing programs

**Market Facts, Inc., Arlington Heights IL**          **12/98-10/99**
**Sampling Analyst**
**Clients: Clorox, Ralston Purina, Procter & Gamble, Pillsbury and Seagram's**

- Assisted in the development of marketing research studies designed to measure current usage, purchase intent, brand satisfaction, and pre-market product testing
- Selected samples from a population representative panel for inclusion in telephone, mail, Internet and focus group research

# Benson Bryers

5921 East Bridalwood ◆ Brooklyn, NY 86423
664.654.1257 ◆ bensonbryers@yahoo.com

## SUMMARY

- Seasoned marketing executive with eight years' experience developing integrated communication plans across both traditional and nontraditional media vehicles
- Extensive experience in market research having developed, executed, and analyzed dozens of qualitative and quantitative studies reaching tens of thousands of consumers
- Strategic business analyst with strong background developing business cases, determining ROI, and interpreting quantitative data for brands including US Cellular, General Mills, and Genentech
- Master's degree from Northwestern University's acclaimed Integrated Marketing Communications program

## EDUCATION

**NORTHWESTERN UNIVERSITY—EVANSTON, IL, December 2006**
- Master of Science in Integrated Marketing Communications (IMC); Overall GPA 3.6/4.0

**Client-Sponsored Consulting Projects**
*Alamo Rental Car*
- Developed business case analyzing metrics for rental car leisure travelers supporting market segmentation as part of 11-week intensive group project
- Selected as project team leader and presented findings to Alamo Chief Marketing Officer delivering winning presentation among 6 competing teams

*Anheuser-Busch*
- Conducted extensive qualitative and quantitative research gauging interest in beer category advertising for experimental AB initiative
- Developed fully integrated program to target consumers and trade to drive beer category sales
- Team placed first at presentation to Anheuser-Busch SVP of Marketing

*General Mills*
- Segmented database of 2.5 million consumers creating four user groups with unique messaging
- Recommendations intended to drive coupon redemption and enhance customer retention

**UNIVERSITY OF CHICAGO BUSINESS SCHOOL—CHICAGO, IL, 2001–2002**
- Took marketing classes Strategic Tools for Marketers, and Advanced Marketing Management

**ROOSEVELT UNIVERSITY—CHICAGO, IL, 1997**
- Bachelor of Arts in Psychology; English/Journalism Minor; Overall GPA 3.7/4.0

## EXPERIENCE

**PRODUCT GROUP INTERN, US CELLULAR, Chicago, IL, Summer 2006**
- Developed a comprehensive awareness program called *New Release Tuesday* promoting **easy**edge suite of new release downloadable data programs

- Determined marketing direction for **easy**edge by marrying market segmentation data for 1.4 million customers with market trends and product usability information
- Expanded awareness campaign to encompass both customer loyalty/retention and churn reduction dramatically enhancing product scope
  - Program launching 10/2/06 in more than 1,500 stores and to 1.2 million existing customers
  - Created internal marketing component for 350 Retail Sales Associates nationwide
- Relaunched and overhauled website www.easyedge.com for 12/1/06 launch

**CO-OWNER**, WINDY CITY DECORATING, INC., Buffalo Grove, IL, 2002–2005
- Increased company revenue 300% in one year after launching integrated direct, online, and trade marketing efforts
- Developed company's first-ever direct marketing campaign targeted to 9,800 high potential households generating 3% response rate
- Managed a team of more than 15 subcontractors and company employees across dozens of projects annually
- Responsible for all company financial management spanning escrow accounts, S-corporation accounting, payroll, and accounts receivable and payable

**MEDIA MANAGER/PLANNER**, ABELSON-TAYLOR, Chicago, IL, 2000–2002
*Abbott, Amgen, Biogen, Eli Lilly, Genentech, Solvay, Takeda, and TAP*
- Planned, implemented, and measured ROI for 13 media campaigns reaching more than 100,000 physicians nationwide
- Developed and analyzed online surveys among thousands of participants to glean target audience insights for winning Genentech and Takeda new business pitches
  - Genentech's Herceptin pitch surveyed 15,000 breast cancer patients with embedded links in 33 different websites and insured highly confidential HIPPA compliance
- Played critical strategic role in consumer research, marketing plan development, and ROI analysis for Herceptin helping generate $8.5MM in incremental revenue for revolutionary breast cancer drug
- Convinced client to launch eight page insert for Amgen's Aranesp—largest ad ever placed by a drug company in a medical journal—in 15 physician magazines exceeding industry average ROI by 29%

**MARKETING & E-COMMERCE ANALYST**, CLASSIFIED VENTURES, Chicago, IL, 1999–2000
- Developed $10MM fully integrated marketing plan for Nielsen's number one real estate website now known as Tribune Interactive
- Negotiated and executed dozens of opportunistic marketing and business development agreements with Yahoo, AOL, and other leading internet companies
- Coordinated affiliate marketing programs with Performix and Cool Savings establishing partnerships with existing Tribune Corporation online content providers
- Created proprietary sales collateral material helping outline sell points for 70-person sales force representing six of the largest newspaper conglomerates in the US

**SAMPLING ANALYST**, MARKET FACTS, INC., Arlington, Heights, IL, 1998–1999
*Procter & Gamble, Clorox, Pillsbury, Seagram's, Ralston Purina*
- Assisted in the development of more than 50 marketing research studies designed to measure usage, purchase intent, brand satisfaction, and pre-market product testing among thousands of consumers
- Selected samples from a population representative panel for inclusion in telephone, mail, Internet, and focus group research across the nation

# First Job After Second Degree

Jessica's resume was all over the place. She had done some teaching in the past, and she had returned to get an advanced degree in education. She also had some random jobs on her resume unrelated to what she wanted to pursue.

We kicked off her resume with a very direct and concise objective. To reinforce her objective, we followed it with her extensive education and credentials.

We did a much better job of highlighting what she actually accomplished in her previous positions. For instance, look at her first job. She just laid out some random phrases about plant tags. When we dug deeper, we found out she had done some fairly impressive tasks, especially as they related to work ethic. We included the number of hours she worked while going to school to highlight her dedication and initiative.

Finally, we included an activities and interests section that highlighted some of her incredible not-for-profit and teaching experiences.

Jessica Janowitz
84 Jasper Street
Jericho Springs, CO 348971
445.814.6421
JessicaJanowitz@msn.com

**Objective:**

To empower students to realize their full potential in our global community and to instill the
excitement and inspiration of learning both in and beyond the classroom.

**Education:**

**Colorado Christian University, Lakewood, Colorado**
Currently enrolled in MACI, Master of Arts in Curriculum and Instruction
Anticipated graduation, late in 2005

**Colorado Christian University, Lakewood, Colorado**
Bachelor of Science in Organizational Management in Christian Leadership
December 2004
GPA: 3.79

**Virginia College, Huntsville, Alabama**
Associate of Science Degree in Network Engineering
June 2002
GPA: 4.00
President's Award for Academic Excellence

**Experience:**

**Gulley's Garden Center, May 2005 to present**
- Maintain inventory for plant tags
- Organize inventory for plant tags
- Transplant and propagate plants

**Celestica Corporation, Colorado, 4/04 to 5/05**
- Mechanical Assembly, Hand loading
- Configure to Order Shipments
- Functional Testing, Electrical Circuit Testing

**Virginia College—Administrative Assistant to Academic Dean, 9/02–7/03**
  **Network Administrator's Assistant, 4/00–5/02**
  **Library Assistant, 4/00–5/02**
- Maintained personnel files for faculty and students, general office procedures
- Proctored computerized and online testing, administered online orientation
- Compiled faculty evaluations, data processing into Word and Excel documents
- Established professional and personal relationships with staff, faculty and students
- Maintained the highest level of confidentiality
- Accomplished and advanced organizational skills

- Detail oriented
- Motivator
- Worked unsupervised
- Built and maintained entire population of computers at Virginia College as Network Assistant
- PC support, updating, configuring, troubleshooting, general maintenance of computers
- Assisted in circulation duties and student research in library, worked in bookstore
- Ability to handle several tasks with efficiency and tact
- Flexible and assumes responsibilities as needed

## Federal Programs, Hunts City Schools—92–93, 02

- Reorganized Native American Education Office in local school system
- Prepared and planned for new curriculum changes due to NCLB directive
- Created new work environment
- Justified inventory, updated computers and files
- Worked unsupervised for duration of government contract
- Planned curriculum and instruction for classes given in K-12 in areas of Native American culture, history, and education
- Assisted in preparing high school students for college and in finding scholarships for their higher education
- Prepared and participated in Native American Festivals and Pow Wows

## Natrona County School System, Casper, Wyoming—Resource Assistant, 8/94–10/99

- Assisted in individualized teaching, encouraging, testing and in the supervising of emotional, behavioral, social, educational and physical growth of special needs students
- Taught Native American history and culture classes to several 4th. Grades in system

## Many Moccasins, Owner, 86–99

- Replication of museum quality Native American artifacts
- Initially, hired half-way house Native Americans to make products
- Eventually, hired identified Native American college student to create products
- Wholesale business selling to numerous museums and retail stores both in the United States and throughout the world

## Certifications in Networking

- A+
- Net+
- MCP
- Experience in Novell and Cisco Routing

# Jessica Janowitz

84 Jasper Street ♦ Jericho Springs, CO 34897
445.814.6421 ♦ JessicaJanowitz@msn.com

## OBJECTIVE

- To obtain a position in Student Affairs at an accredited higher-education institution

## EDUCATION

**COLORADO CHRISTIAN UNIVERSITY**—Lakewood, CO, May 2006
- Master of Arts in Curriculum and Instruction
- Overall GPA 3.8/4.0

**COLORADO CHRISTIAN UNIVERSITY**—Lakewood, CO, December 2004
- Bachelor of Science in Organizational Management and Christian Leadership
- Overall GPA 3.8/4.0

**VIRGINIA COLLEGE**—Huntsville, AL, June 2002
- Associate of Science in Network Engineering
- Overall GPA 4.0/4.0
- President's Award for Excellence in Academics

## EXPERIENCE

**GULLEY'S GARDEN CENTER,** Loveland, CO, May 2005–Present
- Computerized all processes for inventory tracking more than 1,000,000 tags placed in plants
- Overhauled all systems for procurement, distribution, and tracking of tags
- Work 40 hours per week while attending school full time

**CELESTICA CORPORATION,** Loveland, CO, April 2004–May 2005
- Worked 40 hours per week while attending school full-time to finance college education
- Performed final system checks on more than $75M of bridges, switches and routers monthly

**VIRGINIA COLLEGE,** Huntsville, AL, April 2000–July 2003
*Academic Dean's Assistant/Network Administrator's Assistant/Library Assistant*
- Maintained, upgraded, and oversaw more than 300 student and faculty computers and other hardware/software
- Administered and proctored hundreds of online tests
- Conducted more than 100 online, in-person, and over-the-phone school orientations
- Reorganized and streamlined operations for Academic Dean resulting in dramatically enhanced production
- Entered entire library book inventory into new computerized software program, helping expedite check-in/check-out process

### FEDERAL PROGRAMS, HUNTS CITY SCHOOLS, Hunts, AL, 1992–1993, 2002
*Indian Education Teacher*
- Orchestrated new curriculum changes, supplying resources for more than 40 public schools
- Justified $500,000 in inventory including library of 1,000 books
- Helped prepare more than 100 high school students for college and for securing higher education scholarships
- Planned Native American culture, history and education instruction for K–12 classes in 45 schools

### MANY MOCCASINS, Littleton, CO, 1986–1999
*Owner/President*
- Started and ran wholesale business selling replications of museum quality Native American artifacts to 10 museums and 200 retailers both in the US and in Europe
- Grew sales to a peak of $200,000 annually and managed a staff of 15 employees
- Hired, trained, and supervised Native Americans both from halfway houses and from college to make and distribute products
- Managed purchasing for a full range of more than 50 Native American products

### NATRONA COUNTY SCHOOL SYSTEM, Casper, WY, August 1994–October 1999
- Taught Native American history and culture to 4th grade students in 10 elementary schools
- Worked individually with more than 100 special needs children

## ACTIVITIES/SKILLS/INTERESTS

- Vice-President, Nancy Gosslyn Breast Cancer Foundation
- Board Member, Denver Indian Center
- Vice-President, Eagle Lodge Halfway House for Alcoholic Native Americans
- Volunteer, American Cancer Society
- Network Certified in A+, Net+, MCP, and experienced in Novell and Cisco Routing
- Interests include: outdoor activities, crafts, quilting, scrapbooking, singing, and dancing

# FROM STUDENT
# TO PROFESSIONAL

This is it. The big step. It's time for the "show." I'm sure you've heard all the catchy taglines—from classroom to boardroom, from backpack to briefcase. If you have made the move into the working world, you will agree wholeheartedly that life changes a great deal. Your resume is no exception.

Once you start that first job, it is time to change the order of your resume. Your education is no longer your most relevant credential. I know—it's sad, isn't it? You won't be defined exclusively by where you went to college.

As a professional, the first section on your resume should now be experience, and education should drop to the bottom. By placing your experience first, you will make yourself look less like an entry-level candidate vying for an entry-level job.

As we have mentioned before, if you have less than four years of experience, you should have a one-page resume. When you move along further in your career, your college activities become less and less important. Let's be honest, when you're a twenty-six-year-old, not many employers will care that you were captain of the intramural broomball champions six years ago.

You can remove all of your collegiate clubs, honors, activities, and even internships—unless they are very relevant to what you want to do. We've included a couple examples to help you make a smooth transition from student resume to professional resume.

# From Student to Professional

We helped Teresa with her resume when she was graduating from college. After she had a couple years of experience, we freshened up her resume.

We assisted Teresa with the transition from college student to young professional. When you look at Teresa's *before* resume, you assume she is a college student. I know it's hard to give up the past—especially when it was the great days of college—but this is a bad strategy if you want a well-paying job. Too much college on a resume reinforces the notion that you're not ready for the big leagues. Recruiting directors want to hire the most qualified candidates that they can. By starting your resume with a full-time job, you indicate that you have the seasoning to take on a greater challenge.

We also trimmed Teresa's resume down and eliminated many of her college internships. Again, once you have been working for a while, you can pull back from most of your college activities. I would recommend that after about four years you take everything out other than your education. By pulling those collegiate experiences out, you appear less like an entry-level candidate.

# Teresa Townsend

teresa@aol.com ♦ 24 East Tillman Street ♦ Tinseltown, TX 48378 ♦ 678.128.9427

## Objective
To obtain a position in marketing or advertising

## Education
**Bradley University–Peoria, IL: May 2008**
Bachelor of Arts in Communication
Photography concentration
London, England program participant, winter 2003

## Experience
**Account Manager/Project Coordinator,** Burkhart Cain Associates 2004–Present
- Conceptualized, developed and managed multiple client projects totaling over 62% of the firm's gross billing
- Photographed and directed artwork for 150+ projects including print production for collateral pieces and media
- Facilitated vendor/ client relationships
- Managed account for the third largest homebuilder in Indiana with annual gross billings of 4.3 million dollars
- Managed senior retirement community regional campaigns encompassing five states in the Midwest
- Established a new organizational process to help internal structure and work flow
- Managed all client campaigns to ensure placement and deadlines of design and media

**Marketing/Photography Intern,** The Children's Museum of Indianapolis, summer 2003
- Published photograph in November 2003 issue of *Child* magazine with a circulation of 900,000
- Overhauled department's photographic archive system containing more than 40,000 images
- Helped manage $15,000 studio transformation from a film to a digital environment
- Shot and produced eight photographs published in bi-monthly magazine, distributed to over 1,000 donors
- Took dozens of museum pictures used for marketing materials including flyers, direct mail and newsletters

**Photography Intern,** Jewish Federation of Indianapolis, Summer 2002
- Shot several photographs promoting organization's services for fundraising efforts
- Published photographs in monthly newsletters and direct mail pieces used over a two year period
- Efforts held fundraising increase 20% in 2002

**National Extension Team Member,** Sigma Delta Tau Sorority, Carmel, IN, fall 2003
- Selected to work with national sorority headquarters to help launch and transition new chapters nationwide
- Helped establish chapters of the sorority at College of Charleston and Purdue University with over 24 members each
- Organized and submitted incorporation materials to National Panhellenic Conference

**Photography Exhibits,** Peoria, Illinois and Indianapolis, Indiana 2004–2005
- "Dunn through the Lens" a contemporary fine art photographic exhibition of over 30 pieces on display for a month and reviewed in Nuvo magazine a weekly arts publication in the metro Indianapolis area

## Activities/ Interests
- Actress, Singer, Dancer, Indianapolis / Peoria Community Theater, 1996–Present
- Member/Artist Indianapolis Art Center
- Scholarship Chair, Recruitment Chair, member, Sigma Delta Tau Sorority, 2001–Present
- Prevent Child Abuse America, Make a Wish Foundation Volunteer, 2000–Present
- Interests include, singing, traveling, cooking and hot air ballooning

# Teresa Townsend
24 East Tillman Street • Tinseltown, TX 48378
Teresa@aol.com • 678.128.9427

## Experience
**Account Manager,** Burkhart Cain Associates, Indianapolis, IN, 2004–Present
- Managed creative development and execution for more than 10 key agency clients spanning categories including finance, professional services, home building, and state agencies
  - Lead creative team in development of fully integrated campaigns across direct mail, promotions, public relations, outdoor, radio, television, print, and more
  - Personally responsible for clients totaling 62% of agency's billing
- Photographed and directed artwork for 150+ projects including print production for collateral pieces and media consisting of print, television, radio and outdoor advertising
- Oversaw account for the third largest home builder in Indiana with annual gross billings of $4.3 MM
  - Doubled average monthly sales for highly successful Davis Homes 48 hour sale campaign
- Coordinated all efforts for senior retirement community regional campaigns encompassing five states in the Midwest
  - Managed "Where Have the Seniors Gone" integrated campaign resulting in 67% preoccupancy rate
- Overhauled creative workflow process dramatically increasing efficiency and accountability for all client work
- Promoted from Project Coordinator in only nine months

**Photography Exhibits,** Peoria, IL and Indianapolis, IN, 2004–2006
- "A New Slant on Indy" a digitally manipulated exploration of architecture throughout Indianapolis
- "Dunn through the Lens" a contemporary fine art photographic exhibition of over 30 pieces on display for a month and reviewed in *Nuvo* magazine—a weekly arts publication in the metro Indianapolis area

**Marketing/Photography Intern,** The Children's Museum of Indianapolis, Summer 2003
- Published photograph in November 2003 issue of *Child* magazine with a circulation of 900,000
- Overhauled department's photographic archive system containing more than 40,000 images
- Helped manage $15,000 studio transformation from a film to a digital environment
- Shot and produced eight photographs published in bimonthly museum magazine, distributed to over 1,000 donors and members
- Took dozens of museum pictures used for marketing materials including flyers, direct mail and newsletters

## Education
**Bradley University—Peoria, IL,** May 2008
- Bachelor of Arts in Communication
- Photography concentration
- London, England program participant, winter 2003

## Activities / Interests
- Actress, Singer, Dancer, Indianapolis / Peoria Community Theater, 1996–Present
- Member/Artist Indianapolis Art Center
- Scholarship Chair, Recruitment Chair, member, Sigma Delta Tau Sorority, 2001–Present
- Prevent Child Abuse America, Make a Wish Foundation Volunteer, 2000–Present
- Interests include, singing, traveling, cooking and hot air ballooning

# From Student to Professional

It was time for Rachael to grow up.

It isn't until you've read half of the first page of her *before* resume that you realize she's no longer in college. That's certain to doom her chances from the get-go.

Recruiting directors read resumes just like you read anything—top to bottom. Since we've established earlier that you only get about a ten- to fifteen-second scan, you want to make sure to get your reader from the top. Plenty of resumes get pitched in less than five seconds because recruiting directors don't like what they see in the beginning.

I promise you, many of them threw away this resume before they got to the fact that Rachael was a very qualified account executive candidate.

If Rachael is applying for a position as an account executive, then obviously what makes her marketable is her other account executive job. However, when I read this resume, I discover that Rachael was a sorority activities chair back in 1998 before I get to the fact that she's currently an experienced candidate with great relevant accomplishments.

We put it in order, got it on one page, and landed Rachael a job!

# Rachael Rainer

9521 West Roscoe Street, Unit R
Rockford, IL 60204
rachaelrainer@msn.com
213-882-2938

**OBJECTIVE**  Seeking position to apply solid communication and interpersonal skills to the design, development and implementation in an advertising environment. Background and training facilitate a career involving team and interactive situations; conflict resolution; and the ability to overcome challenges and function effectively in diverse, fast-paced environments.

**EDUCATION**  Indiana University, Bloomington, Indiana. Bachelor of Arts Degree (Graduation: May, 2001)
Overall G.P.A. 3.3 / 4.0. Major: Psychology ; Minor: Criminal Justice ; Concentration: Business (Marketing)

Dean's List Fall 2000 (3.5 G.P.A. and above)

Overseas Study Program: Drake University, in affiliation with The Institute for Italian Studies, Florence, Italy (Spring Semester 2000). Completed 12 credit hours of course work. Overall G.P.A. 3.18/4.0.

**LEADERSHIP**  Delta Delta Delta Sorority (January 1998 to May 2001). Offices have included Sorority Rush Party Chair (1999-2000) (orchestrated and managed event to best display house amenities and generate interest in a highly competitive environment); Sorority Winter Formal Chair (1999) (led teams responsible for planning, coordinating, and managing all aspects of annual formal dinner); and Sorority Activities Chair (1998-1999) (collaborated with various fraternities to plan social events; coordinated Homecoming Week activities; and directed house participation in university wide Dance Marathon event).

Panhellenic Association Rho Chi Representative (September 1999-January 2000)
Chosen from 500 applicants as one of 87 student liaisons in the university-wide sorority rush program. Provided leadership, direction and counseling to 25 rushing students, facilitating decision making, reducing anxieties, and ensuring that each student met critical deadlines in a high pressure situation.

## PROFESSIONAL EXPERIENCE

11/04-present  WUNDERMAN, Chicago, IL–ACCOUNT EXECUTIVE, Burger King Account—

7/03-11/04  WUNDERMAN, Chicago, IL–ASSISTANT ACCOUNT EXECUTIVE, Burger King Account—

2/03-7/03  DRAFT, Chicago, IL–ASSISTANT ACCOUNT EXECUTIVE, Burger King Account–Develop estimates and timelines for client. Create job description briefs for internal review. Act as a liaison between client, account and creative teams making sure all needs are fulfilled. Assist franchisees and client partners in acquiring artwork from the agency. Prepare research before and throughout project cycle. Follow up with proper contacts to provide the expected results to projects. Provide support to account team members. Build relationships with members of the Burger King field offices and ensure their requests are completed.

8/01-2/03  CDW Government Inc., Chicago, IL–STATE, LOCAL & EDUCATION ACCOUNT MANAGER—Negotiate and coordinate computing solutions for government and educational institutions. Establish and maintain relationships with new and repeat clients. Promote and advertise company's product line to over 400 prospective clients per week. Continuous review and training of current technology and network design. Completed extensive training.

Spring 2000    Indiana University–RESEARCH ASSISTANT—Assistant to social psychology professor 7 hours per week. Administer tests; and meet with graduate student and professor to synthesize results and analyze findings.

Summer 2000    JAM Productions, Ltd., Chicago, Illinois–INTERN—Variety of activities in intense, fast-paced entertainment environment: assisted event and budget coordinators in organizing plans for corporate and
concert events, researched and located equipment and specialty items for events, prepared revised production schedules. Managed organization at events with duties including pre-show setup, talent stage manager, special needs assistant. Performed office duties as needed, such as receptionist and proofreading sales proposals and legal contracts.

Summers    Green Acres Country Club, Northbrook, Illinois–LIFEGUARD (1998); ASSISTANT POOL MANAGER/LIFEGUARD (1999)—Selected to oversee crew of 15 and serve as liaison to patrons. Worked with manager in clarifying and enforcing safety/use policies, encouraging teamwork and reducing potential conflicts.

# Rachael Rainer

9521 West Roscoe Street Unit R ♦ Rockford, IL 60204
213.882.2938 ♦ rachaelrainer@msn.com

## EXPERIENCE

**WUNDERMAN**, ACCOUNT EXECUTIVE—BURGER KING, Chicago, IL, July 2003–Present
- Manage six creative/production projects and an annual budget of $4MM
- Oversaw complete menu board revamp test across 115 stores in four markets nationwide
  - Wrote creative brief resulting in three separate concepts tested among 600 consumers in focus groups
  - Led production of 75 POS elements with a budget in excess of $1MM
  - Successful test led to additional day-part exploration and expansion
- Spearheaded all aspects of 15 tests, spanning feasibility tests, ops tests, market tests, and ultimate national rollout
  - Successfully launched Chicken Fries throughout entire US resulting an increase of $3MM
  - Introduced Enormous Omelet Sandwich exceeding initial sales performance by $550,000
- Work closely with more than a dozen key cross-functional Burger King clients across product categories including breakfast, desserts, burgers, salads, chicken, and fish
- Partnered with promotional teams at the NFL, AOL, Sprint, FOX TV, and Nickelodeon, launching integrated in-store programs in 7,900 restaurants
- Lead creative development and production on 5–10 national projects monthly with up to 50 POS pieces each
- Worked with internal event marketing team to launch new Chicken Baguette sampling program
- Promoted from AAE in November 2004

**DRAFT**, ASSISTANT AE—BURGER KING, Chicago, IL, February 2003–July 2003
- Helped develop, produce, and launch several new POS projects rolled out nationwide
- Prepared comprehensive competitive analysis tracking all promotional activity for QSR companies including McDonald's, Wendy's and Subway
- Developed artwork for dozens of coupon books requested by franchisees across the country

**CDW GOVERNMENT INC.**, ACCOUNT MANAGER, Chicago, IL, August 2001–February 2003
- Sold $250,000 annually in computer equipment to state, local, and educational organizations

**JAM PRODUCTIONS, LTD.**, INTERN, Chicago, IL, Summer 2000

## EDUCATION

**INDIANA UNIVERSITY**—Bloomington, IN, 2001
- B.A. in Psychology; Criminal Justice Minor; Business Concentration
- Overall GPA 3.3/4.0
- Dean's List Fall 2000

**ITALIAN STUDIES INSTITUTE/DRAKE UNIVERSITY**—Florence, Italy, Spring 2000
- Studied communications and Italian culture

# From Student to Professional

Maria's resume shows us an excellent example of a student resume. In her *before* version, she begins her resume with her education even though that is no longer the most relevant information.

Often, JobBound clients will ask when they should remove their college internships, jobs, or activities from a resume. The answer is typically as soon as you can. You certainly can keep on some relevant internships for a few years after you graduate. In Maria's case, do we really care that she was a member of the marketing club in college more than five years ago? The answer is no.

In her *after* version, you notice that we removed her college experiences except for one internship she held while at school. Recruiting directors are going to be most interested in your most recent jobs and your full-time work experience.

# Maria Martinez

901 W. Michigan Street #9M · Mansionville, MI 38913
789.256.1221 · maria@aol.com

## Career Objective

**ACCOUNT EXECUTIVE:** To obtain an entry level position where strong communication skills, networking abilities, strong personal drive, and high productivity are important. Interested in utilizing bilingual skills in Spanish within a fast paced team oriented work environment.

## Education

**INDIANA UNIVERSITY, Kelley School of Business, Bloomington, Indiana,** Bachelor of Science in Business, Marketing and International Studies majors and Spanish minor, May 2004. Course work includes finance, accounting, marketing research, technology, statistics, and Spanish.

**UNIVERSITY OF SYDNEY, Institute for Study Abroad Program,** Sydney, Australia, February-July 2003. Course work includes gender studies, Australian government, and indigenous studies.

## Skills

**COMPUTER:** Microsoft Office, SPSS, Photoshop, and the Internet.
**LANGUAGE:** Fluent in Spanish.

## Activities

**PHILANTHROPY CHAIRWOMAN, Apparel Merchandising Organization (AMO),** Indiana University, May 2001-May 2002. Organize and promote all philanthropy activities for AMO throughout the year with activities to include clothing drive, car wash, and holiday gift basket preparation/delivery.

**MEMBER, Undergraduate Marketing Club,** Kelley School of Business, Indiana University, September 2000-present. Attend job fairs and presentations given by major corporations; participate in community service activities and social events.

## Experience

**FINELIGHT, Strategic Marketing Communications** Bloomington, IN 09/02- present. Marketing Associate/Quality Control Manager Listen to pre-recorded appointments in Spanish and translate to English while evaluating for quality as well as place calls to potential clients to explain benefits of Elderplan Health Care.

**WET SEAL INC., Arden B.,** Paramus, NJ 12/01-02/02. Sales Associate Attempt to reach an assigned daily target sales amount, responsible for visual merchandising, and locate merchandise using the company wide inventory system.

**NICOLE MILLER** Short Hills, NJ 05/01-08/01. Sales Associate Schedule appointments, create a customer contact program and form a customer base give fashion advice, assist in visual merchandising, create and design window displays, and supervise sales floor. Attempt to reach an assigned sales dollar goal and record actual sales amount daily.

**THE TRICARICO GROUP** Wayne, NJ 11/99-08/00. Accounting Department Representative Organize invoices and architectural drawings for the firm's many retail accounts. Post in the computer charges for faxes, photo copies, and office supplies, and prepare accounts receivable reports.

# Maria Martinez

901 W. Michigan Street, # 9M ♦ Mansionville, MI 38913
789.256.1221 ♦ maria@yahoo.com

## Experience

**Kalamazoo Logistics,** Account Executive—Sales, Strom, MI, July 2004–Present

- Generated more than $250,000 in company revenue from selling nationwide transportation services for one of the world's largest third-party logistics corporations
- Managed more than 200 transactions totaling $450,000 across 75 vendors throughout the country
- Sourced, developed, and nurtured solid relationships with 18 different transportation carriers ultimately representing 80% of personal business
- Ranked second out of 24 sales representatives in four-month contest to create relationships with trucking companies
- Work closely with internal team of dozens of customer reps helping secure freight routes
- Negotiate more than 50 transactions weekly covering all aspects of product shipping including total cost, delivery times, layovers, and rerouting
- Handle over 900 calls weekly
- Utilize foreign language skills on a daily basis working with dozens of Spanish-speaking customers
- Navigate highly complex dual-computer software system tracking 3.2MM transactions daily
- Effectively troubleshoot, resolving dozens of logistical problems during a typical week

**Finelight,** Marketing Associate, Bloomington, IN, September 2003–May 2004

- Made 600 calls qualifying leads and securing appointments for supplemental health care for Medicare patients
- Consistently exceeded company weekly appointment and sales goals
- Evaluated prerecorded Spanish appointments checking for quality control and overall potential customer qualification
- Worked 15+ hours per week while maintaining full course load

## Education

**Indiana University**—Bloomington, May 2004

- Double Major—BS in Marketing and International Business; Minor in Spanish
- Kelly School of Business

**University of Sydney**—Australia, Spring 2003

- Studied Australian government and indigenous culture

## Skills/Activities

- Fluent in Spanish
- All About Dance, Performance Dancer, 2005–Present
  - Performed at Chicago Storm games, Sheffield Garden Walk, and other Chicago events
- Boys and Girls Club of Chicago, Associate Board Volunteer, 2005–Present

# STUDENT RESUME

Student resumes are arranged a little differently, but they follow the same basic guidelines that apply to professionals. You want to focus on specifics and accomplishments. There are hundreds of thousands of college students graduating each year vying for the same jobs. If you want to stand out, you have to market your achievements. For a student, the education should be listed first, and it should be more detailed than the education section in a professional resume. Here are a few basic guidelines for the education section:

## 1. School name first in bold font, followed by city, state and graduation date or anticipated graduation year

- **Dartmouth College**—Hanover, NH, May 2009

## 2. Degree, major, minor, emphasis, concentration, and so forth

- Bachelor of Arts in Journalism; Advertising Major, Media Minor

## 3. GPA

- GPA should only have *one* number after the decimal point. No one wants your GPA carried out to the ten-thousandth percentile!
- If your GPA is 4.0—good for you! Obviously you can list it as 4.0.
- If your GPA is 3.95–3.99, do not round up to 4.0.
- If your GPA is a 3.2 or above, include it; if it is lower, then leave it off.

## 4. List dean's list, honors, awards, and scholarships. Remember to explain any awards or scholarships

- Phi Eta Sigma National Honor Society, membership granted based on superior academics

## 5. Structure study abroad the same as a college entry

• • •

When it comes time to write the experience section of a student resume, it's important to expand the definition of experience. "Experience Required." This is a requirement that plagues many college students. We hear comments like "Every job or internship I apply for says they want someone with experience, so how can I ever get that first job or internship?"

The key is to expand the definition of what is considered experience. Most students think experience comes only from working at a paid job. The truth is you can get great real-world experience from a variety of areas including extracurricular activities, coursework, and even mundane summer jobs.

When you write about your experience, the key is to focus on those transferable skills. Almost any company out there is looking for college students with leadership, initiative, and the ability to solve problems and work with others. They can teach you the details and hard skills for the job; they want to find students with strong raw materials.

In your experience section, don't limit your experience to retail jobs. Did you ever hold a leadership position in a college club? It could have been student government, a sorority, or even the comic book club. The fact that you were selected by your peers to lead an organization is significant. What you did as a leader is also key to this experience. Did you increase membership? Did you overhaul the finances? Did you create a publicity plan that generated coverage by a local paper?

These are the types of skills employers are craving. Don't be afraid to tell them what you have accomplished.

The same goes for meaningful course projects. Don't simply list your classes under a section called "Relevant Coursework." Pick one or two cool class projects and highlight them in your experience section. Again, don't just list the project, but write about your accomplishments.

By expanding your definition of experience and by really highlighting your specific accomplishments, you'll be able to set yourself apart and land a great internship!

Check out the following resume to see how we packaged and marketed one student.

# Student Resume

Tiffany's *before* resume is a classic student resume. First, you can tell she used one of those horrible resume templates. Beware of the resume template! I have never seen a good one, and they can be a nightmare if you need to change anything. The template has too much white space, and right-side indentations are too large.

You will also notice that Tiffany used "I" and long sentences instead of short bullet points. Writing sentences makes the most important part of the resume—the experience—cluttered and difficult to read.

To make space for more important details relating to Tiffany's experience, we removed less significant information such as the list of her coursework and the separate section for accomplishments. Of course, you know your entire resume should be full of accomplishments, not just one designated section.

Tiffany had gained some great experience from a project where her class developed a marketing plan for a real company. Tiffany served as a strategic planner, and she learned skills that were more relevant than her official paid job as a Vector salesperson. This experience wasn't even mentioned on Tiffany's *before* resume!

With a thorough activities and interests section, Tiffany is portrayed as a well-rounded, involved individual.

# Tiffany Leigh
3434 Bulldog Street • Ruston, LA 72967
202.749.3278 • tiffany@hotmail.com

**Objective:**  Seeking to obtain an entry-level position or an internship leading to future employment at a public relations firm.

**Education:**  The Ohio State University, Columbus
Bachelor of Arts in Communication, June 2006
Focus Area: Strategic Communication
Major GPA: 3.3

Relevant Coursework
*Public Relations, Strategic Planning, Public Campaigns, Feature Reporting & Editing, Public Speaking, Interpersonal Communications, Advertising

Accomplishments
*Assisted in research studying the effects of television on behavior
*Member of PRSSA (Public Relations Student Society of America)
*Through classwork, familiarity with writing press releases.
*Assisted in writing a strategic plan for Wooster, Ohio's Secrest Arboretum

**Relevant Experience:**  2005: 10x Media, LLC, Orem, Utah
*Wrote online articles dealing with real estate to increase marketing and website sales potential. These articles were to be written using specific keywords in order to maximize visibility on a search engine.
*I successfully balanced the option to set own work schedule with a tight deadline for submitting articles, and built a trusted relationship with my superiors communicating solely through e-mail

2003: Vector Marketing, Beachwood, Ohio
*Responsible for personal selling to a client list that I created and maintained. This included all steps from designing and implementing a personzalized direct selling plan to generating numerous leads and future customers, to following through with past contacts. I was employed in the top office in Ohio and the Great Lakes Region. As a result, I was invited to and attended numerous training and sales conferences at the regional level.

**Skills:**  *Experience with Macromedia Fireworks and Dreamweaver, as well as MS Word, Excel and Powerpoint
*Through classwork, familiarity with writing press releases
*Intermediate college-level coursework completed in the Spanish language

*Will gladly relocate

---

# Tiffany Leigh

3434 Bulldog Street • Ruston, LA 72967
202.749.3278 • tiffany@hotmail.com

## Education

**The Ohio State University**—Columbus, June 2006
- Bachelor of Arts in Communication
- Strategic Communication Focus; Film Studies Minor
- Major GPA 3.3; Dean's List

## Experience

**Editorial Intern,** 10x Media, LLC, Orem, UT, Summer 2005
- Researched and wrote more than 100 community snapshots used by several national real estate companies to drive website traffic
- Performed extensive Internet research to secure community information including public transportation, housing, schools, commerce and other demographic information
- Trusted by company management to work remotely and to establish independent work schedule

**Strategic Planner,** Secrest Arboretum, Ohio State University, Spring 2006
- Crafted comprehensive 25-page strategic plan with group of five other students as part of nine-week classroom project
- Met with senior executives from Secrest Arboretum to determine direction for development of strategic communication plan intended to increase attendance and to drive interest in renovated property
- Delivered final presentation to three Arboretum managers and executives

**Sales Representative,** Vector Marketing, Beachwood, OH, Summer 2003
- Delivered in excess of 200 personalized presentations offering complete line of high-quality Cutco knives
- Ranked in the top half of office based on sales of more than $3,000
- Helped office achieve number one ranking in Ohio and in all of Great Lakes region
- Invited to attend three state/regional sales meetings based on outstanding job performance

**Research Assistant,** Ohio State University, Spring 2005
- Assisted with complex research study gauging the affects of television viewing on children
- Distributed dozens of 100-question surveys to OSU faculty and staff
- Compiled information tracking responses from qualitative portion of survey

## Activities/Skills/Interests

- Public Relations Student Society of America (PRSSA), 2004–2006
- Habitat for Humanity Volunteer, 2005
- Proficient in SPSS
- Interests include: sports, travel, film, Ohio State athletics

# CONCLUSION

There you have it: a look inside the mind of a recruiting director. You just had the veil lifted from one of the most secretive processes in the working world: How does a recruiting director read a resume?

I hope you found the book interesting and informative. It is impossible to read this book and not have a better understanding of how to write your resume and get a job. As you saw from reading all the *before* resumes, most job seekers do not craft their resume in the right way. They do not target their resume to the recruiting director, and they do not sell their unique accomplishments.

That is why this information is so useful. Job seekers do not normally think like recruiting directors, but now you can. You just learned exactly what it takes to create the perfect resume.

If you read the book from cover to cover, you will have noticed a few consistent themes. To highlight:

## 1. Focus on accomplishments versus job descriptions

Hands down, this is the single most important thing you can do on your resume. *Everyone* writes job description resumes. People describe not only what they did, but what anyone has ever done in that job.

You have to make sure your resume is full of accomplishments. What are the results of your actions and what exactly did you do? Now is not the time to be shy. Now is not the time to be conversant in the details. Let the reader know in no uncertain terms what you did.

## 2. Be specific

Recruiting directors want to see numbers; they want to see names and data. As you witnessed, the good resumes were filled with numbers that contextualized results. We also include brand names whenever possible. These can make you sound more impressive and allow the reader to know what makes you great.

## 3. Trim it down

Shorter is better than longer. You should never have anything more than a two-page resume if you are looking for a business job. Students should never have more than a one-page resume. The best place to trim—especially for more seasoned job seekers—is the stuff more than ten to fifteen years old. You can list these jobs on your resume, but you do not need to get into excruciating detail.

## 4. Make yourself an easy hire

As I have said before, most recruiting directors want to put a round peg into a round hole. Look at the job description for the position you are applying for and align your skills and accomplishments to that description. For more experienced job seekers, a summary of qualifications can be a great place to do that. More importantly, make sure all of your bullet points for each job are targeted in the order that you list them. If you are going for a job that is more in the finance field and you did a few financial projects in your last marketing job, list the financial accomplishments first.

A great resume and a successful job search are all about making you the most obvious person to hire. Remember, to recruiting directors your resume is actually *you*. They do not know you other than on that sheet of paper in front of them. They will look at it for ten to fifteen seconds and decide if you can be the one.

Everything you do with your resume needs to make it obvious that you are the ideal candidate for the job. Now that you have read this book, you have all the tools to do this.

•   •   •

Remember to check out the appendix. We've included some tools to assist you. There is an action verb list if you are running out of ideas for beginning your bullet points. We have a resume checklist to make sure you don't forget any of the tips we mentioned. This book doesn't address cover letters in depth, but we threw in a few cover letters as an added bonus to help you get your well-written resume noticed. Make sure you keep reading.

Good luck!

# APPENDICES

# Powerful Action Verbs

| | | | |
|---|---|---|---|
| Accelerated | Composed | Drafted | Identified |
| Accomplished | Computed | Earned | Illustrated |
| Achieved | Conceptualized | Edited | Implemented |
| Activated | Conducted | Educated | Improved |
| Administered | Consolidated | Eliminated | Incorporated |
| Advertised | Constructed | Employed | Increased |
| Advised | Consulted | Enhanced | Inspected |
| Allocated | Contacted | Enforced | Installed |
| Analyzed | Contributed | Engineered | Instituted |
| Appraised | Controlled | Established | Integrated |
| Assessed | Converted | Evaluated | Introduced |
| Assisted | Coordinated | Examined | Judged |
| Attained | Corresponded | Executed | Launched |
| Authorized | Created | Expanded | Led |
| Awarded | Critiqued | Expedited | Maintained |
| Authored | Customized | Facilitated | Managed |
| Balanced | Compiled | Finalized | Masterminded |
| Budgeted | Decided | Formed | Maximized |
| Built | Delivered | Formulated | Merged |
| Calculated | Designated | Gained | Modified |
| Chaired | Designed | Generated | Negotiated |
| Checked | Determined | Governed | Observed |
| Coached | Developed | Grossed | Obtained |
| Collaborated | Diagnosed | Guided | Operated |
| Collected | Directed | Handled | Orchestrated |
| Communicated | Discovered | Headed | Organized |
| Compiled | Displayed | Helped | Overhauled |
| Completed | Documented | Hired | Oversaw |

| | | | |
|---|---|---|---|
| Participated | Purchased | Revised | Supervised |
| Performed | Ran | Screened | Surpassed |
| Pinpointed | Rated | Selected | Surveyed |
| Piloted | Reconciled | Served | Taught |
| Pioneered | Recorded | Shaped | Tested |
| Planned | Recruited | Sold | Trained |
| Prepared | Reduced | Solved | Tutored |
| Presided | Regulated | Spearheaded | Updated |
| Processed | Rehabilitated | Sponsored | Upgraded |
| Produced | Reorganized | Standardized | Used |
| Projected | Repaired | Started | Utilized |
| Promoted | Researched | Streamlined | Won |
| Proposed | Resolved | Strengthened | Worked |
| Provided | Restored | Structured | Wrote |
| Publicized | Reviewed | Studied | |

# Resume Writing Checklist

## Visual Appeal

❑ Font size and style is appropriate and easy to read

❑ Section headings and bullets are consistently lined up and spaced

❑ Margins are not less than .75 of an inch to prevent overcrowding

❑ White space is not more than 25 percent to maximize space

❑ Section headings, spacing, and margins combine to make resume visually appealing for fifteen-second scan

❑ Text is bolded, highlighted, underlined, bulleted, or indented where necessary to make specific items stand out

❑ Resume is printed on high-quality paper—white, ivory, or light-colored

## Organization and Layout

❑ Did not use a resume wizard or Word template

❑ Included most relevant and compelling experiences first

❑ Used bullet points, not complete sentences, to describe experiences

❑ Length of resume reflects experience level (one page if less than four years of experience, never more than two pages for business job)

## Contact Information

❑ Name and current address

❑ Non-work email address

❑ Best phone number where you can be reached 9:00 a.m. to 5:00 p.m.

## Education

❑ Highest level of education is listed first

❑ Included school name, city, graduation year, or anticipated graduation date

- ❏ Listed degrees, minors, or concentrations
- ❏ Recorded GPA if it is higher than a 3.2
- ❏ Listed any relevant academic awards, honors, scholarships
- ❏ Included any study abroad programs

## Experience

- ❏ Listed title, company, city, state, and dates of employment
- ❏ Focused on results and scope of job **accomplishments**
- ❏ Used powerful action verbs
- ❏ Emphasized skills and accomplishments most relevant for the desired job first
- ❏ Limited usage of company jargon and acronyms
- ❏ Provided as many numbers, data, specifics, and achievements as possible

## Activities, Professional Associations, Interests

- ❏ Included any relevant affiliations or activities with leadership role and dates
- ❏ Listed hobbies or interests to show a well-rounded character

## Accuracy

- ❏ Double-checked for typos and grammatical errors
- ❏ Had resume proofread by at least two other people

# The Cover Letter:
# A Teaser Ad for Your Resume

Job seekers across the nation often lament writing cover letters, and recruiting directors across the nation often lament reading cover letters. Why? Because the standard, typical cover letter is downright boring. It's basically a prose version of a candidate's resume. Now, why would a recruiting director want to read your resume in sentence form?

The reason that cover letters are so boring is because all of them are written the same way. Job seekers have been misguided in the instruction that all cover letters should follow the same format. Everyone is taught that a cover letter should be a single-spaced, full-page, four paragraph letter, organized as follows:

Paragraph 1: How you heard about the job

Paragraph 2: Why you want the job

Paragraph 3: Your qualifications for the job

Paragraph 4: How you will follow up on the job

Practically every single person writes the *exact same* cover letter! This format sucks out all the creativity and interest.

The cover letter offers you an amazing opportunity to set yourself apart and to tell your unique story. This letter not only shows the recruiting director a sample of your writing and communication skills, but it also shows that you're interested in the job and are willing to take the time and effort to write something.

There is one trick when it comes to writing a cover letter: Make it different. Think about your cover letter as a teaser ad for your resume. You don't want it to tell your life story, but you do want to attract interest in your resume.

You also want to keep it short. Just as with resumes, you want your cover letter to be shorter rather than longer. Challenge yourself by making some sentences just a few words and making some paragraphs one sentence. Write it very personally, and be conversational. Of course, you want the document to look and sound professional, but you don't have to make it overly stuffy.

The key is to catch recruiting directors' attention in the first sentence or two so they actually read on and give your resume extra review time. You must be careful though—there's a fine line between what you think is clever and what a recruiting director thinks is juvenile!

Here's a good sample cover letter for an advertising account manager. Can you read the first line without reading the rest of the letter? You'll quickly see the difference between this one and the typical cover letter.

•  •  •

Dear Ms. Marhula,

I learned much of what I need to know about account management from my family.

I'm actually an only child, but I grew up with more than 40 cousins living within one mile of me.

Traits like adaptability, getting along with others, rolling with the punches and being competitive, all became second nature to me. If I didn't stand up for what I believed in, if I didn't mesh with different personalities, and if I didn't have a thick skin, I would've had trouble surviving in the family!

It's those exact traits that have made me successful in the field of advertising. As an experienced account executive, I've forged wonderful working relationships with our clients and become a true partner with all of our internal departments—often by using the same skills I learned from family dynamics. I have to be honest, when I'm working with our creative department, it doesn't seem too different from dealing with a pack of raucous cousins!

I'm very excited about a career at Landon Marketing. Your work, your client list and your reputation in the industry have all impressed me.

I'll plan to contact you in a week's time to follow up. I hope to have the chance to become part of the Landon Marketing "family."

Regards,
Joe Templin

• • •

This certainly isn't the perfect cover letter for everyone, but it does give you a sense of what to do. Of course, if you are entering a creative field, you definitely want to use your cover letter to showcase your inventive thinking and writing. Even if you are going into a conservative field like banking or accounting, you can benefit from writing a short, interesting cover letter. In those cases, you can speak to why you became interested in the field or why you love the industry. Here are six categories that you can use as starting points for writing your cover letter. For each, we also share an example of a captivating first sentence.

## 1. How you got interested in the field

After spending an insightful summer painting with my two cousins with autism, I knew I wanted to be an art therapist.

## 2. Why you like the particular job or company

I began admiring your company at age six. Even before I could comprehend your articles, I would "read" *Southern Living* magazine with my mom on our front porch swing.

## 3. Special skills or experience you have related to the field

While teaching high school English in New Orleans after Hurricane Katrina, I found that I learned just as much as I taught.

## 4. A great opportunity you had

It's not every day that an intern gets to go on a business trip to Asia with the city mayor.

## 5. Personal connection

I had the pleasure of meeting with Carolyn Little, who reinforced my desire to work at your state-of-the-art hospital.

## 6. Explain a possible "red flag" on your resume

Why would an established investment banker give up a lucrative career and go back to school to be an editor? It's easy. Passion.

As a reminder, keep your cover letter short and personal, and let some of your personality shine through.

Now let's take a look at a few other examples from some experienced professionals.

• • •

## Special skills or experience in the field

Jason was a passionate, high-level marketing executive. He needed a creative cover letter that parlayed his creativity but also showcased his special experiences in building brands and businesses.

By marketing and selling himself, Jason shows he has the ingenuity, background, and ability to market a company successfully.

We decided to use one word to begin Jason's cover letter: Building. Since this cover letter was for a marketing position, this one word excites a little curiosity. This analogy helps paint a strong picture of Jason's passion for business and his work.

Since Jason was applying for a VP position, we highlighted some of his major accomplishments and showed the large scale and wide breadth of his past experiences. What recruiting director wouldn't want someone who could grow the business by 500 percent? We played up his significant, special skills to show that Jason is a driven, passionate leader who can begin building the business from day one.

Take a look at the cover letter, and notice how each sentence leaves a little hook so you want to read the entire letter!

• • •

# Jason Kroll

817 East 35th Street, Apt. 318 • Ulysses, TX 89816

928.826.8611 • jason@utexas.edu

May 10, 2009

37774 Kennedy Drive

Austin, TX 34421

Dear Mr. Kelso:

Building.

It's what I do for a living.

No, not in the traditional hammer and nail sense, but in the business sense—whether it's building a marketplace for a product I'm selling, building a series of original products, or building a business.

Six years ago, the world of internet advertising was unproven and untapped. I created a sales and marketing plan of attack for this fledgling media, and ultimately built an incredibly strong client base and revenue stream that helped our company grow 500% in six years.

In working closely with my clients and with a project management team, I built a series of innovative programs and products that respond to an ever-changing web-based marketplace. As the technology has evolved, I've been able to adapt to the changing playing field.

Finally, I built a business of more than 180 clients that includes senior managers and decision makers at some of the world's largest consumer brands and advertising agencies.

I'm excited to learn more about Angelo Worldwide, and I'm thrilled at the chance to build your business. I look forward to following up about the Vice-President of Marketing Services job.


Regards
Jason Kroll

• • •

## Explain a possible "red flag" on your resume

Samantha had a long career in sales, but she had worked for several different companies. When recruiting directors picked up her resume, they could see this "job hopping" as a potential red flag.

In Samantha's case, she had switched companies, but she remained in the same line of business. Therefore, we decided to address the situation head-on. Instead of tiptoeing around the fact that Samantha had changed companies numerous times, we stated that fact in her cover letter.

We also found the positive attributes that had come from those decisions, and we played up the fact that Samantha had exposure to a huge client base. She's actually gained a wide scope of experience in her line of business by working for several companies.

We also didn't dwell on the possible problem. We mentioned it, and moved on. There is no need to dramatize the situation, but the mere fact that you mention it makes it less taboo. It also gives you a chance to briefly and succinctly explain your story. This same theory goes for other "red flags" as well. You can address them in your cover letter, but do not dwell on them. Check out Samantha's cover letter to see how we employed the technique.

• • •

# Samantha Gail

**9927 Dudstone Street • Danes, IL 71187**

**958.995.6942 • samantha@aol.com**

June 15, 2008

2378 North Avenue
Gladstone, OH 28283

Dear Ms. Gribbin:

Passion. Dedication. Industry know-how.

These are the attributes that drive me, and these are the attributes that I bring to my work. I've worked for several different companies, and I see each job as a valuable learning experience that adds to my knowledge base.

I'm passionate about the job that I do. When representing a line or opening a territory, I've always started from the ground up. No one ever gave me a $30MM brand and said grow it to $40MM. They gave me a new brand or a new territory and watched as I drove it to success.

I'm dedicated to performing my best. I'm a "roll up your sleeves" kind of person who makes work a priority and who believes wholeheartedly in customer service.

I have extensive industry know-how. With more than 15 years in the field, I'm well-known and well-respected by manufacturers, retailers, and other reps of all sizes—from the big box retailers to the mom-and-pops.

I'd like the opportunity to share more of my passion, dedication and know-how in person. I look forward to following up soon.

Regards,
Samantha Gail

• • •

## Why you became interested in the field

Through her first sentence, Sarah shows that her current career path is an interest and a passion she's had since she was a child. Many people say that it takes a special person to be a good teacher, and that it's almost a calling. Sarah is able to paint a picture of her "calling." The decision to be a teacher wasn't a fallback idea or a "why not?" career choice. Being a teacher is something Sarah has wanted for years. What principal or school board wouldn't like that?

Sarah had a great love for helping students and pushing them to the next level, and we wanted to convey that in her cover letter. By making some paragraphs only one line, we really call attention to them. When you have a full-page of block, single-space paragraphs, it's a little difficult to read and nothing jumps out at you.

Sarah not only had passion, but she had the initiative and determination to make a difference. We wanted to highlight that point in her cover letter, so we mentioned the new curriculum that she created from scratch. That experience was on her resume, but we knew it would catch some attention in the cover letter. Sarah doesn't just go through the motions; she goes above and beyond the call of duty in her job.

Again, your cover letter could be the thing that gets your resume and you considered for the job. Your resume gives the facts and the credentials, and your cover letter gives you a chance to tell a story and round yourself out.

At the end, we mentioned the school's name and reinforced how Sarah would be a good fit.

• • •

# Sarah Hartman

**29456 Bright Lane • Renaissance, GA 71549**
**854.229.1235• sarah@hotmail.com**

July 20, 2008

9292 Quiet Oaks
Biloxi, MS 29292

Dear Ms. Swarner:

When growing up, I always played "school" with my younger sister, and I was always the teacher.

There's no better feeling than knowing you helped a child learn.

Touching lives, supporting growth, and facilitating the interaction of children are what have drawn me to teaching for the past seven years.

My experience has taught me that to be successful you must be patient, creative, and driven—three of my greatest strengths. I love working with children, and I love inspiring learning. There's no better feeling than seeing one of your students finally "get it."

Creative lesson plans and boundless energy are what I consider to be my hallmarks. I had the privilege of launching an entirely new curriculum at Bellaire Middle School. It was certainly a challenge, but with all new course materials, an all-school play and a trip to a Spanish language theater group, I knew the students were doing so much more than just going through the motions.

I'm anxious to tell you more about my qualifications, and why I'd like to be a part of St. Alphonsus School. I'll plan to follow up in a week's time. In the meantime, feel free to contact me at 854.229.1235.

Regards,
Sarah Hartman

# INDEX

in-depth, 18
layoff issue in, 111
preparation for, 112
skill in, 111–12
when to conduct, 130
Irrelevant jobs
bullet points for, 213, 216
eliminating, 76, 78–82
IT. *See* Information Technology
Italics, 22

Jargon
abbreviations and, 114, 115
industry, 225, 226
use of, 158, 159–60
Job(s)
irrelevant, 76, 78–82, 213, 216
switching, 76
Job boards, 24
JobBound
accomplishment resume v. job description, 191–95
after advanced degree and, 223–25, 227
career change, strategy for, 30–31, 34–35
college internships removed by, 252–54
condensing resume by, 158–61, 169–72
contract work and, 78, 81–82
custom-tailored resumes, 25
education, highlighted and, 232, 235–36
extracurricular activities and, 114, 116
greatness, focusing on, 39–41
internal promotion, selling for, 53–55, 58–59
marketing candidate, 119–20, 122
promotion resume by, 131–35
Public Relations skills, 39
quantifying resume, 164, 167–68
Job changer
in cover letter, 76
frequent, 5, 75–92
positive aspects of, 77
for promotion, 129, 131
Job description
accomplishments v., 10–13, 191–95, 207, 209, 261, 262
accurate fit for, 60
example of, 137, 138–39
specific, 191, 194–95
Job experience. *See* Work experience
Job hopping, 88
clarification of, 76
Job listings, on company websites, 113
Job qualifications. *See* Qualifications

Job search
boss, informing about, 129
business email using, 130
for dream job, 187–209
follow-up to, 147
inside contacts in, 147
interviews, 130
no responses to, 145–47
online, 113
professionalism in, 130
rejection as part of, 147, 148
research for, 54
in rut, 145–86
while employed, 129–31
Job seekers, 25–26
recent graduates, 9, 15
seasoned, 8–9, 262
students, 114
Job titles, 39, 40
consolidating, 71–74
showcasing, 83, 86–87

Kraft Foods, 83, 86, 144

Layoff, 111–27
anticipation of, 196
career reassessment after, 112, 119–20
company assistance after, 119–20, 122
company considering, 196
landing work after, 112–13
mindset after, 93–94
skills enhanced after, 94
transition made after, 93, 119
Leadership skills, 30–31
in college club, 257
in consulting, 121, 122
proving, 206
Length, of resume, 149, 150–55. *See also*
One-page resume; Two-page resume
condensing, by JobBound, 158–61, 169–72
less is more, 71, 74
for student, 243, 248–51, 262, 263
Leo Burnett Advertising, 1
Leveraging
company assistance, 119–20
experience, 106
Life transitions
college to professional, 245, 247
after layoff, 119
returning to work after, 93
LinkedIn, 25

marketing, 233, 235
marketing and communications, 49–50, 69
organizations, 123, 126
in public relations, 185
Programmer/analyst, 58–59
Project Manager, 150, 156
  over 16 years experience, 197, 199
  for software implementation, 176–77,
    179–80
Promotion
  advanced degree for, 223–24
  internal, 25, 53–74
  job change for, 129, 131
  justifying, 54
  in less than one year, 204
  positioning for, 60
  resume by JobBound, 131–35
  seeking, in company, 129
Property Manager, 100, 103
Public Relations (PR)
  expert, 213, 214, 216
  job in, 39, 41

Qualifications. *See also* Summary of qualifications
  section
  key to, 15–16
  lacking in, 5
  matching, 3, 6–7, 16, 27, 60, 262–63
  when needed, 15–16
Quitting job, 130–31

Readability, 142, 143
Real-world experience, 256, 257
Recruiting directors
  call backs and, 146
  chances taken by, 28–29
  compelling points for, 36, 38
  easy hire for, 262–63
  eliminating resumes, 196
  entry-level candidates and, 245, 247
  first glance of resume for, 196
  gap and, 94–95
  graduate degree information for, 223
  as human resources professional, 158
  identifying with, 25–26
  jargon with, 158
  job hoppers and, 76
  job qualifications match for, 3, 6–7, 16, 27,
    262–63
  lengthy resumes and, 149, 262
  one-minute review and, 196
  one- or two-page resume for, 10

proof of success for, 3, 54
recent job interest for, 201
relevancy for, 83
reliance on numbers by, 137, 262
scanning resumes, 8, 30, 164, 181, 248, 249,
  262–63
specifics spelled out for, 65, 262
thinking like, 261–63
writing for, 218, 221, 252, 261
Recruitment
  as low priority, 146
  revamping process of, 191, 194, 195
References section, 20, 207
Rejection, in job search
  attitude toward, 147
  dealing with, 148
Religious groups, 20
Relocating, 201
Results, highlighting, 66
Returning to work, after freelancing, 96
Rheem, 65
Round peg in square hole, 27, 262

Salary increase, 129
Sales
  associate, 227, 253
  cabinetry, 137, 138–41
  representative, 138, 140, 141
Salesman, asset to company v., 137, 138–39
Scholarships
  attention to, 224
  listing on student resume, 256
Schoolteacher
  highlighting experience of, 237, 240
  to HR professional, 36, 38
School, transfer from, 225
Seasoned candidate
  with fiduciary accomplishments, 218, 221
  with fifteen plus years experience, 211–12, 216,
    262
Sections, condensing, 181, 183–83, 186
Selling candidate, 53. *See also* Candidate;
  Marketing
  short, 213
Senior Account Manager, 67–70
Senior Planner, advertising, 115
Senior Vice President, Event Marketing,
  89, 91
Sentence, full in resume, 9, 149
Serif fonts, 22. *See also* Font
Severance packages, 119
Showcasing titles, 83, 86–87

# ABOUT THE AUTHORS

**Brad Karsh** is the president and founder of JobBound (www.job
bound.com), a company dedicated to helping candidates land the
jobs of their dreams. An industry expert in the career field and an
accomplished public speaker and author, Brad Karsh has been featured on *Dr. Phil*, *CNN*, and *CNBC* and has been quoted in the *Wall
Street Journal*, *Washington Post*, *New York Times*, *USA Today*, and
many others. Brad is a job advice columnist for both *Yahoo!* and
*AdAge*, and he is author of *Confessions of a Recruiting Director:
The Insider's Guide to Landing Your First Job* (Prentice Hall Press,
2006).

Prior to starting JobBound, Brad spent fifteen years at Leo Burnett Advertising in Chicago. He left in 2002 as the VP/director of
talent acquisition, responsible for all the agency's hiring. While at
Burnett, Brad evaluated more than 10,000 resumes, interviewed
more than 1,000 candidates and hired hundreds of new employees.
Brad has become a national authority on the job search process.

Brad graduated from Wesleyan University in Middletown, Connecticut, with a BA in history and currently resides in Chicago with
his wife Lisa and son Milo.

**Courtney Pike** is the director of communications at JobBound. In more than five years of experience in the development and career counseling field, Courtney has shared her passion, vision, and expertise. Courtney is a solutions-oriented career development and communications professional who has brought leading-edge career initiatives to JobBound. She has combined her love of learning and development with her creativity in communications to help propel JobBound to the top of the market. Courtney received her bachelor of arts degree in English and public relations from Spring Hill College in Mobile, Alabama. Courtney currently resides in Chicago.